D1711636

THE FAMILY
Evaluation and Treatment

AMERICAN COLLEGE OF PSYCHIATRISTS

Officers (at time of 1979 Annual Meeting)

Gene Usdin, M.D., *President*

Warren S. Williams, M.D.
President-Elect

Shervert H. Frazier, M.D.
First Vice-President

John C. Nemiah, M.D.
Second Vice-President

Henry H. Work
Secretary-General

Charles E. Smith, M.D.
Treasurer

Sidney Malitz, M.D.
Archivist-Historian

Program Committee for 1979 Annual Meeting

Robert L. Williams, M.D., *Chairman*

Allan Beigel, M.D.

Pietro Castelnuovo-Tedesco, M.D.

Thomas H. Holmes, M.D.

Harold Lief, M.D.

Morris A. Lipton, M.D.

George H. Pollock, M.D.

Peter F. Regan, M.D.

Publications Committee

Jerry M. Lewis, M.D., *Chairman*

Charles K. Hofling, M.D., *Vice-Chairman & Editor-in-Chief*

Ransom J. Arthur, M.D.

Harold Hiatt, M.D.

Maurice J. Martin, M.D.

Hyman L. Muslin, M.D.

Michael R. Zales, M.D.

Henry H. Work, M.D. (*ex-officio*)

The Family

Evaluation and Treatment

Edited by
CHARLES K. HOFLING, M.D.
Professor of Psychiatry,
St. Louis University School of Medicine

and

JERRY M. LEWIS, M.D.
Psychiatrist-in-Chief,
Timberlawn Psychiatric Hospital;
Clinical Professor of Psychiatry and
Clinical Professor of Family Practice and Community Medicine,
University of Texas, Southwestern Medical School at Dallas

BRUNNER/MAZEL, *Publishers* • New York

SECOND PRINTING

Library of Congress Cataloging in Publication Data

American College of Psychiatrists.

The family.

Proceedings of the 1979 annual meeting of the American College of Psychiatrists, held Feb. 7-11, 1979, Costa Mesa, CA.

Includes bibliographical references and index.

1. Mentally ill—Family relationships—Congresses. 2. Family psychotherapy—Congresses. I. Hofling, Charles K. II. Lewis, Jerry M., 1924-
III. Title.

RC455.4.F3A44 1980 616.8'915 79-21933
ISBN 0-87630-233-1

Copyright © 1980 by THE AMERICAN COLLEGE OF PSYCHIATRISTS

Published by
BRUNNER/MAZEL, INC.
19 Union Square
New York, New York 10003

All rights reserved, including the rights of reproduction in whole or in part in any form.

MANUFACTURED IN THE UNITED STATES OF AMERICA

Contributors

YRJÖ O. ALANEN, M.D.

Professor of Psychiatry, University of Turku, Finland

DAVID P. BARASH, Ph.D.

Associate Professor of Psychology and Associate Professor of Zoology, University of Washington, Seattle

DONALD A. BLOCH, M.D.

Director, The Ackerman Institute of Family Therapy, New York City, New York

SAUL L. BROWN, M.D.

Clinical Professor of Psychiatry, University of California at Los Angeles, School of Medicine

CHARLES K. HOFLING, M.D.

Professor of Psychiatry, St. Louis University School of Medicine; Visiting Professor of Psychiatry, University of Cincinnati College of Medicine

JERRY M. LEWIS, M.D.

Psychiatrist-in-Chief, Timberlawn Psychiatric Hospital; Clinical Professor of Psychiatry and Clinical Professor of Family Practice and Community Medicine, University of Texas, Southwestern Medical School at Dallas; Director, Research and Training, Timberlawn Psychiatric Research Foundation

THEODORE LIDZ, M.D.

Professor of Psychiatry, Yale University School of Medicine

HAROLD I. LIEF, M.D.

Professor of Psychiatry and Director, Division of Family Studies, University of Pennsylvania

JAMES GRIER MILLER, M.D., Ph.D., F.A.C.P.

President, University of Louisville

JESSIE L. MILLER, M.S.

DAVID REISS, M.D.

Professor, Department of Psychiatry and Behavioral Sciences, George Washington University School of Medicine; Director, Center for Family Research

MARSHALL D. SCHECHTER, M.D.

Professor of Psychiatry and Director, Division of Child and Adolescent Psychiatry, University of Pennsylvania

ALBERT J. SOLNIT, M.D.

Sterling Professor of Pediatrics and Psychiatry and Director, Child Study Center, Yale University

GENE USDIN, M.D.

Clinical Professor of Psychiatry, Louisiana State University School of Medicine

Contents

Preface

This volume, which addresses itself to an area of considerable current interest to all mental health professionals, is the eleventh publication of the American College of Psychiatrists. The College, founded in 1963, provides recognition for leaders in American psychiatry who have made significant contributions to the field. Its continuing academic function is to provide an open scientific forum and to promote and maintain professional standards of excellence, actively furthering the continuing professional growth of its members.

Members of the College represent varied schools of thought comprising all facets of the profession: practitioners, teachers, administrators, and researchers. The orientation always has been pluralistic, essentially using a psychosociobiologic approach. The format of the annual scientific meetings is one of presentations followed by small group discussions. This has provided a valuable educational experience for those involved. The student and scholar, latent in even the most senior psychiatrist, seem to be rekindled by this type of learning experience. Above all, the organization seeks to maintain the ideal of excellence.

Publications of the College represent the carefully edited scientific proceedings of its annual meetings, thus making available to all mental health professionals recent concepts and findings.

The College has expanded its *raison d'être* to provide continuing medical education for nonmembers by developing publications, by presenting regional continuing education workshops, and by becoming increasingly involved with other organizations related to continuing graduate and postgraduate education.

This volume examines the family in health and illness, bringing together mental health professionals of different orientations and disciplines. The family is discussed as an interacting system, detailing what makes for family health as well as illness. The authors emphasize recognition of the need for family assessment and, when indicated, professional intervention. This is followed by a review of the various concepts and techniques to improve family health or minimize and avoid significant family illness. The book has the recurrent motif, one that is becoming more and more apparent to psychiatrists, that the human family is not just one of several cultural options, but a basic, almost organic, ingredient of normal psychological growth—basic to the very definition of the human individual.

I hope that readers of this volume will find much to interest them and, especially, that they will discover in these pages concepts and techniques that will be useful to them in aiding their patients as well as improving their own family life.

GENE USDIN, M.D.
President, 1978-79
American College of Psychiatrists

Introduction

> In my judgment, one of the basic reasons we have had crime, lawlessness, and disorder in the United States has been the breakdown of the family unit.
>
> ROBERT F. KENNEDY (1)

> No matter how many communes anybody invents, the family always creeps back.
>
> MARGARET MEAD (2)

Breakdown of the family or some kind of unquenchable vitality? The condition of the family as a prime cause of generally deplored aspects of our civilization or as a victim of surging social forces? No doubt the points of view inherent in these questions all have validity. In any case, a deep concern about the status of the family is of almost palpable intensity in America and the West generally and seemingly in many other parts of the world as well. It is felt in all walks of life and is constantly reflected in all media of communication.

Moreover, this concern of our culture is not merely a conscious (and, in some aspects, an unconscious) concern; it has become a self-conscious concern. Mothers, fathers, and children are not merely striving to conform to—or rebel against—certain accepted modes, but they are increasingly aware of doing so. (This is not necessarily to say that most laymen of our time are prone to experiencing especially deep personal or interpersonal insight; often what is said in justification or condemnation of functions and attitudes is in the nature of rationalization or even at the level of the cliché.) In accord with, and perhaps partly helping to further, this *Zeitgeist,* there has been a striking increase of interest on the part of social and behavioral scientists, notably including psychiatrists, in studying and attempting to help families and family members as such. This scientific interest has never been greater or more serious than it is today, and the present volume is an instance of it.

Since, with a few exceptions, the essays comprising this book deal with the present, the recent past, and the immediate future, a few words of historical background may not be out of place in the interests of perspective. There appears to be wide agreement that these are difficult times; that stresses upon society in general and the family in particular are great. One hears it said that the family, at least as we know it, is in a struggle for survival. What tends to be forgotten or overlooked is that, broadly speaking, society and the family specifically have always been engaged in serious struggles. (As Walter J. Ong has put it conversationally: "Times are bad; but then they've always been bad" (3).) This is said not at all to discount the many specific stresses characteristic of our times. The lessening influence of custom and tradition, the increased frequency with which families make geographic moves, the lessened practical usefulness of children and old people, the development of greater social fluidity, the accelerated rate of material changes, the accelerated rate of changes in the relationships between the sexes and between various ethnic groups—all these, as well as other sources of stress, are perfectly evident. Moreover, if—without taking them too literally or too arbitrarily—one finds some heuristic value in the vast metaphors of Spengler and Toynbee and their followers, one may be prepared to believe that our century represents a more significant watershed in history than would many randomly selected centuries of the past.

Yet, such recognitions need not commit one to a basically pessimistic view of the family today and its potentialities. They do not so commit the authors of the present essays. In their studies of families they maintain a high degree of objectivity. In their studies of family therapy there is still a basic objectivity, but there is also a note of optimism and even affection. Our authors seem to like families, to want them and their members to move in the direction of health, and to evince considerable determination to assist in this process.

It is true, however, particularly for psychiatrists, that even a brief look at relatively recent historical studies of the family and of childhood may prove of value. Since most of us have experienced an education heavily weighted toward the natural sciences, we tend to share with laymen, if only subliminally, a belief in certain myths about Western families which are rather far from the truth. For example, we tend to believe in a long golden age of the family, stretching back for centuries from some time in the fairly recent past. To speak simplistically, our image is likely to be that of a closely linked extended family, with the mother devoting herself almost exclusively to housewifely duties, the father going to work in field or artisan's shop, the children (allowed to grow up slowly) doing simple chores around the house, and a number of kindly grandparents available to lend a hand with the care of the children and other household tasks. The idea seems to be that, after a long time, this idyllic state collapsed more or less recently (perhaps under the impact of the industrial revolution, perhaps in response to more modern technological developments, such as those in transportation and communication).

While the work of social and cultural historians, and particularly of psychohistorians, is still in its relatively early stages, enough has been accomplished to show the above picture to be an idealized and sentimental one. It is not that the several individual aspects of the picture never existed—but the idea that all of them existed together for a very extended period of time and that our generation is the first to witness the decomposition of this fabric is mythical. In his seminal work *L'Enfant et la vie familiale sous l'ancien régime* (4), Philippe Ariès, through iconographic, literary, and demographic studies, has shown that the evolution of the patterns and perceptions of childhood and family life, which are often considered to have existed almost from time immemorial, was extremely gradual.

> In the 10th Century artists were unable to depict a child except as a man on a smaller scale. How did we come from that

ignorance of childhood to the centering of the family around the child in the 19th Century? (R. Baldrick, trans.)

Ariès also suggests that, though the patterns and perceptions arrived at in aristocratic and upper-middle-class circles by the early 19th century had widened to include most of European and American society by the mid-20th century, they had not changed nearly as much as generally supposed.

Other scholars have exposed other aspects of the myth. For example, Wrigley writes (5):

> . . . The co-resident family group from Elizabethan times onward normally consisted only of the basic reproductive unit of husband, wife, and children, or a remnant of the same. . . . Occasionally a grandparent was also present, but lateral extension of the co-resident unit was very rare in the ordinary ranks of society, and vertical extension uncommon. . . .

When one considers the limited life expectancy in renaissance and early industrial times, one can readily believe that there has probably been more contact between grandparents and grandchildren in the 20th century than ever before (6).

Or think of the supposedly very modern concept that a woman's life cannot or should not be limited to activities pertaining to the roles of wife and mother. Actually, it was only during a brief period of our history and only within the more prosperous groups of our society that the limited idea was economically feasible, or even conceivable.*

The work of the social and psychohistorians is, however, not limited to the exposure of idealizing and sentimental myths for what they are. They shed light on some of the problems of the late 19th and the 20th centuries, e.g., the perhaps unrealistically large expectations in emotional terms we have come to have of the family. As Hareven has put it:

---

* The idea of a wide choice of extrafamilial vocations for women is, of course, a relatively modern one. In earlier times women worked in the fields if in rural settings and at handcrafts (or later in shops or factories) if in bourgeois settings. But, of course, so did men.

> In Western society today, the major burdens of family relationships are emotional, while in the nineteenth century [and earlier] they were heavily weighted toward economic needs and tasks. . . . Relationships between husbands and wives, parents and children, distant kin, and even family members and strangers were based on socially sanctioned mutual obligations that transcended personal affection and sentiment (7).

The vastly greater *socialization* of life in earlier times, while it created stresses of its own, clearly imposed lesser demands on the family as the gratifier of psychosocial needs. The idea of the home as a haven, quite distinct from and set over against a complex and often distressing social milieu, is clearly a rather recent one. When a child at the age of seven was apprenticed to a fellow town-dweller to learn a trade, or was made a member of the agricultural labor force of the lord of the manor, times were no doubt "bad," but they were bad in ways for which the family was not expected to supply the answers. As the lives of most of us have become more individualized and private, family stresses have changed, and it is no wonder that they are not fully understood, let alone mastered.

To an increase of such understanding and a furthering of such mastery the essays in the present volume are dedicated. In a general way, one may divide these presentations into three categories: 1) those which are primarily devoted to a psychosocial understanding of the modern family in health and illness (with clear clinical implications); 2) those which offer a broad background for, or a broad approach to, the more focused studies; and 3) those which are primarily concerned with the treatment of families and their members. The Stanley R. Dean Award lecture fits best conceptually into the first of these categories, and the methodical reader may wish to read it in this context. However, by reason of College tradition and of its being exclusively concerned with the families of schizophrenics, it has been placed in a separate section at the end of the volume.

In what may be considered the theme essay of this book, Lewis offers an overview of the systems approach to families and then probes in detail problems in the appraisal of what he terms "family competence," an apt phrase for an overall quality of stability and adjustment capacity of the family as an entity. Areas deserving further research are indicated, and illustrations of interpersonal psychopathology are given.

Lidz, using time-tested psychoanalytic concepts and drawing upon his own fundamental research, relates continuing family influences to the psychological development of the individual, thus bridging areas which have too often been considered rather separate from one another.

Solnit widens the focus, introducing sociological and legal factors bearing on the status of the family and supporting his assessment with appropriate statistics. He introduces and discusses issues pertaining to the evaluation of individuals within the matrices of the families of which they are members, thus preserving a continuity with the Lewis and Lidz essays.

Reiss offers a review of family assessment methods, with a detailed illustration of his favorite. By "choice points," he refers to technical "options now available to clinicians and researchers in doing effective evaluations of the family." He discusses options, both "substantive" and "technical," currently available to clinicians and investigators in evaluating families. Reiss' exposition is dialectical; for purposes of clarification he sets up a series of contrasting approaches, first those involving ways of looking at families and then those involving technics of doing the assessments. For example, the development view is contrasted with the cross-sectional; in family-environment transactions, the contrast is between focusing on shaping processes within the family or on societal forces influencing the family—and so on. Among technical options, assessment may take place before or during intervention, in the home or in an institution, concentrating on particular features or concentrating on rigidly standardized measurements. (There is, however, no insistence that these various contrasting options cannot often be synthesized.)

Brown's essay, closing the first section, could almost as logically have opened the third. It is a transition paper, arguing for a differentiation between family interviewing (emphasis on assessment and building cooperation) and family therapy (emphasis on effecting major changes). Family interviewing, as described and illustrated by Brown, clearly has both therapeutic potential and (one assumes, often) a therapeutic effect, as, of course, is true of individual evaluative interviews—a circumstance which merely illustrates the truism that a well-done assessment is likely to be therapeutic.

In the next section, Miller and Miller offer a relatively detailed presentation of general living systems theory with particular reference to its applicability to the functional components of the family. Terms not in the ordinary working vocabulary of many psychiatrists are explained with clarity. The Millers make a good case for what they call the "neutrality" of the concepts thus described (e.g., the avoidance of pejorative connotations), and they demonstrate how the theory facilitates an instructive comparison of one system with another.

Barash discusses behavior pertaining to families from a broad evolutionary perspective. In an essay replete with illustrative examples of both infrahuman and human behavior, he demonstrates the very considerable extent to which patterns of mate-selection, breeding, and nurturance are explicable in terms of natural selection. As do the other authors, Barash acknowledges the significance of factors outside the field of his particular interest. He is concerned with revealing the biological underpinnings of psychosocial phenomena, not with exclusivity.

Bloch's essay, which opens the third section, serves several functions. It briefly surveys several schools of thought which have led to modern family therapy; it distills some of the basic characteristics of family therapy; it considers and illustrates indications and contraindications for family therapy; and it offers a sympathetic view of the stresses that impinge upon a professional entering this field of treatment.

Schechter and Lief's contribution consists of two interlocking presentations. In the first portion, Schechter offers a detailed example of a family therapy with a designated adolescent patient, including the evaluation of patient and family preliminary to the therapy. Lief adds a dimension in his portion, which describes his work with the parents (and particularly the father) of the adolescent, carried out prior to Schechter's therapy. While offering an engrossing clinical study, these essays illustrate some widely generalizable principles, indicating that the material was carefully selected.

The third section is concluded by the minimally edited transcription of a teaching exercise in which members of the College interrogated from the floor some of the authors of the papers here presented. The authors' group consisted of Bloch, Brown, Lewis, and Lief. The discussion was lively, as panel members reacted to one another as well as to the audience's input. In looking at this material the reader may get a sense of the atmosphere in which the separate presentations were offered.

Alanen's Stanley R. Dean Award Lecture describes his investigative work over a period of some 20 years on schizophrenia as a manifestation of disturbed intrafamilial psychic processes. Building on the work of Lidz, Lymann Wynne, and other pioneers, Alanen and his associates have carried out a series of studies which, while placing the subjects under intensive and subtle scrutiny, nevertheless yield data which lend themselves to statistical treatment. The therapeutic implications of what have been basically ongoing studies of pathogenesis are clearly noted.

In sum, the American College of Psychiatrists endeavors in this volume to present an exciting and representative current view of the work of psychiatrists and their colleagues in understanding families and assisting them and their individual members to move in the direction of greater health.

CHARLES K. HOFLING, M.D.

REFERENCES

1. KENNEDY, R. F., quoted in J. P. Bradley, L. F. Daniels, and T. C. Jones (Eds.), *The International Dictionary of Thoughts.* Chicago: J. G. Ferguson Publishing Company, 1969.
2. MEAD, M., quoted in *Reader's Digest,* June, 1972.
3. ONG, WALTER, J., S.J., personal communication.
4. ARIÈS, P.: *L'Enfant et la vie familiale sous l'ancien régime,* Paris Librairie Plon, 1960; published in the United States as *Centuries of Childhood: A Social History of Family Life,* R. Baldrick, trans. New York: Alfred A. Knopf, 1962, 10.
5. WRIGLEY, E. A.: Reflections on the history of the family. In: *The Family,* spring, 1977 issue of *Daedalus* (Vol. 106, No. 2, of the *Proceedings of the American Academy of Arts and Sciences*), 77.
6. HAREVEN, T. K.: Family time and historical time. In: *The Family,* spring, 1977 issue of *Daedalus* (Vol. 106, No. 2, of the *Proceedings of the American Academy of Arts and Sciences*), 62.
7. *Ibid.,* 64.

THE FAMILY
Evaluation and Treatment

Part I

1

The Family Matrix in Health and Disease

Jerry M. Lewis, M.D.

Introduction

Psychiatry has a long history of interest in the family of the patient. During the past several decades, however, clinical and research activity has greatly increased. Much of this increase has resulted from the application of systems concepts to the study and treatment of the family. Systems concepts emphasize the need to study the family as a social organism greater than the sum of the individual family members' personalities and values. One focus is on what transpires between the members of the family and is concerned, in particular, with repetitive patterns of interactions that reflect the underlying rules that govern life in the family. Although a full discussion of systems concepts as they are applied in working with families is beyond the scope of this report, a suggestion of their usefulness may be gathered from the following clinical vignette.

> The Jaspers were known as a "hard luck" family. Harold, the father, a rigid, unyielding draftsman, had, at 39, multiple facial tics, hypertension, and angina on exertion. Maude, his 37-year-

old wife, weighed 211 pounds. She was chronically depressed and had been taking a tricyclic antidepressant for two years. Much of the time she simply sat and thought about everything that seemed wrong with her life.

The daughter, Susie, age 19, had severe, labile diabetes. In the preceding year she had been hospitalized seven times, most often for acidosis that appeared to follow stressful life events. Harold, Jr., or "Buddy," had a lengthy record of arrests at age 16. He was aggressive, manipulative, and firmly identified with a delinquent gang.

Studying each of these four family members individually would reveal an abundance of intrapsychic pathology. The father would be seen as a compulsive character with much underlying oral deprivation and rage that was barely controlled. The mother's preoedipal personality configuration resulted in excessive dependent needs, inadequate assertiveness, and markedly ambivalent object relationships. The diabetic daughter was a remote, alexithymic person with marked immaturity. The son's personality appeared to be crystallizing around a character disorder that included avoidance of closeness, the exploitation of others, and impulsive, aggressive acts. Each family member was significantly disabled. This individually based approach is traditional and has great explanatory value. It does not, however, tell us much about the family as a system, nor does it provide us with all of the understanding possible about the behavior of family members.

To obtain data about the family system requires a procedure that promotes interaction among the family members. The clinician's observations would focus on the nature of the interactions, particularly on those repetitive exchanges that appear to be patterns. Such a procedure yielded the following data about the Jasper family:

Harold Jasper dominated the family's discussion. He did so by establishing each focus of attention, repeatedly interrupting the others, and using hostile sarcasm to quell minor displays of opposition to his controlling behavior. His wife, Maude, was silent, sighed heavily, and sat close to Buddy, reaching out occasionally to pat his knee. Buddy's anger was thinly concealed. Although the focus of much of the discussion was on Buddy and the "bad" company he kept, the boy responded, for the

> most part, only with smirks and clenched fists. Susie had taken a chair apart from the other family members. She participated in the discussion without evidence of affective involvement.

The clinician concluded that the Jasper family system was significantly dysfunctional. Noteworthy were the dominant-submissive nature of the parental relationship, the evidence of a mother-son coalition aligned against the father, the absence of closeness except in that coalition, the suggestion of chronic conflict, the prevailing mood of anger, the affective withdrawal and/or extrusion of the daughter, and the ineffectiveness of family problem-solving. The family appeared rigid in structure with little evidence of adaptive flexibility. However, despite the family's pain and despair, their conversation was clear; it was easy to understand the meaning of their communications, even the nonverbal ones.

This interactional view is no more the whole picture of the Jaspers than were the brief individual descriptions. It does suggest the type of data given attention in this conceptual stance. To focus on the *process* of family communication complements the insights gained through individual evaluation. Each adds depth to the clinical understanding. This point needs emphasis because it is tempting to assume a singular conceptual stance and focus only on data that confirm our initial hypotheses. At the level of clinical intervention, this is somewhat analogous to what, in a different context, Havens described as the mad surgeon who takes out each patient's gallbladder regardless of the nature of the illness (1). It is, then, with the central construct of the need to consider multiple etiologic systems—biologic, developmental, intrapsychic, family, social, and cultural—that this paper approaches the family in the matrix of health and illness.

Overview of the Systems Approach to the Family

The literature regarding family systems is extensive, and no attempt will be made to review it. The focus will be on several trends that seem important to the writer. The initial research activity that appeared to excite many professionals centered on the reports of three groups working in the area of schizophrenia. Bateson and the Palo Alto group (2), Lidz and his group at Yale (3), and Wynne and Singer at the National Institute of Mental Health (4, 5) were working in the area of communication deviance. The work of these three groups suggested that communication in families containing a schizophrenic member involved idiosyncratic processes and meanings that were specifically related to the schizophrenic member's thought disturbance. Although part of the excitement generated by this work was related to its new conceptual base, the family, some of it appears to derive from the idea of specificity, e.g., that a specific deviance in family communication was involved in the etiology of a member's specific psychopathologic syndrome, schizophrenia. Although Lidz, in particular, stressed that such families revealed severe disturbances in *all* areas of family life (6), the response of many to the research of these three groups was the hope of discovering a simple, linear, direct, causal relationship that, in turn, would lead to effective treatment. Such hopeful excitement seems to reappear repeatedly in the development of both biologic and psychologic systems of understanding and intervening in psychiatric disorders.

The work of early family therapy pioneers such as Ackerman (7) and Bowen (8) added to the stirring interest, and family systems and family therapy became for some a revolution that displaced or minimized the insights obtained from biologic and developmental perspectives.

The movement of family systems research into the more rigorous confines of clinical research, however, brought with it increasing difficulty. Often the exciting insights derived from the earlier and more naturalistic research could not be translated into measurable processes without reducing the earlier concepts to a shadow of their original brilliance. The selection of families for controlled research brought investigators face to face with the uncertain reliability of individual diagnosis. Nowhere was this clearer than in the area of schizophrenia. It appeared necessary to separate index patients with schizophrenia into two groups, the process and reactive, or poor and good prognosis groups. Significant differences in family variables were found for these two groups (9). Singer and Wynne suggested that two forms of family communication disturbance were distinct, and they termed these "amorphous" and "fragmented" (10, 11).

Research moved in other directions, but most often the basis for grouping families remained the diagnosis of an individual family member. Families containing patients with neurotic, depressed, delinquent, or psychosomatic disturbances were compared with those whose members had other diagnoses, or had members for whom no clearly diagnosable psychiatric disorder was apparent. Although differences between the groups were often apparent, the interpretation of such differences was clouded by the selection process, the failure to demonstrate homogeneity within groups (including families usually selected as controls) (12), and the need to consider that some of the families' differences were responsive to the presence of a patient in the family.

The increased complexity of this research has resulted in some waning of the initial excitement. The idea that family interactions in themselves were sufficient to account for individual psychiatric dysfunction has been tempered by hypotheses that include two or more etiologic systems. Reiss, for example, has emphasized that, with few exceptions, family systems researchers have not integrated their findings with nonfamily variables that almost certainly are involved in the etiology of schizophrenia (13).

Other promising developments come from the study of high risk families and the study of groups of families over considerable periods of time. The longitudinal approach is illustrated by the work of Baumrind (14), who is exploring the effects of different patterns of parental authority on the development of instrumental competence in children. This type of research involves variables from two perspectives: 1) the child's *developmental* tasks and 2) the nature of the *family* interactions which provide the context in which those tasks are approached. French, from a clinical framework, emphasizes the need for the clinician to attend to multiple systems—the pre-operational thought of the young child, for example, and the nature of the family processes (15).

One aspect of the work of Goldstein and Rodnick exemplifies the study of families at high risk for the development of schizophrenia in a family member (16). Using the deviations in parental communication studied by Wynne and Singer, they have demonstrated that high risk families can be identified prior to the onset of severe psychopathology in the child. Their follow-up evaluations are proceeding at five-year intervals. This type of study avoids many of the difficulties involved in selecting families containing an already identified patient.

Goldstein and Rodnick, in their review of the family's contribution to schizophrenia, state that there seems to be a statistical relationship between disordered family relationships and the presence of schizophrenia, but that it is not clear whether the relationship is specific for schizophrenia as contrasted with other psychiatric disorders (16).

Although the research trends have had an impact upon the practice of family therapy (indeed, many of the researchers were family therapists), the field of family therapy has grown much more rapidly, and many of its practitioners appear to be little influenced by the findings from more rigorous and controlled research. For some, family therapy appears to have sufficient power to be the preferred treatment for all psychiatric syndromes—as if the insights and interventions derived from biologic, developmental, and other systems soon will be unnecessary. Many factors appear to nourish this optimism. By and large, family therapists disallow the importance of insight as a process crucial to change, stress the importance of the here-and-now, focus on the family as the sick organism and the individually identified patient as only one symptom of the family's sickness, and are optimistic about the capacity for change in basic family relationship patterns. Often the role of the family therapist is aggressive, attacking, and manipulative—a behavioral pattern both alien and offensive to most clinicians trained in individual psychotherapy. As a consequence, collaborative efforts between the two groups of therapists are few, and data-based guidelines regarding the indications and contraindications for family therapy are difficult to evolve.

Of course, both outcome evaluation and process research are needed. Gurman and Kniskern have studied over 200 reports of the outcome of family and marital therapy in which treatment was focused explicitly on altering interactions of family members (17).

Several particularly pertinent findings emerge. They divided the studies into 1) those reporting gross improvement rates, 2) comparative studies, and 3) studies with control groups. In the gross improvement rate studies, 60 to 75 percent of the couples were seen as improved from therapy, and deterioration was seen in 5 to 10 percent of the cases. Deterioration occurred far more often in marital therapy (11.6 percent) than it did in family therapy (5.6 percent).

In their review of comparative studies, Gurman and Kniskern reported that marital therapy was demonstrated to be so superior to individual therapy for marital problems as to make individual therapy of questionable value in that situation. Family therapy appears to be equal or superior to all other forms of treatment for individuals and families with problems involving family living.

In the controlled studies, marital and family therapies were superior to no-treatment controls in 18 studies. In 11 studies there were no differences, and in two studies marital and family therapies resulted in worsening of the situations as contrasted with the control groups. Despite broad differences in the quality of study design, solid trends are revealed. The results from the gross improvement rate studies and the comparative and controlled studies are consistent: Marital and family therapies have considerable potency and, in some instances, their results compare favorably to those seen in individual therapy. Many questions, of course, remain. For example, are these therapies equally effective with severely disturbed, moderately disturbed, and mildly disturbed families? Can the striking results of Minuchin and his group in the areas of bronchial asthma, anorexia nervosa, and labile diabetes (18) be replicated? Can gains be made in the identification of crucial therapeutic processes involved in successful family therapy? We must await future outcome and process research. For purposes of this report, it appears important to emphasize that in these two related fields—family systems research and family therapy—we have entered into the era of more rigorous design and assessment. There appears little doubt that family interactions can, in some cases, provide considerable explanatory power and that, in some instances, family or marital therapy may be the treatment of choice.

As in other branches of science, however, we must continuously appraise our models and, when they are no longer as useful as others, modify or discard them. In considering the family in the matrix of health and illness, I wish to propose a model of family competence constructed from research data that lends itself readily to a consideration of the role of biologic and developmental variables. This model proposes that families can be distinguished by their general or overall level of functioning, and that this global measure may play a role in determining the susceptibility of family members to both physical and mental illness. The model suggests that, at any given level of family functioning, there may be specific patterns of family organization, communication, and conflict which predispose to specific illnesses in family members. An initial or sole focus on the search for specific patterns may be obscured by the impact of the family's general level of functioning on susceptibility to a wide range of disturbances. Indeed, the model proposes that often nonfamily biologic, developmental, and cultural variables play a decisive role in the nature of the specific disorder developed.

The Continuum of Family Competence

This method of family assessment searches for quantitative differences between families who differ widely in their overall levels of competence. It presumes that there are certain basic tasks facing families; some do them well, and others do them poorly. This model acknowledges that, in the selection of the basic tasks, value judgments are used. These must be explicit, and consideration must be given to those circumstances that render the value judgments unusable. In our research, we accept the concept that the family is first a survival system—a mechanism for insuring the actual physical survival of its members (12). If actual physical survival is a daily family task, we presume that certain patterns of organization and communication will work better than others. In other words, there would be an optimal family structure for that context.

Our completed research has involved us, however, with families for whom daily survival was not a central task. We have studied families for whom favorable socioeconomic realities appeared secure. In these middle- and upper-middle-class families, we assumed that the two central tasks are the maturation and stabilization of the parental personalities and the production of autonomous children. Although these two tasks find wide acceptance as critical functions of the family, obviously they are dependent upon historical and cultural influences. In the population we studied, it was the extent to which a given family accomplished these two tasks that determined its level of competence. Certain patterns of interactions were associated with an optimal level of competence, whereas other patterns were correlated with failure to accomplish one or both tasks. Families were rated first at an overall level (global health—pathology) and then on continua describing more specific variables. For example, the optimal families were characterized by clear structure with flexibility, dysfunctional families by clear but rigid structures, and severely dysfunctional families by unclear structure. Therefore, one continuum (overt power) ranges from flexibility to rigidity to chaos.

Structure and other variables are measured by the use of five-point rating scales, the Beavers-Timberlawn Family Rating Scales, for which adequate reliability measures were established (12). They are used by trained raters who watch 10 to 50-minute segments of videotaped family testing in which families are presented with verbal problems to solve. (The rating scales may also be used in the assessment of the family in the clinician's office.) The variables themselves arise from a theoretical framework articulated by my colleague, W. Robert Beavers (12). After describing the variables found to be useful in the assessment of families across the continuum of competence and describing representative families, we can look at the nature of individual psychopathology, if any, in famliy members at a given level.

Interactional Variables Associated with Family Competence*

The rating scale variables occupy a point midway between the often rich insights of the skilled clinician observing a family and the detailed, micro-analytic counting techniques in which each

---

* See appendix for rating scales.

communication sequence is evaluated from many perspectives. The level of assessment represented by the rating scale has some of the richness of the clinical level along with quantification, which is the merit of the micro-analytic techniques.

1) *Overt Power* is one of three variables that measure the structure of the family. It is concerned with issues of leadership, authority, control, and interpersonal influence. The scale itself ranges from chaos, to degrees of dominance, to a leadership pattern, to shared leadership.

2) The *Parental Coalition* scale assesses the nature of the parental relationship in terms of the apparent strength or weakness of that coalition. It involves both the instrumental and the affective components of the relationship.

3) The *Closeness* scale is based on the concept that one must be separate to be close. It combines the appraisal of two variables: (a) separateness or individual boundaries; and (b) interpersonal distance. The scale ranges from those families with distinct boundaries and high levels of closeness, to those with distinct boundaries and great interpersonal distance, to those families with vague and indistinct boundaries among members.

4) *Family Mythology* assesses the congruence between a family member's family image and the rater's appraisal of the family. Obviously complex, it reflects the observable level of validation or the shared denial within the family.

5) *Goal-Directed Negotiation* refers to the ways in which a family solves problems. Efficient negotiation involves the exploration of each member's opinions and feelings, the search for a consensus, or the ability to compromise. For example, a family would not be efficient if a single member quickly solved a family problem, because this process would eliminate the opportunity for the negotiation of a shared solution, thus eliminating consideration of the contributions of all other members of the family group.

6) *Clarity of Expression* is one of four variables related theoretically to the development of autonomy in family members. It ranges from communications that are very clear to those in which hardly anyone is ever clear.

7) *Responsibility* involves the degree to which the family system

encourages members to accept the responsibility for individual actions, feelings, and thoughts. Raters using this scale become sensitive to the tendency in some families to deny and project responsibility.

8) *Invasiveness* involves rating the family regarding the number of intrusive statements. Intrusions, invasions, or "mind reading" involve one person's telling (not asking) another family member what that other member thinks or feels. When this interactional process occurs, it is very detrimental to the developing autonomy of children. It rarely, if ever, occurs in healthy families, but may be pervasive in the most severely dysfunctional.

9) *Permeability* involves the degree to which the family acknowledges the messages from all family members. Such acknowledgments may be verbal or nonverbal, and families range from those that are very open and responsive to such communications to those where communications fall on deaf ears.

10) *Range of Feelings* rates aspects of the breadth of a family's affective system. It measures the degree to which the family encourages or tolerates the expression of feelings of all kinds.

11) The *Mood and Tone* scale measures the quality of what can be called the family's basic mood. Unless a family is under stress, it has a characteristic affective tone or temperament. This may range from warm, affectionate, and optimistic, to polite, to hostile, to depressed, to pessimistic or hopeless.

12) The *Unresolvable Conflict* scale reflects the impact of conflict on the problem-solving capacity of the family, that is, the observer's judgment about whether or not—or to what degree—the family appears unable to resolve conflict.

13) The *Empathy* scale measures the degree to which the family responds to family members' feelings with understanding. ("I know what it's like to be mad, to be sad, or to be glad.") The observer is asked to rate the degree to which the family system is sensitive to communication of feelings.

14) The *Global Health-Pathology* scale measures the family's overall level of competence or, in earlier language, health or pathology.

In one study involving 70 families containing an identified adolescent patient and 33 research volunteer families, there were highly significant correlations between each of the 13 interactional scales and independent ratings of global family competence. These Spearman correlations ranged from 0.30 to 0.79, and the sum of the scales correlated 0.90. Each of the correlations was significant at a probability level of $< .005$ (12).

There was also a significant correlation between the family global competence ratings and an independent measure of the identified adolescent patient's level of psychopathology (Pearson $r =$ p. 52, $p < .005$) (12). This correlation is particularly significant when one considers that the measure of global family health or pathology is a here-and-now measure and does not directly tap biologic and developmental determinants of adolescent psychopathology.

Families at Different Levels of Competence

The following brief descriptions of typical families convey something of the quality of family life at different points on the continuum of family competence. The data for the descriptions were obtained by using both research and clinical methods, including family system testing, exploratory family interviews, home visits and individual exploratory interviews, and psychological testing of family members.

Optimal Families

These families may vary widely in style, but their relationship patterns and ways of communicating add weight to Tolstoy's observation that happy families are much alike (19). The parents have been married 20 years and have evolved a relationship in which power is shared. Each sees the other as competent, and leadership in the family is shared. Either parent is capable of providing leadership. The parents have achieved high levels of psychological intimacy; these husbands and wives repeatedly mentioned the ability to "talk about anything." There seemed to be an unusually affectionate bond, high levels of sexual satisfaction, and highly evolved individuality. Differences were respected; ego boundaries were clear and associated with high levels of closeness.

As might be anticipated, there were no competing coalitions. Relationships with their own parents or friends were most often warm and satisfying, but they did not have the intensity of the marital relationship. There was an absence of emotionally charged father-daughter or mother-son coalitions within the family; nothing suggested unusually charged or powerful coalitions that competed with the marital relationship.

The families were close, yet the children were individuals in their own ways. The family appraised their strengths in much the same way that observers did. In striving to understand their good fortune, each parent assigned the major responsibility to the other.

These families relied often on negotiation as an approach to problems or conflicts, and they were efficient in its use. They were clear in their communication, despite high levels of spontaneity. Family members took responsibility for thoughts and actions, and the system as a whole had high levels of permeability. Invasions were rare.

Optimal families expressed a wide range of feelings. There were high levels of empathy and nothing to suggest unresolvable conflict. The basic family mood was warm, affectionate, humorous, and optimistic.

The studies of the individuals who comprise these families strongly suggest high levels of psychological maturity. The fathers were successful in their vocations, indicated that major satisfactions came from being mentors to younger people, and worked hard and for long hours. They had, however, something left over for their families. As a group they were persons who liked structure and organization and yet could play. They were not remote or detached. In Vaillant's hierarchy of ego defenses, they used both neurotic and mature defenses (20). Most drank moderately; none used tranquilizers or sedatives; and they shared high levels of physical health.

The wives in these families showed comparable levels of psychological maturity. Most of them were full-time in the home; only a few were employed. They found major satisfactions within their marriages and families, but many had extensive interests outside the home. They were warm, open women. They described themselves as most fortunate in their choices of mates. Although many of these couples were very "physical" in the sense of high levels of sexual activity, others were less active sexually. Regardless, however, of the frequency of sexual intercourse, the wives reported being orgastic and having high levels of satisfaction.

The children were accomplishing age-appropriate developmental tasks in cognitive, social, and intrapsychic realms. As a group they were friendly, open, active, often athletic, and in both interviews and testing were seen as healthy. A striking finding in this group of families was the impact of birth order. Older children, regardless of gender, tended to more self-discipline and productivity, and younger children, regardless of gender, were more apt to be less self-disciplined but more expressive and openly affectionate. This finding is in contrast with that in less well-functioning families in which these characteristics were more closely related to gender than birth order.

These family systems appeared to offer family members a high level of emotional support and, at the same time, encourage individuality and autonomy. They are rarely, if ever, seen in clinical practice, and their very existence as a group is often doubted by mental health professionals who usually experience intimately only their families of origin, their here-and-now families, and families in trouble who seek their professional services. As a group, these families tell us something about what, under favorable circumstances, is possible in family life.

Competent But Pained Families

These families are less well adapted than the optimal or healthy families, but are significantly different from clearly dysfunctional families. The distinguishing characteristic of such a family is the failure of the parental marriage to meet the wife's emotional needs. She experiences herself as emotionally deprived as a result of her husband's affective unavailability. "I never know what he is feeling," and "He is not interested in my feelings," are common complaints.

To observers, these women appeared sour and angry. As a group they tended to be obese, had frequent physical complaints, saw their physicians often, and were apt to be receiving antianxiety agents. Often they formed an intense coalition with a child, parent, or friend who appeared to function as an ally.

The husbands appeared much as described by these unhappy women. Although as successful vocationally as husbands in optimal families, they were more detached, less open with feelings, and tended to see interpersonal relationships as less rewarding than instrumental accomplishments. They recognized their wives' unhappiness, but did not accept responsibility for much, if any, of it. Rather, they focused on how difficult their wives were to be with. "She's always complaining, has let herself go physically, and only wants to talk about problems," is a typical statement.

As is apparent, each spouse is able to see only the other's role in their shared failure to achieve intimacy. As a consequence, their relationship appears stalemated, and there is an undercurrent of hostility. Despite this flaw in their marriages, these couples have high levels of involvement with their children and are committed to the importance of the family.

In most of these families, one parent tends to be moderately dominant. There is no clear pattern of shared leadership. The wives often have a coalition with one child. Ego boundaries are distinct, but there is not the degree of closeness seen in optimal families. Members of competent but pained families most often accurately assess the assets and liabilities of their families. There is some tendency to scapegoat externally—"We have some problems, but they're nothing compared to our neighbors," is a typical example.

These families often have good negotiating skills and are efficient problem-solvers if the problems are external and do not impinge too directly on the marital pain.

They encourage autonomy by high levels of expressive clarity, reasonable permeability to each other, and general acceptance of responsibility for individual behavior.

In the family affective system there is some restriction in the range of feelings expressed. It is as if the family gingerly skirts some intense affects—perhaps to avoid touching on the pain of the parents' relationship. Although warmth and caring (particularly of the children) are obvious, there is less humor and joy. Empathy is present to a moderate degree. Parental conflict is subdued, but its impact on the family is obvious. However, many family strengths and the parents' shared commitments to the importance of their parenting task preclude any serious splitting of the family unit. In many ways, these families just miss higher levels of competence. The wives seem to accept their unhappy adaptations, yet none was an identified patient. Clearer understanding of this process, however, awaits the results of follow-up studies now in progress.

The children appear healthy. They are achieving appropriate developmental milestones and function well socially and educationally. None is symptomatic. In fact, raters cannot distinguish them from the children from optimal families on the basis of independent readings of interview transcripts and MMPI responses, a circumstance suggesting that it does not require an optimal family to produce healthy children.

Dysfunctional Families

We observed two patterns of family organization among the dysfunctional families: the dominant-submissive and the conflicted. Both patterns are characterized by rigidity; there is a fixed, "is now, was then, and ever will be" quality to family life.

The dominant-submissive pattern is one in which one parent dominates and controls every aspect of family life. His or her dominance may be accepted fairly passively, or it may be circumvented by acting-out behavior, most often outside the home.

Although both parents demonstrated clear individual ego boundaries, the parental coalitions were strained by the gross inequality in parental power. Whether or not the submissive spouse was openly resentful, there was little closeness or intimacy. Indeed, family members were distant with each other. The exceptions most frequently involved a coalition between either the submissive spouse and a child or two of the children. Those coalitions, although providing some closeness, were oppositional in the sense that they were against the dominant parent.

Often these families see their situation as normal, and they explain any difficulty by blaming a person or condition outside the family, or scapegoating one family member who is blamed for everything that is wrong with life in the family.

These families do not negotiate. The dominant parent makes every decision, paying little, if any, attention to the opinions and feelings of others. They blame others rather than accept responsibility. Their communications were clear, but they are relatively impermeable to each other. Although the dominant parent may presume to "mind read" other family members, such invasions do not reach the frequency and intensity seen in severely dysfunctional families.

The expression of feelings was often masked (particularly in the presence of the dominant parent); the pervasive family mood was either hostile or sad; there was little to suggest that empathy is valued or used; and the conflict, however muted, was omnipresent.

This family pattern may be seen occasionally in research volunteer families in which there is no identified patient. The pattern, however, is frequently seen in the families of psychiatric patients. Clinical experience suggests that it is a common pattern in the families of hospitalized adolescents. The patient's symptomatology is most often one of three types: 1) the severe neurotic adolescent with, for example, an incapacitating phobic or compulsive syndrome; 2) the adolescent with a serious behavior disturbance with rebelliousness and acting-out against authority; or 3) the adolescent with acute reactive psychosis. Often the identified patient and the submissive parent are involved in a coalition against the dominant parent.

Although either parent may present as an identified patient, clinical experience suggests that it is more likely to be the submissive parent. Depression is common.

The second type of dysfunctional family is the chronically conflicted one. In this pattern of family organization, the parents constantly war with each other. Each parent seeks to dominate the other; neither will share power, and neither is willing to accept a submissive role. They maintain the struggle by any technique, device, or manipulation. The children are sucked into the conflict, sometimes in stable coalitions with one parent, but often in brief, transient coalitions, first with one parent, then the other. Although individual boundaries are clear, there is neither closeness nor trust.

Despite the endless conflict, many such families deny difficulty—often by relying on both internal and external scapegoating. They cannot negotiate because each problem precipitates another round of conflict. The parents, having never worked out an acceptable answer to the question, "Who has the right to decide what?" cannot work together, and children do not learn to solve problems.

These families communicate with moderate clarity, are often impermeable to each other, and avoid responsibility by reliance on blaming. Hostile, attacking feelings are expressed, but most other feelings cannot be expressed, and empathy is not seen. The family mood is hostile, and the conflict appears endless.

Such families may volunteer as controls in family research, and some contain no identified patient. The pattern is seen frequently, however, in families containing a disturbed adolescent. Most often the identified patient is a person with a character or personality disorder in which intimacy is avoided, others are to be used and manipulated, and there is much well-defended sadness and emptiness. Adolescents with reactive pyschoses are sometimes seen in such families.

These two forms of dysfunctional families are common in clinical practice. Although both types may vary in intensity of dysfunction, the patterns seem rigidly fixed. There is, however, nothing bizarre about them. Family members do not appear chronically psychotic; the meaning of family communications is usually clear to the clinician. They seem, in many ways, to be similar to some of the families termed "skewed" or "schismatic" by Lidz, Cornelison, Fleck, and Terry (6), although they describe blurring of individual boundaries in some such families. These families also appear similar to the families of "good prognosis" schizophrenics described by Mishler and Waxler (9) and to the "depressive position" families in which Skynner (21) found whole-object relationships, containment of ambivalence rather than splitting, the greater differentiation of self than found in more primitive families.

It is tempting to generalize and suggest that in dysfunctional families the parents' attempts to solve the issue of their power or influence led to relinquishment of any hope of closeness or intimacy. As a consequence, regardless of whether or not family members experience a diagnosable psychiatric disorder, many are limited in their capacities for relating. Thus they fail to achieve the emotional strength available to those more fortunate individuals who spend their lives in families sustained by closeness and intimacy.

Severely Dysfunctional Families

At the levels of least competence are those families who neither support maturation and growth for the parents nor encourage autonomy in the children. Families at this level of dysfunction reveal one of two patterns. The first is a pattern dominated by the influence of one parent and in which that parent's view of the world is idiosyncratic. The dominant parent is often psychotic or borderline. As a consequence, there is considerable clouding of meaning and high levels of invasiveness. In other ways, such families show many of the characteristics of the dominant-submissive dysfunctional family. This pattern of severely dysfunctional families is much like the families described by Lidz and co-workers (6) as "skewed."

The second pattern is the chaotic family. No member has enough influence to provide leadership. The family demonstrates amorphous or vague and indistinct boundaries between members. Bowen has described this as the "amorphous ego mass" (8). As a consequence, it is often difficult for the clinician to know the meaning of family communication. When presented with problems, the family tends to avoid, deny, and only rarely come to closure and solve problems. Expressive clarity is low, invasions common, and members are frequently unreceptive to each other. There is a cynical or hopeless family mood; feelings are avoided; fusion of individual members obscures conflict.

These chaotic families often appear strange and bizarre to others. They do not relate to the surrounding world, and often the only real connections are to the parents' families of origin. Clumped together, they drift in a world of meaning all their own. Obtaining an individual sense of selfhood is terribly difficult in such a system.

These families attracted the attention of early researchers in the area of family approach to schizophrenia. They are seen as "pseudomutual" (22), "enmeshed" (23), and "poor prognosis" (9). Skynner describes them as occupying the paranoid/schizoid oral position of family organization (21). He sees them as characterized by part-object relationships, splitting, projection, and confusion over boundaries.

In contrast to dysfunctional families, these severely dysfunctional families are relatively rare in clinical practice. They are not found in research volunteer populations and, when seen clinically, are noted to contain one or more members with schizophrenic illnesses (often with many process features) or persons with severe borderline syndromes.

This conceptualization of the continuum of family competence and the description of the characteristics of families occupying points on the continuum have clinical usefulness. They offer the clinician a way of organizing observations in order to evaluate a family's structure and competence. However, one should bear in mind that when an individual or family comes to a clinician it is often a time of stress for the family. Whether the stress is illness within the family, loss of a loved one, economic deprivation, or the challenge of a family developmental stage (for example, children leaving home), the family as a system will undergo change. It becomes important, therefore, for the clinician to distinguish the family's basic patterns from its response to stress. Anthony is among those who have described the family's response to stress (24). He suggests that there is a change from a pattern of clear structure with flexibility to rigid patterns of relating and responding. If the stress is not dealt with, the organization may disintegrate to chaos, with the family drifting aimlessly like a ship without a rudder. Anthony's description of the movement from flexibility to rigidity to chaos observed in the families he studied parallels the structural patterns described in the continuum of competence and adds weight to the validity and clinical usefulness of the concept.

Areas for Future Research

The Role of the Family in Individual Patienthood

Although most professionals acknowledge the role of multiple variables in the determination of individual psychiatric illness, much of the research exploring the interactions between variables attends to one group of variables (e.g., the developmental pathology) with precision and sophistication, while attending to other groups of variables (e.g., the family system) with a much more primitive technology. It is like looking at one variable under a high-power microscope and the other with the naked eye. In response to this dilemma, Reiss and Wyatt (25) have suggested a format for research in schizophrenia that includes both biologic and family variables that are theoretically related to the schizophrenic disorder in the individual family member.

This cogent call for precision in the measurement of family variables must, however, take into consideration the evidence that a family's general level of competence may predispose to a variety of psychopathological syndromes in family members. If, for example, families containing reactive schizophrenic adolescents demonstrate parental relationships that are markedly skewed in the direction of one parent's dominance, that pattern cannot be assumed to be specific for schizophrenia unless it is absent in comparably dysfunctional families containing, for example, a child with a severe psychosomatic disorder. There are many similarities in family patterns reported to be specific for families containing members with different psychiatric syndromes. It is likely that many of these observations confuse findings that describe the family's general level of functioning with variables thought to be specific for a particular psychiatric disorder in some families, but a systems approach suggests that nonfamily variables may play the decisive role in determining the nature of psychopathology in other instances.

It is with these distinctions in mind that I suggest that an initial evaluation of the general competence of the family may assist in developing answers to three basic questions: 1) Will psychiatric disorders develop in any members of a family? 2) In which member or members of a family are psychiatric disorders most likely to develop? 3) What psychiatric disorders will develop in members of a family?

1) Whether any members of a family experience a psychiatric disorder is, of course, a complex issue. On the average, however, individuals with strong support systems of all types have protection from the development of serious psychiatric illness. The protection is not complete, of course, for other variables (genetic, developmental, etc.) may create such vulnerability that living in a competent family is not sufficient. Longitudinal research studying the in-

dividual health of family members from a wide range of family competence is needed.

It is extremely important not to assume that families which contain no identifiable psychiatric patients are equally competent and supportive. Our work suggests that research volunteer families screened for significant individual psychopathology show much variation (12). The assumption that they are both homogeneous and normal and can, therefore, be used as controls with which to contrast families containing psychiatric patients will obscure differences between competent or healthy families and those with serious levels of dysfunction. This is a critical issue, for example, in the interpretation of the adoptive studies in research on schizophrenia. It is important to remember that children of schizophrenic parents who are placed in adoptive families are placed in family systems that may range from competent to significantly dysfunctional.

Our data suggest a direct relationship between the competence of the family and the presence and severity of individual psychopathology. The Pearsonian correlation in one sample was 0.52 ($p < .005$). What appears needed are longitudinal studies of large numbers of families of varying degrees of competence to establish firmly the relationship between the role of the family as a support system and the development of individual psychopathology. Once this issue is clearly resolved, a number of crucial questions should result. For example, is a particular parental communication style the specific factor in severely dysfunctional families that accounts for the development of schizophrenia rather than other severe psychopathology in a child? Does severe individual psychopathology (e.g., schizophrenia or a severe borderline syndrome) develop through genetic, developmental, or other influences in individuals from competent families? How do families at varying levels of competence deal with the presence of severe illness in a family member? These and other questions await answers.

2) The question as to which family member is most likely to become a patient also points the way to future research. Nonfamily factors can often be decisive. Genetic factors, temperament, or developmental trauma can play the crucial role in the development of psychiatric disorders in a member of the family. Sometimes, how-

ever, family interactional variables may be involved in the "selection" of a patient. The most common hypothesis is that one family member is "selected" or "volunteers" for the sick role. The establishment of this role and its capacity to occupy the family's attention are presumed to divert attention away from an even more serious problem (most often in the parental relationship). The scapegoated family member is seen, therefore, as part victim, but also noble in his or her sacrifice for the welfare of the family. The idea of assignment and acceptance of the sick role is an attractive clinical hypothesis. Direct proof is lacking, but there is clinical and anecdotal evidence to suggest that removing the scapegoat's illness may lead to further deterioration in the parental relationship and that, conversely, improving the parental relationship may ameliorate the scapegoat's symptoms.

Another approach to understanding why one particular family member develops a psychiatric disorder concerns the issue of the type and degree of connection individuals feel to a family—whether they feel more, or less, attached to the family. Moss (26) has suggested that individuals are attached to social systems in only a limited number of ways. These include: 1) the identified person for whom the social system is a major feature of the individual's identity and information-processing; 2) the alienated person for whom the social system no longer provides a meaningful sense of connection; 3) the autonomous person for whom the social system is important but not essential for identity and information-processing; and 4) the anomic person for whom the social system is incomprehensible (this results in a type of attachment with only marginal participation).

Family systems research needs to develop increasingly precise methods of measuring role assignments and styles of attachment. Clinical experience suggests the promise of these areas of research. An example is the stable but obsessive-compulsive person from a severely dysfunctional family in which all other members demonstrate overt thought disturbances. The obsessive-compulsive family member may have been assigned the stable, productive role early in life or may never have been as attached to his or her family as other family members. (Whereas being less attached to a competent family may contribute to psychopathology, a similar lack of attachment to a severely dysfunctional family may protect against severe psychiatric disturbance.) It appears reasonable to assume that in some instances family factors play a role in the development of a psychiatric disorder in a certain family member.

3) The final question involves the nature of the psychiatric disorder which develops in a family member. There is evidence that both family and nonfamily factors may play a role. Siblings may inherit different propensities for psychiatric disturbances. For example, not all children in a family with a genetic loading for schizophrenia may share equally in that vulnerability. It is also clear that critical early developmental experiences may vary tremendously in the children of a single family. One child may experience early interactions with a calm and secure mother, who, with a second child, may be significantly depressed because of the recent loss of one of her own parents.

In addition to these nonfamily variables, there may be specific types of family disturbances that significantly influence the nature of individual psychopathology within the family. One would look for studies that explored the role of such specific family variables in, for example, the etiology of schizophrenia. Here, the attention might be on the role of parental communication styles, family attentional mechanisms, or the establishment of individual boundaries. The design of such studies would have to take into consideration the facts that there is often more than one identified patient in the same family and that the patients frequently have dissimilar psychiatric disorders.

Although evidence is strong that family variables are involved in understanding whether a member of a family will develop a psychiatric disorder, which member is most vulnerable and what disorder will develop, it is equally clear that the attempt to answer these questions on the basis of family factors only is most often an oversimplification of complex events. Future family systems research must involve systems other than the family in the effort to understand the role of the family in the etiology of individual psychopathology.

The Family and Physical Illness

Another research area of considerable promise is the role of family factors in the development of physical illness in family members. Although time does not allow a full review of the literature which suggests the promise of this area, a few representative studies will be mentioned.

In an integrated, biopsychosocial model of illness (27), serious consideration is given to the psychosocial factors that contribute to the development of illness. The bulk of this work has involved individuals, and the focus has been the role of life change (28, 29, 30), life stress (31, 32, 33, 34, 35, 36), object loss (37, 38, 39, 40), or reactions to change, stress, and loss, as in the "giving-up—given-up" syndrome (41, 42). This exciting direction in psychosomatic research appears concerned primarily with the general susceptibility of individuals to all illness, rather than the earlier and narrower search for specific psychosocial variables associated with specific illnesses. However, most of the studies make no systematic attempt to evaluate the role of the family in altering susceptibility to illness.

There are reports which suggest that understanding the role of the family system in influencing family members' general susceptibility to all illness may complement the studies of individual psychosocial variables. Over 30 years ago, Richardson, an internist, wrote of the family as the *unit* of illness. He suggested that unusually rigid family systems increased family members' vulnerability to all illnesses and observed that, when faced with chronic illness or repetitive, acute illness, it is important for the physician to consider whether the illness can be understood best by considering the individual or the family as the unit of illness (43). In the early 1960s, Peachey and Kellner independently reported about family patterns of illness and the tendency for many families to experience illnesses in clusters followed by periods of no illnesses (44, 45). The clusters of illnesses were not comprised of illnesses for which a common pathogen was necessary.

In 1964, Dingle and co-workers published their findings from a public health study of 86 families over a ten-year period, which involved the assessment of 25,000 illnesses (46). This investigation did not include formal evaluation of family variables, but the authors noted the tendency for different families to have stable levels of illness. Some families had consistently high rates, and others consistently low ones. They concluded that, although they could not separate the effects of heredity and environment, it was apparent that the family unit was an important entity in understanding illness.

During the 1960s and early 1970s there were also attempts to search for specific family patterns associated with the classic psychosomatic diseases. Meissner made an attempt to formulate the psychosomatic process in families at both the level of the family affective system and the nature of the individual patient's psychopathology and attachment to the family (47). Jackson reported findings from families containing a patient with ulcerative colitis and suggested a specific family interactional pattern (48). Grolnick reviewed the literature and suggested a cluster of four or five family factors, including rigidity and difficulty with object loss, as being more or less specific for psychosomatic disturbances (49). These valuable studies appeared to search for specific family factors involved in the causation of specific diseases without attending to the more general role of family factors in influencing individual susceptibility to all diseases. What appeared specific for certain diseases may have been more closely correlated with susceptibility to all diseases.

Minuchin and his co-workers described an "open system" model of psychosomatic illness in children and reported exceptional results in a family approach to the treatment of children with labile diabetes, intractable asthma, and anorexia nervosa (18). Their model of a family with psychosomatic disturbances stressed that three factors are necessary for the development of severe psychosomatic illness in children: the presence of a psychologically vulnerable child; a family characterized by enmeshment, overprotectiveness, rigidity, and lack of conflict resolution; and the sick child's role in allowing the family to avoid facing other problems. This work is unusually rich and multifactorial, and it demonstrates logical connections between the characteristics of the model and the nature of the treatment interventions. It does not, however, attempt to investigate whether the family factors are specific to psychosomatic illness in children or are factors associated with high levels of all illnesses in family members. This is an important area for further investigation, in part because of the excellent therapeutic results.

Other writers have suggested the role of family factors in influencing susceptibility to illness. Moss has presented a theoretical system which offers many leads (26). Weakland has proposed that family interactions may be related to illness in several ways (50). These include influencing the course and outcome of a given illness, rather than its beginning. Another possible relationship is that certain family interactions may constitute conditions sufficient for the precipitation of a specific illness. The third possibility is that family interactions, while neither necessary nor sufficient, could act as a predisposing influence. Finally, Weakland suggests that some forms of family interaction may increase susceptibility to illness generally, with the specific illness that develops dependent on factors other than family interactions.

This area is a promising one for future research. Such efforts might do well to deal first with the possible role of family members' general susceptibility to all illnesses before proceeding to study specific patterns associated with specific illnesses. Our research found that families who could discuss death and dying in personal terms following an experimental stimulus subsequently reported fewer episodes of illness and more "all well" days than those families who could not (12). This prospective work is preliminary, utilizes a small, homogeneous sample, and requires replication with different and larger samples. The role of repetitive patterns of family interactions in influencing family members' susceptibility to all illnesses is a promising direction for future family research.

Interpersonal Psychopharmacology

The nature of group interactions may influence an individual's response to psychoactive agents. For example, if an individual is in a friendly group and having fun, a single cocktail may produce a pleasant glow. If the individual is drinking alone or is one of a sad and dispirited small group, the same amount of alcohol may only deepen the gloom. There are similar anecdotal reports about the use of marijuana. The questions these reports raise are whether or not being a part of certain types of group interactions influences an individual's response to psychotropic agents and, if so, what are the characteristics of the interaction that influence the response?

Animal studies suggest that the individual's response to psychotropic agents may be altered by the presence and structure of a group. Lasagna and McCann, for example, demonstrated that the LD_{50} of amphetamine for mice was profoundly influenced by whether the drug was administered to isolated mice or to mice crowded together (51). It took only one-seventh the amount of amphetamine under the crowded circumstances. Either phenobarbital or chlorpromazine protected against the increased lethality associated with crowding without, however, influencing the LD_{50} for isolated mice. Brown demonstrated that phenobarbital and pentobarbital in doses large enough to produce hypnosis in isolated mice resulted paradoxically in stimulation of spontaneous activity when mice are grouped together (52).

In humans, the impact of group or interpersonal factors on individual response to psychotropic agents can be studied by focusing on the doctor-patient relationship (as in the study of the placebo effect), by investigating the impact of the ward milieu on hospitalized psychiatric patients' responses to psychotropic agents, and by studying the ways in which family variables may influence family members' responses to psychotropic agents. Although there are studies in each of the three areas, often they have suffered because of the difficulty of identifying and measuring the characteristics of the group or interpersonal relationships. Family systems research offers the investigator an approach which, in part, meets these problems. There are numerous opportunities to focus research efforts in ways that may clarify the complex person-drug-context interactions, thus furthering our understanding of both response to and failure to respond to psychotropic drugs.

Studies of the impact of family variables on the response to psychotropic agents suggest that for some schizophrenic patients certain family variables may play an important role. One indirect approach measured the impact of family factors on relapse rates for schizophrenic patients, both with and without psychotropic drugs. Brown and his colleagues demonstrated that families who are over-involved with the patient in hostile and critical ways are associated with a 58 percent relapse rate, which contrasts with a 16 percent relapse rate in patients returning to families who are supportive and accepting (53, 54, 55). Sixty-six percent of patients on placebo relapsed after returning to hostile, over-involved families, but that relapse rate could be cut to 46 percent by the use of psychotropic medication. The relapse rate of patients returning to warm, supportive families (16 percent) was not influenced by the use of medication.

In replicating these studies, Vaughn and Leff (56) demonstrated additional important findings. The relapse rates for patients from the different types of families were not a function of the patients' level of behavioral disturbance, a circumstance which suggests that families with high levels of hostile, critical over-involvement were not primarily responding to greater behavioral disturbance in the schizophrenic family member. A second finding is that psychotropic drugs appeared more effective in preventing relapse if the amount of face-to-face contact between patient and family (high on negative emotions) was low. Finally, the inclusion of a control group of depressed patients demonstrated the same relationship between hostile, critical over-involvement and relapse. This finding suggests that the family variables correlated with relapse are not specific for schizophrenia but may be general or nonspecific factors that operate negatively with a variety of psychiatric disorders.

Cohen and co-workers took a more focused approach to the impact of family variables on the response to psychotropic medication (57). They demonstrated that schizophrenic patients from families low in conflict and tension showed significantly greater reduction in aggression in response to chlorpromazine than did patients from high tension and conflict families. This work suggests that schizophrenic patients from families in which conflict and tension are high and part of the family norm are less likely to respond to chlorpromazine with reduced aggression.

These studies should be considered suggestive; there are methodological problems as well as a variety of possible interpretations. They do point the way, however, to promising areas of research. Some of these are:

1) Is the impact of the family on the response to psychotropic medication a result of the broad factor of overall level of family competence? Do patients from severely dysfunctional families respond less well than patients from less disturbed families?

2) Is the impact of the family on the response to psychotropic medication a result of a specific family variable (e.g., level of conflict, level of empathy, or closeness)? Such a specific factor may operate regardless of the family's general level of competence.

3) Can the family's understanding of psychiatric illness influence the response to medication? Can the family's attitude about taking medications influence the response to psychotropic agents?

4) Can different family variables influence responsiveness to different psychotropic agents? If, for example, specific family variables influence the response to chlorpromazine, would the same or different variables be involved in that small percentage of manic-depressive patients who fail to respond to lithium?

5) Can the response of a family member to a psychotropic agent alter the family structural pattern? A family characterized by rigid structure might respond to a family member's psychiatric disorder by moving toward chaos. Would a clear and positive response of the patient's symptoms to a psychotropic agent reverse this alteration in family structure?

These questions are only representative. What is needed initially, of course, is the conclusive demonstration that family variables do influence the individual's responses to psychotropic agents. If that is accomplished (and there is much to suggest that it can be), there are a number of studies that will help us to explore in logical sequence the specific person-drug-context interactions.

Conclusion

In this paper, I have emphasized several aspects of the role of the family in health and illness. The first is that the clinician will often develop an incomplete understanding of psychopathology unless he or she attends the role of concurrent family interactions. At the same time, the hope that an individual's psychiatric disorder can be understood completely by attending only to family interactions will lead to an equally incomplete understanding.

A second point involves the concept of a quantitative approach to family competence. The level of family competence can be assessed by a consideration of a small number of interactional variables, and I suggest that such an approach has clinical utility.

A third point is that family interactions and the level of family competence should be considered as only one of a number of factors involved in the determination of the general susceptibility of family members to all illnesses—both physical and mental. The search for specific family variables involved in the etiology of discrete psychopathological states should not confuse those factors with the variables involved in determining general susceptibility.

Finally, I have noted a few of the many research areas that appear to contain great promise.

The family has come in for its share of justifiable criticism aimed at the institutions of our culture. Too many people, for example, are deprived of a family. However, those who cry that the family is dying have neither studied competent families nor adequately considered the role of the family in the maintenance of health. We are only beginning to understand the ways in which family dysfunction can make life a living hell. At the same time, we are only starting to understand the ways in which the family contributes both to health and to the meaning of life.

REFERENCES

1. HAVENS, L. L.: *Approaches to the Mind: Movement of the Psychiatric Schools From Sects Toward Science.* Boston: Little, Brown & Co., 1973.
2. BATESON, G., JACKSON, D. D., HALEY, J., and WEAKLAND, J.: Toward a theory of schizophrenia. *Behav. Science,* 1:251-264, 1958.
3. LIDZ, T., CORNELISON, A., TERRY, D., and FLECK, S.: Intrafamilial environment and the schizophrenic patient: VI. The transmission of irrationality. *Arch. Neurol. Psychiat.,* 79:305-316, 1958.
4. WYNNE, L. C. and SINGER, M. T.: Thought disorder and family relations of schizophrenics: I. A research study. *Arch. of Gen. Psychiat.,* 9:191-198, 1963.
5. WYNNE, L. C. and SINGER, M. T.: Thought disorder and family relations of schizophrenics: II. A classification of forms of thinking. *Arch. Gen. Psychiat.,* 9:199-206, 1963.

6. LIDZ, T., CORNELISON, A., FLECK, S., and TERRY, D.: The intrafamilial environment of schizophrenic patients: II. Marital schism and marital skew. *Am. J. Psychiat.*, 114:241-248, 1957.
7. ACKERMAN, N. W.: *The Psychodynamics of Family Life.* New York: Basic Books, 1958.
8. BOWEN, MURRAY: Family relationships in schizophrenia. In: A. Auerback (Ed.), *Schizophrenia—An Integrated Approach.* New York: Ronald Press, 1959.
9. MISHLER, E. and WAXLER, N.: *Interaction in Families.* New York: John Wiley & Sons, 1968.
10. SINGER, M. T. and WYNNE, L. C.: Thought disorder and family relations of schizophrenics: III. Methodology using projective techniques. *Arch. Gen. Psychiat.*, 12:18, 1965.
11. SINGER, M. T. and WYNNE, L. C.: Thought disorder and family relations of schizophrenics: IV. Results and implications. *Arch. Gen. Psychiat.*, 12:201-212, 1965.
12. LEWIS, J. M., BEAVERS, W. R., GOSSETT, JOHN T., and PHILLIPS, V. A.: *No Single Thread: Psychological Health in Family Systems.* New York: Brunner/Mazel, 1976.
13. REISS, D.: Families and the etiology of schizophrenia. Fishing without a net. *Schizophrenia Bulletin,* No. 14, 8-11, Fall, 1975.
14. BAUMRIND, D.: The contributions of the family to the development of competence in children. *Schizophrenia Bulletin,* No. 14, 12-37, Fall, 1975.
15. FRENCH, A.: *Disturbed Children and Their Families.* New York: Human Sciences Press, 1977.
16. GOLDSTEIN, M. J. and RODNICK, E. H.: The family's contribution to the etiology of schizophrenia; Current status. *Schizophrenia Bulletin,* No. 14, 48-63, Fall, 1975.
17. GURMAN, A. J. and KNISKERN, D. P.: Research on marital and family therapy: Perspective and prospect. In: S. L. Garfield and A. E. Bergin (Eds.), *Handbook of Psychotherapy and Behavior Change: Empirical Analysis* (2nd Ed.). New York: John Wiley & Sons, 1978.
18. MINUCHIN, M., BAKER, L., ROSMAN, B. L., LIEBMAN, R., MILMAN, L., and TODD, T. C.: A conceptual model of psychosomatic illness in children. *Arch. Gen. Psychiat.*, 32:1031-1038, Aug., 1975.
19. TOLSTOY, L.: *Anna Karenina,* Part I, Ch. I. New York: The Modern Library, p. 3, translated by Northan Haskell Dole.
20. VAILLANT, G. E.: Theoretical hierarchy of adaptive ego mechanisms. *Arch. Gen. Psychiat.*, 24:107-118, 1971.
21. SKYNNER, A. C. R.: *Systems of Marital and Family Psychotherapy.* New York: Brunner/Mazel, 1976.
22. WYNNE, L. C., RYCKOFF, I. M., DAY, J., and HIRSCH, S. I.: Pseudomutuality in family relations of schizophrenics. *Psychiatry,* 21: 205-220, 1958.
23. MINUCHIN, S.: *Families and Family Therapy.* Cambridge, Mass.: Harvard University Press, 1974.

24. ANTHONY, E. J.: The impact of mental and physical illness on family life. *Am. J. Psychiat.*, 127:138-146, 1970.
25. REISS, D. and WYATT, R. J.: Family and biologic variables in the same etiologic studies of schizophrenia: A proposal. *Schizophrenia Bulletin*, No. 4, 64-81, Fall, 1975.
26. MOSS, G. E.: *Illness, Immunity, and Social Interaction: The Dynamics of Biosocial Resonation.* New York: John Wiley & Sons, 1973.
27. ENGEL, G.: The need for a new medical model: A challenge for biomedicine. *Science*, 196, 4286; 129-136, April 8, 1977.
28. RAHE, R. H., MEYER, M., SMITH, M., KJAER, G., and HOLMES, T. H.: Social stress and illness onset. *J. Psychosom. Res.*, 8(1):35-44, 1964.
29. RAHE, R. H., MCKEAN, J. D., JR., and ARTHUR, R. J.: A longitudinal study of life-change and illness patterns. *J. Psychosom. Res.*, 10:355-366, 1967.
30. RAHE, R. H.: Life change measurement as a predictor of illness. *Proc. Roy. Soc. Med.*, 61:1124-1126, 1968.
31. CANTER, A., IMBODEN, J. B., and CLUFF, L. E.: The frequency of physical illness as a function of prior psychological vulnerability and contemporary stress. *Psychosom. Med.*, 28:344-350, 1966.
32. HINKLE, L. E., JR., PINSKY, R. H., BROSS, I. D. J., et al.: The distribution of sickness disability in homogeneous groups of healthy adult men. *Am. J. Hygiene*, 64:220-242, 1956.
33. HINKLE, L. E., JR., CHRISTENSON, W. N., KANE, F. D., OSTFELD, A., THETFORD, W. N., and WOLFF, H. G.: An investigation of the relation between life experiences, personality characteristics, and general susceptibility to illness. *Psychosom. Med.*, 20:278-295, 1958.
34. HINKLE, L. E., JR. and WOLFF, H. G.: The nature of man's adaptation to his total environment and the relation of this to illness. *Arch. of Internal Med.*, 99:442-460, 1957.
35. MEYERS, R. J. and HAGGERTY, R. J.: Streptococcal infections in families: Factors altering individual susceptibility. *Pediatrics*, 29:539-549, 1962.
36. MUTTER, A. Z. and SCHLEIFER, M. J.: The role of psychological and social factors in the onset of somatic illness in children. *Psychosom. Med.*, 28:333-343, 1966.
37. LESHAN, L. and WORTHINGTON, R. E.: Loss of cathexis as a common psychodynamic characteristic of cancer patients: An attempt at statistical validation of a clinical hypothesis. *Psychological Reports*, 2:183-193, 1956.
38. PARKES, C. M. and BROWN, R. J., JR.: Health after bereavement, a controlled study of young Boston widows and widowers. *Psychosom. Med.*, 34:449-461, 1972.
39. REES, W. D. and LUTKINS, S. G.: Mortality of bereavement. *British Med. J.*, 7:13-16, 1967.

40. Schmale, A.: Relationship of separation and depression to disease. *Psychosom. Med.*, 20:259-277, 1958.
41. Engel, G. L.: A psychological setting of somatic disease: The "giving-up, given-up" complex. *Proc. of Roy. Soc. of Med.*, 60: 553, 1967.
42. Engel, G. L. and Schmale, A. H.: Psychoanalytic theory of somatic disorder. *J. Am. Psycho-Anal. Assn.*, 15:344-365, 1967.
43. Richardson, H. G.: *Patients Have Families*. New York: Commonwealth Fund, 1945.
44. Peachey, R.: Family patterns of stress. *General Practitioner*, 27:821, 1963.
45. Kellner, R.: *Famiy Ill Health*, Springfield, Ill.: Charles C. Thomas, 1963.
46. Dingle, J. H., Badger, G. F., and Jordan, W. S., Jr.: *Illness in the Home: A Study of 25,000 Illnesses in a Group of Cleveland Families*. Cleveland: The Press of Western Reserve Univ., 1964.
47. Meissner, W. W.: Family dynamics and psychosomatic processes. *Fam. Proc.*, 5(2):142-161, 1966.
48. Jackson, D. D.: Family homeostasis and the physician. *Calif. Med.*, 239-242, Oct., 1965.
49. Grolnick, L.: A family perspective of psychosomatic factors in illness. A review of the literature. *Fam. Proc.*, 11(4):457-486, 1972.
50. Weakland, J. H.: Family somatics—a neglected edge. *Family Process*, 16(3):263-272, 1977.
51. Lasagna, L. and McCann, W.: Effect of tranquilizing drugs on amphetamine toxicity in aggregated mice. *Science*, 125:1241, 1957. Also in Andres Goth (Ed.), *Medical Pharmacology*. St. Louis: The C. V. Mosby Co., 1978.
52. Brown, B. B.: *Intern. Physiol. Congr.*, 20, 133-134, 1956. (Abstr.)
53. Brown, G. W., Birley, J. L. T., and Wing, J. K.: Influence of family life on the course of schizophrenic disorders: A replication. *Brit. J. Psychiat.*, 121:241-258, 1972.
54. Brown, G. W., Carstairs, G. M., and Topping, G.: The post-hospital adjustment of chronic mental patients. *Lancet*, II, 685, 1958.
55. Brown, G. W., Monch, E., Carstairs, G. M., and Wing, J. K.: The influence of family life on the course of schizophrenic illness. *Brit. J. Prev. Soc. Med.*, 16:55, 1962.
56. Vaughn, C. E. and Leff, J. P.: The influence of family and social factors on the course of psychiatric illness: A comparison of schizophrenic and depressed neurotic patients. *Brit. J. of Psychiat.*, 129:125-137, 1976.
57. Cohen, M., Freedman, N., Engelhardt, D. M., and Margolis, R. A.: Family interaction patterns, drug treatment. *Arch. Gen. Psychiat.*, 19: 50-56, 1968.

Appendix

BEAVERS-TIMBERLAWN FAMILY EVALUATION SCALE

Family Name .... Rater ....

Segment .... Date ....

Instructions: The following scales were designed to assess the family functioning on continua representing interactional aspects of being a family. Therefore, it is important that you consider the entire range of each scale when you make your ratings. Please try to *respond on the basis of the videotape data alone,* scoring according to what you see and hear, rather than what you imagine might occur elsewhere.

I. *Structure of the Family*

A. Overt Power: Based on the entire tape, check the term that best describes your general impression of the overt power relationships of this family.

1	1.5	2	2.5	3	3.5	4	4.5	5
Chaos		Marked dominance		Moderate dominance		Led		Egalitarian
Leaderless; no has enough power to structure the interaction.		Control is close to absolute. No negotiation; dominance and submission are the rule.		Control is close to absolute, Some negotiation, but dominance and submission are the rule.		Tendency toward dominance and submission; but most of the interaction is through respectful negotiation.		Leadership is shared between parents, changing with the nature of the interaction.

B. Parental Coalitions: Check the terms that best describe the relationship structure in this family.

1	1.5	2	2.5	3	3.5	4	4.5	5
Parent-child coalition				Weak parental coalition				Strong parental coalition

C. Closeness

1	1.5	2	2.5	3	3.5	4	4.5	5
Amorphous, vague and indistinct boundaries among members				Isolation, distancing				Closeness, with distinct boundaries among members

II. *Mythology:* Every family has a mythology; that is, a concept of how it functions as a group. Rate the degree to which this family's mythology seems congruent with reality.

1	1.5	2	2.5	3	3.5	4	4.5	5
Very congruent		Mostly congruent				Somewhat incongruent		Very incongruent

III. *Goal-Directed Negotiation:* Rate this family's overall efficiency in negotiating problem solutions.

1	1.5	2	2.5	3	3.5	4	4.5	5
Extremely efficient		Good				Poor		Extremely inefficient

IV. *Autonomy*

A. Clarity of Expression: Rate this family as to the clarity of disclosure of feelings and thoughts. This is not a rating of the intensity or variety of feelings, but rather of clarity of individual thoughts and feelings.

1	1.5	2	2.5	3	3.5	4	4.5	5
Very clear				Somewhat vague and hidden				Hardly anyone is ever clear

B. Responsibility: Rate the degree to which the family members take responsibility for their own past, present, and future actions.

1	1.5	2	2.5	3	3.5	4	4.5	5
Members regularly are able to voice responsibility for individual actions				Members sometimes voice responsibility for individual actions, but tactics also include sometimes blaming others, speaking in 3rd person or plural				Members rarely, if ever, voice responsibility for individual actions

C. Invasiveness: Rate the degree to which the members speak for one another, or make "mind reading" statements.

1	1.5	2	2.5	3	3.5	4	4.5	5
Many invasions				Occasional invasions				No evidence of invasions

D. Permeability: Rate the degree to which members are open, receptive and permeable to the statements of other family members.

1	1.5	2	2.5	3	3.5	4	4.5	5
Very open		Moderately open				Members frequently unreceptive		Members unreceptive

V. *Family Affect*

A. Range of Feelings: Rate the degree to which this family system is characterized by a wide range expression of feelings.

1	1.5	2	2.5	3	3.5	4	4.5	5
Direct expression of a wide range of feelings		Direct expression of many feelings despite some difficulty		Obvious restriction in the expressions of some feelings		Although some feelings are expressed, there is masking of most feelings		Little or no expression of feelings

B. Mood and Tone: Rate the feeling tone of this family's interaction.

1	1.5	2	2.5	3	3.5	4	4.5	5
Usually warm, affectionate, humorous and optimistic		Polite, without impressive warmth or affection; or frequently hostile with times of pleasure		Overtly hostile		Depressed		Cynical, hopeless and pessimistic

C. Unresolvable Conflict: Rate the degree of seemingly unresolvable conflict.

1	1.5	2	2.5	3	3.5	4	4.5	5
Severe conflict, with severe impairment of group functioning		Definite conflict, with moderate impairment of group functioning		Definite conflict, with slight impairment of group functioning		Some evidence of unresolvable conflict, without impairment of group functioning		Little, or no unresolvable conflict

D. Empathy: Rate the degree of sensitivity to, and understanding of, each other's feelings within this family.

1	1.5	2	2.5	3	3.5	4	4.5	5
Consistent empathic responsiveness		For the most part, an empathic responsiveness with one another, despite obvious resistance		Attempted empathic involvement, but failed to maintain it		Absence of any empathic responsiveness		Grossly inappropriate responses to feelings

VI. *Global Health-Pathology Scale: Circle the number* of the point on the following scale that best describes this family's health or pathology.

10	9	8	7	6	5	4	3	2	1
Most Pathological									Healthiest

2

The Family and the Development of the Individual

Theodore Lidz, M.D.

It may seem an overstatement and even strange to suggest that many of the most significant changes that are taking place in the concepts of personality development, psychopathology, and psychotherapy derive simply from the appreciation that the child grows up in a family. After all, the family has everywhere been the primary agency for providing for children's biological needs, while simultaneously guiding their development into integrated persons, capable of directing their own lives in the society in which they are brought up. Perhaps the point is that the family is so ubiquitous that its critical functions in personality development have, until recently, been largely overlooked. When, some 25 years ago, my colleagues and I began our systematic studies of the families in which schizophrenic patients had grown up, we could find little to guide our efforts in the psychiatric literature.

Functions of the Family

Over the years, it has become clear that it has been the neglect of the central position of the family in human development that has been responsible for many of the theoretical confusions that have beset psychiatry and psychoanalysis. Now psychiatric developmental theory seems to be entering a new phase in which the place of the family takes on greater salience. Under the influence of Margaret Mahler and indirectly of Erik Erikson, developmental theory has begun to focus on the separation-individuation process (1, 2). Although Mahler has confined her studies to the mother-child relationships during the first three or four years of life and the studies have not considered the total impact of the family transactions, the general orientation can be extended to include how children manage the critical tasks as they progressively find their places as boy or girl members of the family, venture from the family into peer groups and school, become caught up in the impact of sexual drives and conflicts concerning independence, and finally gain integrated ego identities. The process of separation-individuation which requires a gradual replacement of family support by intrapsychic structures cannot, of course, be studied without paying careful attention to the total family milieu, for much of the process depends upon the nature of the family transactions in which the child is developing.

In general, dynamic psychiatric theories of personality development have largely derived from and remained related to psychoanalytic theory. Psychoanalysis has drawn attention to the impact of the family upon its offspring's personality development. It has emphasized how the mother's ways of nurturing can promote libidinal fixations, how the oedipal transition leads to superego formation, as well as various other matters that are central to the study of personality development. However, it has focused primarily upon early childhood experiences, and upon the interaction between a parent and child rather than on the family transactions. Psychoanalysis as a theory has not considered the influence of the total family environment upon the entire family group and each member of it. The genesis of different personality types, as well as the choice of neurosis or psychiatric syndrome, has been attributed to fixations at various levels of pregenital libidinal development. As object relations theories developed, they considered that early libidinal fixations impaired the capacities for object relationships, and that most subsequent emotional and interpersonal difficulties result from such fixations.

In the intensive, long-term studies of schizophrenic patients and their families carried out at Yale (3), it became apparent that the patient's nurturance had often been impaired during the first months of life because of maternal depression; such findings did not explain the etiology of schizophrenic disorders, for similar difficulties are found in other psychiatric and psychosomatic conditions. Whatever aspect of the family setting and family transactions was examined, something was found to be seriously amiss. A great deal of the family life had been markedly disturbed or distorted in each of these families from before the patient was born and persisted through the time the patient was hospitalized in adolescence or early adult life. Although the concepts of fixation and regression were important, it seemed essential to take into consideration the ways parents interact with the child and with each other over the years. The flaws in nurturant care or the early trauma that have been considered as the causes of fixations could be predisposing rather than determining factors and might be even more important as symbols of what continued throughout the patient's formative years.

A number of studies of patients with different types of psychopathology have been leading to a major shift in dynamic developmental theories (4-22). An infant does not develop into an integrated and self-sufficient adult simply because serious fixations have been avoided. Development is not just a matter of the nurturance of inborn directives and potentialities; rather, it requires positive directives from a suitable interpersonal environment and social system. The necessary positive molding forces of the interpersonal environment have been largely overlooked because they are built into the institutions and mores of all societies and into the ubiquitous family, which has everywhere knowingly or unknowingly carried out the task of directing the child's potential into an integrated personality.

In brief, infants do not develop into reasonably integrated individuals unless there is considerable positive input from those who raise them throughout their developmental years. I have sought to describe these fundamental requisites elsewhere and will only summarize them here (23, 24).

Any basic psychology of personality development and maldevelopment must recognize that the human has a method of adaptation and survival different from any other organism because the evolution of the species rested upon the selecting out of mutations that increased the capacity for using tools, and particularly that tool of tools, language. Because of the capacity for symbolic functioning, humans were released from motivation by instinctual patterns, drives, or by conditioning *alone* and could be motivated and directed by future goals and thus be capable of ego functioning. Because humans could verbally communicate to others what they learned, learning became cumulative and peoples developed cultures. Although, like those of all other animals, the human physiological mechanisms are suited to a relatively limited physical environment, humans could increasingly modify the environment to their needs. To live in very different physical and social environments, they had to assimilate the necessary adaptive techniques from those who raised them. Unless we appreciate that humans have a dual endowment—a genetic inheritance with which they are born and a cultural heritage into which they are born and which they must assimilate from those who raise them—we can never understand human development and maldevelopment correctly. This is a fact that is vital to a viable science of personality development and must form the basis of any scientific psychiatry.

Human infants must learn their basic adaptive techniques, and everywhere they learn them from the families that raise them or from some planned substitute for the family. The family conveys these techniques, often unknowingly, while it nurtures and protects the child. Indeed, even though the family is a social rather than a biological structure, it is an essential correlative of the human's biological makeup, and any attempt to understand the child's development without due consideration of the family in which it takes place is bound to err, for it eliminates an essential of the developmental process. The ready acceptance of the neat phrase, "The child is born to live in an average expectable environment" (25), has aggravated a basic misunderstanding of the developmental process. Infants are not, in fact, born to live in such an environment; they are born to live in a rather limited environment, but they can live in the Arctic or in a desert if the culture and the family that carries the cultural techniques have learned to modify the environment to human needs. Hartmann (25) took a more comprehensive view when he wrote, "Human action adapts the environment to human functions, and these the human being then adapts to the environment which he has helped create."

The biological makeup of human beings requires that they develop in a social system and assimilate a culture. The complete dependency of infants and very small children requires that they be raised by persons to whom the children's welfare is as important as their own. Children's dependency and prolonged attachment to parental persons provide major motivations and directives for their development into members of society. The family forms the earliest and most persistent influence, encompassing the still unformed infant and small child, for whom the parents' ways and the family ways are *the* way of life, the only ways the child knows. All subsequent experiences are perceived, understood, and reacted to emotionally according to the foundations established within the family. The family ways and the child's patterns of reacting to them become so thoroughly incorporated in the child that they can be considered determinants of the constitutional makeup, difficult to differentiate from the genetically determined biological factors with which they interrelate —a circumstance that greatly complicates the study of physical development as well as of personality development. Subsequent influences will modify the influence of the family, but they can never completely undo early core experiences.

The family, however, has essential functions aside from childrearing: It subserves essential needs of the spouses as well as needs of the society. The family not only fills a vital need of every society by carrying out the basic enculturation and socialization of its new recruits, but also subserves other societal functions. The family constitutes the basic unit of society: It forms a group of individuals which society treats as an entity; it constitutes an economic unit; and the network of kin helps stabilize even post-industrial societies. The family provides roles for its members both within the family and in the larger social system, and influences status, motivation, and incentives that affect the relationships between individuals and the society.

The nuclear family, however, is formed by a marriage and serves in many ways to complete the lives of the husband and wife and to provide them with a new stabilizing family milieu of mutually interdependent persons. These three sets of functions of the family—for the children, the society, and the spouses—are intimately interrelated, and some conflicts among them are inevitable. Although we are focusing upon the family and the personality development of children, the intricate relationships among the marital relationship and the fulfillment of the parents' needs and the capabilities of a family to carry out its child-rearing functions properly cannot be neglected.

There is, of course, considerable difference between a marriage without children and a family. In a marriage, the spouses can assume very diverse types of role relationships and find very different ways of achieving a satisfactory reciprocity. The customary roles of husband and wife can be reversed with the wife earning the livelihood and the man doing the cooking and housekeeping; each can remain in their parental homes; one or both may find sexual outlets outside of the marriage; one spouse may fill a parental rather than a marital role for the other. The ways in which spouses relate are virtually countless. However, when the arrival of a child turns a marriage into a nuclear family, the spouses' ways of relating must shift to make room for the children, and limits are set upon how the couple can relate if they are to provide a proper developmental setting for their children.

Just what is required of parents and the family they form in order to provide a proper developmental setting is difficult to analyze. The transactions of a family are diaphanous and difficult to grasp. Some requirements are universal because they concern the essential biological needs of children, and some are necessary to prepare children to live properly in a particularly society. Our ethnocentric orientations can make it difficult to distinguish between the two. Then, too, the functions of the family can be analyzed in different ways. The approach taken here derives largely from the study of families in which child-rearing has gone seriously awry. As with the study of human physiology, it is often first possible to detect essentials of the process when the smooth flow breaks down and creates pathology. The intensive study of the dynamics of the family has been going on for only 25 years or so, and the topic is large and complex. This paper seeks to provide an outline that may serve to guide further studies and to form a framework for the understanding of the unique transactions of any given family.

Although a marital relationship is complex, it can be studied and understood in terms of the interaction between two persons. A family, in contrast, cannot be grasped simply in interactional terms for it forms a true small group with a unity of its own. In all true groups the actions of any member affect all. Members must find reciprocally interrelating roles or conflict ensues. The group requires shared objectives and leadership toward achieving them. The group exacts loyalty, requiring that all members give some precedence to the needs of the group over their own desires. Small groups, even threesomes, tend to divide into pairs that exclude others from significant relationships and which impair or disrupt the group unity. In the family, such characteristics of groups are heightened because of the intimate relationships between members and their lengthy interdependence. Clarity of roles, boundaries, and communication, as well as cohesive structure and effective leadership, are necessary to promote unity and minimize divisive tendencies.

Characteristics of the Family

The family, however, is a very special type of group with characteristics imposed upon it by the biological differences of its members, as well as by the particular purpose it serves. Recognition of these characteristics leads to an appreciation of some of its structural requisites and operations (26).

1) *The nuclear family is composed of two generations, each with different needs, prerogatives, and obligations.*

The parents, raised in different families of origin, seek to merge themselves and their family backgrounds into a new unit that satisfies the needs of both and completes their personalities in a new relationship they hope will be permanent. Aside from permitting each spouse to move into a family in which affection and sex can be unified, in contrast to the spouses' roles in their original families, marriage provides each spouse with the opportunity to achieve again the security afforded by a union in which one's welfare is of paramount importance to another. Each seeks completion through a complementary relationship with a member of the other sex, for, in a general sense, neither a man nor a woman can be complete alone. The completion is not only sexual, for the two sexes, at least in the past, have been raised to divide the tasks of living and to complement each other in nonsexual ways as in producing and raising children.

The new family they form differs to a greater or lesser degree from their families of origin, and thus requires malleability in both partners. The new relationship requires the intrapsychic reorganization of each spouse to take cognizance of the partner and to appreciate that a spouse's orientation differs from his or her own. The behavior of each spouse is modified by the id, ego, and superego of the other. Wishes and desires of a spouse that can be set aside must be differentiated from needs that cannot be neglected.

The parents are properly dependent upon one another, and children must be dependent upon parents, but parents cannot properly be dependent upon immature children. The parents serve as guides, educators, and models for offspring. They provide nurturance and give of themselves so that the children can develop. Though individuals, as parents they function as a coalition, dividing roles and tasks. Since the parents are basic love objects and objects for identification for their children, who they are, how they behave, and how they relate to each other are of utmost importance to the child's personality development—a matter that seems obvious but which has largely been overlooked or neglected in the study of child development.

Children, in contrast to parents, receive their primary training in group living within the family, remaining dependent upon the parents for many years, forming intense emotional bonds to them, assimilating from them and taking on their characteristics; yet they must learn to live within the family so that they are able to emerge from it to live in the broader society and to start families of their own.

2) *The nuclear family is also composed of two genders, which traditionally have had differing but complementary functions and roles.* As the roles and functions are no longer so clearly divided in many families, the division of the tasks of living and child-rearing often requires conscious agreement, which can create difficulties for the parents, and perhaps ultimately for the children. However, in most families traditional roles still remain a significant factor in determining the way in which parents achieve reciprocal role relationships. The primary female role derives from woman's biological makeup and is related to bearing and nurturing children and the maintenance of a home needed for that purpose. This leads to an emphasis upon interest in interpersonal relationships and emotional harmony—an affiliative or expressive-affectional role. The male role, originally related to man's muscular strength, is concerned with the support and protection of a family and establishing its position in the larger society, an instrumental-adaptive role. Of course, in performing affiliative functions, a mother carries out many instrumental functions, and most fathers, even in highly traditional families, relate expressively to family members.

3) *The relationships between family members are held firm by erotic and affectional ties.* The parents, seeking to form a permanent union, are not only permitted but expected to have sexual relationships. In contrast, all direct sexual relationships within the family are prohibited to the children. Erogenous gratification from parental figures accompanying nurturant care is needed and fostered, but must be progressively frustrated as the child's need for such primary care diminishes, lest the bonds to the family become too firm and prevent the child's investment of interest and energy in the extrafamilial world. The de-eroticization of children's relationships to other family members before their adolescence is a primary task of the family.

4) *The family forms a shelter for its members within the larger society.* Theoretically, at least, members receive affection and status within the family by ascription rather than through achievement, an arrangement which provides some emotional security in the face

of the demands of the outside world. However, the boundaries between the family and the rest of society cannot be rigid; rather, they must be semipermeable—the family must follow and transmit the societal ways to a considerable degree to enable its children to function within the society when they emerge from the family.

These fundamental characteristics of the nuclear family and correlaries derived from them set requisites for spouses, their marital interaction, and their parental behavior if the family is to provide a suitable setting for the harmonious development of their offspring into reasonably integrated adults.

Essential Aspects of the Child-Rearing Process

On the basis of the characteristics of the family that have been outlined, the essential aspects of the child-rearing process can now be examined. It had been noted earlier that the child does not grow up to attain a mature, workable personality simply through the nurturance of inborn directives and potentialities, but requires positive direction and guidance in a suitable interpersonal environment and social system. The family must foster and direct the child's development by carrying out a number of interrelated functions. Such family functions can be discussed in many different ways. Here they shall be considered under five major headings: 1) the parental nurturant functions, including the affectional, which must meet the child's needs and supplement his or her immature capacities in a different manner at each phase of development; 2) the dynamic organization of the family which forms the framework for channeling the child's drives and directing the child into becoming an integrated individual; 3) the family as the primary social system in which the child learns the basic social roles, the value of social institutions, and the basic mores of the society; 4) the task of the family of transmitting to the child the essential instrumental techniques of the culture, including its language; and 5) the need for the family to communicate in a manner that fosters mutual understanding and cooperation, as well as reasonable clarity of directives and meanings. These five categories overlap and interpenetrate, but considering them separately affords a means of study of how a family functions.

Parental Nurturant Functions

The nurturance of the infant and child is one function of the family that has been specifically recognized by most developmental theories; since it has been the focus of intensive study, it does not require extensive elaboration here. The parental nurturance must meet children's needs and supplement their immature capacities at each phase of their development—from the total care given the helpless neonate to fostering an adolescent's movement toward independence from the parents. It concerns more than filling the child's physical needs: It involves the emotional needs for love, affection, and a sense of security; it includes providing opportunity for the utilization of new capacities as the child matures. Proper nurturance requires parents to have the capacities, knowledge, and empathy to alter their ways of relating in accord with the child's changing needs. The degree of constraint provided a nine-month-old is unsuitable for a toddler, and the physical contact appropriate between a parent and a five-year-old would be unsuitable for a young adolescent. The ability to establish and maintain age-appropriate boundaries between the parents and child constitutes an important aspect of parenthood related to the capacity to appreciate that the child is a separate individual with different needs, feelings, and perceptions.

The capacity to nurture or be maternal is not an entity. Some parents can properly nurture an almost completely dependent infant but become anxious and have serious difficulties with a toddler. Some have difficulties in allowing the child to form the eroticized ties essential to the development of the preoedipal child, and others have difficulties in frustrating the child's eroticized attachment during the oedipal phase. These parental problems at specific periods in a child's development may lead to developmental fixations in the child. Children, however, usually have the same parents throughout childhood, and the parents' ways of interacting with each other and with the child over time are often more significant in establishing personality traits or personality disturbances in offspring than are fixations at a specific developmental period.

Although the mother is usually the primary nurturant figure to the small child (and usually the family expert in child-rearing), her relationship with the child does not transpire in isolation but is influenced by the total family setting. It is obvious, though often overlooked, that a mother's capacity to nurture properly is influenced profoundly by her marital interaction with her husband. The demands of another child, the relations between her children, and the father's relationships with the children can influence profoundly her maternal behavior. Her capacities to give of herself to a child are affected by the emotional input that she receives from others, and in most contemporary families there is no one other than the husband from whom she can receive the necessary emotional sustenance.

Children's attachments to their parents, which develop as concomitants of their nurturance, provide major motivations for their development into social beings and furnish parents with the leverage to channel the children's drives. The wish and need for parents' love and acceptance and the desire to avoid rebuff and punishment lead children to seek to conform to expectations when such are consistent and reasonable. Through the wish to be loved by a parent, as well as to become someone like the parent, the child gains major developmental directives.

The quality and nature of the parental nurturance children receive profoundly influence their emotional development—not only their vulnerability to frustration, but also the anger, aggressivity, anxiety, hopelessness, and helplessness they experience under various conditions. As Erikson has pointed out, nurturance influences the quality of the basic trust children develop, in others as well as in themselves (2). It influences their sense of autonomy and the clarity of the boundaries established between themselves and the parents. It contributes to their self-esteem as members of their own sex. It lays the foundation for trust in the reliability of collaboration and the utility of verbal communication as a means of solving problems. The physiological functioning of children can be permanently influenced by the manner in which the parental figures respond to their physiological needs. It is apparent even from these brief comments why so much attention has been directed to the parental nurturant functions and how profoundly they influence personality development. They are, however, only one aspect of what children require from their parents and family.

The Family Structure and the Integration of the Personality

It is apparent that the integration of the developing personality is profoundly influenced by the dynamic organization of the family. The organization of the family varies from culture to culture; the instrumental leadership of the nuclear family may be divided between the father and the mother's oldest brother, as in the Trobriand Islands, or rest to a great extent in the father's oldest brother, as in the Fijis. The mother's influence on the children may be dominant for the first 8 to 12 years of a boy's life and then be almost completely displaced, as in the highlands of New Guinea. It is difficult to generalize, but the nuclear family everywhere may follow certain organizational principles because of its basic functions and the biological makeup of its members. The family members must find reciprocally interrelating roles or distortions in the personalities of one or more members will occur. The division of the family into two generations and two genders lessens role conflict and tends to provide a conflict-free area in which the immature child can develop, while directing the child to grow into the proper gender identity which forms the cornerstone of a stable ego identity.

All groups need unity of leadership, but the family contains two leaders—a father and a mother. Unity of direction and organization requires a coalition between the parents which is possible because of the different but interrelated functions of the father and the mother. In order for the family to develop and maintain a structure conducive to fostering the integrated development of its offspring, the spouses must form a coalition as parents, maintain boundaries between the generations, and carry out the fundamental functions related to their gender-linked roles. Though these requirements may sound simple, they are not easy to maintain, and the consequences of failure to fulfill them can be far-reaching.*

A coalition between the parents is necessary not only to give unity of direction, but also to provide each parent with the support essen-

* Some may take issue with the concept that the maintenance of gender-linked roles is essential. The roles need not be conventional, but it is important to realize that we do not yet know the consequences of attempts to obliterate or reverse differences in maternal and paternal roles.

tial for carrying out his or her principal functions. The mother, for example, can better limit her erotic investment in a child to maternal feelings when her sexual needs are being satisfied by her husband. Coalitions are usually more readily achieved when spouses fill complementary rather than similar roles. The tendency of small groups to divide up into dyads that create rivalries and jealousies is diminished markedly if the parents form a unity in relating to their children. The child's tendency to compete with a parent—the essence of the oedipal situation—is overcome if the parental coalition is firm. This frustration of the child's fantasies assists in redirecting him or her to the reality that requires repression of such wishes. If the parents not only form a coalition as parents but also as a married couple, the children are provided with adult models who treat one another as alteregos, both striving for the partner's satisfaction as well as for their own. Such children are very likely to grow up valuing marriage as an institution that provides emotional gratification and security.

Children properly require two parents: a parent of the same sex with whom to identify and who serves as a role model to follow into adulthood, and a parent of the opposite sex who becomes a basic love object whose love and approval are sought by identifying with the parent of the same sex. However, a parent can fill neither role effectively for a child if denigrated, despised, or treated as a non-entity or enemy by the spouse. If the parents are irreconcilable, they are likely to confuse the child's development because the child is apt to internalize contradictory directives and be caught in a double-bind, feeling rejected by one parent when seeking to please the other. A child may then sometimes follow a negative directive by seeking to be different from the parent of the same sex in order to gain the affection of the other. A need to be different does not provide as much direction as does accepting a parent of the same sex as a model to emulate and follow into adulthood. Parents can form a reasonably satisfactory coalition in respect to their children despite marital discord and, to some extent, despite separation. They can agree about how the children should be raised; further, each can support the other to the children as a worthwhile person and good parent even if not a suitable marital partner for the self. Some of the most destructive effects of divorce upon children occur when one parent vilifies the other to a child.

When serious failures of the parental coalition occur, the growing children may invest their energies in the support of one parent or seek to bridge the gap between the parents rather than investing their energies in their own development. A child sometimes becomes a scapegoat as his or her problems are turned into the major overt source of dissent between the parents. Often, such children come to feel responsible for the parents' conflicts. Children may willingly oblige and assume the role of villian in order to mask the parental discord so that they may retain the two parents they need. When parents fail to achieve a parental coalition, the children can become prey to conflicting motivations, directives, emotions, and standards that interfere with the development of a reasonably well-integrated personality.

The generation boundaries. The failure of parents to achieve a coalition can lead also to breaches in the generation boundaries within the family. The division of the nuclear family into two generations lessens the danger of role conflict and gives the child freedom from competition with a parent and, hence, increased freedom for development. The parents are the nurturing and educating generation and provide both adult models and objects of identification for the child. Children require the security of dependency to be able to utilize their energies in their own development. If they must provide the major emotional support for the parents, their personalities become stunted and they are apt to suffer "ego foreclosure" (27). A different type of affectional relationship exists between parents than between parent and child. When a parent uses a child to fill needs that are not met by a spouse, the child can seek to widen the gap between the parents. Finding an essential place in completing the life of a parent may interfere with the necessary turning to the extrafamilial world for self-completion. The situation is complicated, both because of the intense relationship which normally exists between a mother and her very young "preoedipal" child, and because of the normal slowness of the separation-individuation of the child from the mother. The boundaries between generations help both mother and child overcome the bond and help the child to find a proper place as a male or female member of the family and then to move on to invest energy and attention in peer groups and schooling.

The generation boundaries may inadvertently be breached by parents in a number of ways. The mother may fail to establish boundaries between herself and her child by not differentiating adequately between her own feelings and needs and those of the child. A parent may inappropriately use a child to fill needs unsatisfied by a spouse. A parent may behave more like a child than a spouse and become rivalrous with the child for the attention and affection of the other parent. The most obvious disruption of generation lines occurs in incestuous and near-incestuous relationships in which a parent gains erotic gratification from a child. In all such situations, the oedipal situation remains more or less unresolved, and the excluded parent's jealous and hostile feelings lead to the child's fears of retribution and retaliation that are not simply projections of his or her wishes to be rid of the parent. In such situations, the child's aggressive and libidinal impulses directed toward parents are increased rather than undergoing repression and gradual resolution and, ultimately, are controlled only through strongly invested defensive mechanisms.

Gender-linked roles. Security of gender identity is a cardinal factor in the achievement of a stable ego identity. This refers primarily to a person's self-concept and security in being male or female, as well as the ways of relating to others, but not to the capacities to carry out various occupations or functions within the environment. Of all factors entering into the formation of personality characteristics, the sex of the child is the most decisive, despite changes in child-rearing and the increased opportunities available to women in recent years. Confusions and dissatisfactions concerning sexual identity can contribute to the etiology of many neuroses and character defects, as well as perversions. Probably all schizophrenic patients are seriously confused concerning their sexual identity. A child does not attain gender-linked attributes simply by being born a boy or girl, but through role allocations that start in infancy and then through role assumptions and identifications as the child grows older.

The maintenance of the appropriate gender-linked roles by parents plays a major role in guiding the child's development as a boy or girl.

Although the parents in most contemporary families need to share parental functions, as well as the economic support of the family, some differences between mothers and fathers need to be maintained to direct a child's development. The problem is more subtle than the father filling the instrumental role and the mother the expressive role. Even in traditional families, mothers perform instrumental functions in running the home and making decisions concerning the children, and fathers usually fill affectional-expressive functions with their wives and children. Although the functions are changing, clear-cut role reversals furnish offspring with culturally deviant images of masculinity and femininity. The inability of the mother to fill an affiliative role or the father to provide instrumental leadership can create serious difficulties. As Parsons and Bales pointed out, a cold and unyielding mother is more deleterious than a cold and unyielding father, while a weak and ineffectual father is more damaging than a weak and ineffectual mother (26). More specifically, a cold and aloof mother may be more detrimental to a daughter who requires experience in childhood with a nurturant mother to attain feminine and maternal characteristics, and an ineffectual father may be more deleterious to a son who must overcome his initial identification with his mother and early dependency upon her to gain security in the ability to provide for a wife and family.

A child's difficulties in identifying with a parent of the same sex may derive from the parent's unacceptability to the spouse whose love the child seeks. Simply because she is a woman, the mother may be basically unacceptable to a father with homosexual proclivities. The daughter attempts to gain the father's approval by seeking to be boyish, by being intellectual, or through some other means that do not threaten him by feminine appeal. Similarly, if the mother is consciously or unconsciously rivalrous with all men, a son can readily learn that masculinity will evoke rebuff from her, and the fears of engulfment or castration by the mother become greater and more realistic sources of anxiety than fears of retaliatory castration by the father. Other intrafamilial difficulties can interfere with a child's gaining a secure gender identity. If parents convey the wish for the child to be of the other sex, or if the child needs to avoid incestuous entanglements, secure gender identity may not develop. In general, however, the attainment of a proper gender identity by the child is assured if the parents adequately fill their own gender roles and each is accepted and supported in living out these roles within the family.

The relationship between the dynamic organization of the family and the integration of the offspring's personality is a topic that has just begun to be studied. Still, a little consideration leads to the recognition that each aspect of personality formation is influenced profoundly by the family organization.

Socialization

The differentiation between socialization and enculturation is somewhat arbitrary, and the processes clearly overlap. Socialization concerns teaching the child basic roles and institutions of the society through the family transactions, whereas enculturation deals with that which is transmitted symbolically from generation to generation.

The form and functions of the family evolve with the culture and subserve the needs of the society of which it is a subsystem. It is the first social system that children know and, living in it, they gain familiarity with the basic roles as they are carried out in the society: the roles of parents and children, of boy and girl, of man and woman, of husband and wife. They learn how these roles impinge upon the broader society and how the roles of others impinge upon the family and its members. Although roles can be considered as units of a social system, they also become part of the personality and give cohesion to personality functioning. Individuals do not learn patterns of living entirely on their own, but in many situations learn roles and then modify them to their specific needs and personalities.

Within the family the child also learns about a variety of basic institutions, including the family, marriage, extended family systems, and institutions of economic exchange. Values are inculcated by identification, superego formation, teaching, example, and interaction. The wish to participate in or avoid participation in an institution such as marriage can be a major motivating force in personality development. It is the function of the family to transmit to the offspring the prescribed, permitted, and proscribed values of the society and the acceptable means of achieving goals.

Within the family's social system, children are involved in a multiplicity of social phenomena that leave a permanent imprint upon them. Some of these are the value of belonging to a mutually protective unit, the rewards of renouncing one's own wishes for the welfare of a collectivity, the hierarchies of authority, and the relationship between authority and responsibility. The family value systems, role definitions, and patterns of relating become part of the children's personalities far more than what is consciously taught to them.

Enculturation

Enculturation concerns the acquisition of the techniques for survival and adaptation which are not inherited genetically but are assimilated as part of the cultural heritage. In a complex industrial and scientific society, the family obviously can transmit only the basic adaptive techniques to its offspring, and many of the instrumentalities of the culture must be conveyed by schools and other specialized institutions. In order to survive, each society has developed a set of instrumental techniques and institutions that modify the environment to human needs.

The cultural heritage includes such tangible matters as styles of dress and housing and the ways of hunting and farming, and less tangible but vital conceptualizations as religious beliefs, ideologies, and ethical values that are accepted as axiomatic and are defended by various taboos. Enculturation is a topic that has received increasing attention in antipoverty programs where it has become apparent that the cultural deprivation of children is no less important than their social and economic deprivations. Deprived children cannot learn readily because they have not been provided with the symbolic wherewithal for abstract thinking and with enough breadth of experience to reason adequately in guiding their own lives. There is evidence that a significant proportion of mental retardation derives from cultural deprivation rather than biological inadequacies. Religious beliefs, so important in determining a person's way of life and value systems, are handed down primarily in the family; and Gilbert and Sullivan could well ask, "Why is every child alive/Born either a Liberal or a Conservative?"

The recognition of the relativism of cultural belief systems and standards, which has come with the attainment of higher education by a large proportion of the population, the intermingling of peoples of different ethnic backgrounds, and the advent of television, has decreased the assuredness persons have in the value systems with which they have been brought up and has opened the way for inner conflict concerning directives for living. Marriages that cross ethnic, religious, and social class lines may leave the parents uncertain of what belief systems and what adaptive techniques to convey to their offspring. Further, while there may well be common features in the lives of the impoverished and dispossessed everywhere—"the culture of poverty"—many families are in the lowest socioeconomic group because they have over several generations become incapable of transmitting a culture—an integrated set of instrumental techniques and guidelines for living.

The transmission of language. The topic of enculturation cannot be encompassed even in meager outline here, and only a single aspect, the transmission of language, will be considered: This is done not simply as an illustration but because the totality of the enculturation process depends so greatly upon language. Language is the tool by means of which humans internalize their experiences, think about them, try out alternatives, and conceptualize and strive toward future goals rather than simply seek immediate gratifications. After the first years of life, the acquisition of almost all other instrumental techniques depends upon language. Collaboration with others, so critical to human adaptation, depends upon the use of a shared system of meanings. Indeed, the capacity to direct the self, to have any ego functioning at all, depends upon having verbal symbols with which to construct an internalized symbolic version of the world which one can manipulate in imaginative trial and error before committing oneself to irrevocable actions. The inculcation of a solid foundation in the language of the society is one of the crucial tasks of the family.

To understand the importance of language to ego functioning, it must be appreciated that in order for individuals to understand, communicate, and think about the ceaseless flow of their experiences, they must be able to divide their experiences into categories (28). Each culture is distinctive in the way in which its members categorize their experiences, and each child must learn the culture's system of categorizing to be able to communicate with others in the society and to be able to think coherently. No one can start from the beginning and build a personal system of categorization.

Categories are formed by abstracting common attributes from experiences or objects that are never precisely identical, bestowing some sort of equivalence upon them, and thus providing the world with some coherence and regularity that enable prediction (29). The vocabulary of the language is the catalogue of the categories into which the culture divides its world and its experiences. Thus, the words of the language have a predictive capacity upon which we base much of our action; without the predictive capacity derived from the meaning of words, the world would remain far more aleatory for us. We expect "Spring" to recur annually; we know something called "candy" will be sweet.

The proper learning of words and their meanings and of the syntax of the language is essential to ego functioning and to human adaptation, but there is no assurance that it will be taught or learned correctly. The correctness and the stability of children's language rest primarily upon the teaching of the members of their families. The process depends upon reciprocal interaction between children and their tutors, the consistency between the teachers, the cues they provide, the sounds to which they respond or remain oblivious, and the meanings which they reward consistently or sporadically—or indicate are useless, ineffectual, undesirable, repugnant, or punishable. Learning language, so vital to being human as well as to survival, is a very complicated matter that cannot be elaborated upon here, but it is apparent that the family transactions are a critical factor in the process. Whether or not meanings and syntax of the language are learned correctly depends largely on the parents. Unfortunately, parents may be irrational and highly inconsistent, or convey aberrant usages because of their own defense mechanisms, or in other ways convey a distorted or impoverished language system to the children.

Intrafamilial Communication

The importance of the family in teaching language to its children leads to the importance of intrafamilial communication. The proper functioning of the family depends greatly on the clarity with which members can communicate their wishes, needs, feelings, and dissatisfactions, and how they can resolve their differences. The absence of means of communicating and resolving conflicts with others, as well as the presence of chronic conflicts and dissatisfactions within the family, greatly affect children's development (30).

Communication within the family is often nonverbal and tacit as well as verbal. The shared background and consistency in responding and reacting to various situations obviate the need for explanations and spoken directives in many circumstances. Parental expectations often become implicit for a given situation. However, nonverbal messages are more likely to be misunderstood than verbal messages. Bernstein has shown that lower-class children are likely to suffer serious limitations in their cognitive development because of the paucity of verbal communication in their homes, where directions are often given by single words, by isolated phrases, or by slaps and blows (31).

It now seems likely that the parental *styles* of communicating are major factors in the development of differing personality types and character traits, as well as personality disorders, in their children. A new dimension was added to the study of personality development and psychology when Bateson et al. formulated the double-bind hypothesis of the etiology of schizophrenic disorders (6). Additional insight was gained when my colleagues and I described the irrationalities of the family environment in which schizophrenic patients grew up (32). They were taught to misperceive, deny the obvious, and distrust "outsiders," if not one or the other parent. Wynne and Singer documented that at least one parent of a schizophrenic patient has an amorphous or fragmented style of communicating (33-36). Similarly, Johnson and Szurek have shown that parents of delinquents had communicated the wish that the child live out impulses a parent had desired to realize but had been unable to put into action (37). Parents of upper-middle-class delinquents often teach by "do as I say, not as I do," and often seem to say, "It doesn't matter so much what you do; it's the way things look that counts." They may use language to gloss over transgressions and make things look satisfactory.

One of the major functions of conjoint family therapy, which is also one of the advantages it has over individual therapy, concerns the clarification of communication between family members. Families are helped to transmit feelings clearly to others, to make the covert overt, to have members recognize that others have different perspectives, expectations, feelings and needs, to clarify paradoxical communications, and to open the way for resolution of differences and conflicts that have been hidden or ignored by making them explicit and available for resolution. Much remains to be learned about intrafamilial communication, but focusing upon it has clearly opened new therapeutic potentialities.

Summary

Personality development cannot be understood abstracted from the family matrix in which it takes place. Although child-rearing techniques and the emotional quality of the nurturance provided the child have been the major focus of attention in the past and are of critical importance, they do not encompass the topic. Children require positive input from those who raise them in order to develop into reasonably self-sufficient and integrated individuals. The structuring of their personalities depends greatly upon the dynamic organization of the family in which they are raised. The proper understanding of social roles and institutions is affected by how parents fill their roles and relate to one another, as well as to the remainder of society. Children acquire characteristics through identification, but also by reactions to family members and by finding reciprocal roles with them. Superego development derives from the internalization of the directives of two parents and will be inconsistent if the directives are contradictory or if the parents do not form a workable coalition in respect to the children. Children must assimilate the basic instrumental techniques of the culture in which they grow up and the parents are the major conveyors of these ways of adaptation to their children. Ego functioning, the capacity to direct the self into the future, depends upon the acquisition of language, and the adequate acquisition of language depends greatly on the family tutors and the nature of the intrafamilial communications. Although we have not been able to explore fully the pervasive influence of the family upon personality development, and are only beginning to appreciate properly its pervasiveness, it becomes clear that numerous sources of deviant personality development become clear when we consider the implications of this approach.

In the study of personality development and in the search for guidelines to assure stable emotional development, the emphasis upon what parents should or should not do to the child, for the child, and with the child at each phase of development has often led to neglect of the very significant issues of who the parents are, how they act and communicate, how they relate to each other as well as to the child, and what sort of family they have managed to create.

REFERENCES

1. MAHLER, M., PINE, F., and BERGMAN, A.: *The Psychological Birth of the Infant.* New York: Basic Books, 1975.
2. ERIKSON, E.: Growth and crises of the "healthy personality." *Psychological Issues,* Vol. 1(1), Monograph 1, 1950.
3. LIDZ, T., FLECK, S., and CORNELISON, A.: *Schizophrenia and the Family.* New York: International Universities Press, 1965.
4. LIDZ, R. W. and LIDZ, T.: The family environment of schizophrenic patients. *Amer. J. Psychiat.,* 106:332-345, 1949.
5. LIDZ, T., CORNELISON, A., et al.: The mothers of schizophrenic patients. In: T. Lidz, S. Fleck, and A. Cornelison (Eds.), *Schizophrenia and the Family.* New York: International Universities Press, 1965.
6. BATESON, G., JACKSON, D. D., HALEY, J., and WEAKLAND, J.: Toward a theory of schizophrenia. *Behav. Sci.,* 1:251-264, 1956.
7. SINGER, M. and WYNNE, L.: Differentiating characteristics of the parents of childhood schizophrenics, childhood neurotics, and young adult schizophrenics. *Amer. J. Psychiat.,* 120:234-243, 1963.
8. DELAY, J., DENIKER, P., and GREEN, A.: Le milieu familial des schizophrenics: 1. Proposition du problème. *L'Encephale,* 46: 189-232, 1957.
9. DELAY, J., DENIKER, P., and GREEN, A.: Le milieu familial des schizophrenics: 2. Méthode d'approche. *L'Encéphale,* 49:1-21, 1960.

10. DELAY, J., DENIKER, P., and GREEN, A.: Le milieu familial des schizophrenics: 3. Résultats et hypothèses. *L'Encéphale*, 51:5-73, 1962.
11. MISHLER, E. and WAXLER, N.: *Interaction in Families*. New York: John Wiley & Sons, 1968.
12. LAING, R. and ESTERSON, A.: *Sanity, Madness and the Family*. London: Tavistock Publications, 1964.
13. PAVENSTEDT, E. (Ed.): *The Drifters: Children of Disorganized Lower-Class Families*. Boston: Little, Brown, 1967.
14. MINUCHIN, S., et al.: *Families of the Slums*. New York: Basic Books, 1967.
15. KNIGHT, R. P.: The dynamics and treatment of chronic alcohol addiction. *Bull. Menninger Clinic*, 1:233-250, 1937.
16. CHASSEL, J.: Family constellation in the etiology of essential alcoholism. *Psychiat.*, 1:473-503, 1938.
17. BRUCH, H. and TOURAINE, G.: Obesity in childhood: V. The family frame of obese children. *Psychosom. Med.*, 2:141-206, 1940.
18. BRUCH, H.: *Eating Disorders: Obesity, Anorexia Nervosa, and the Person Within*. New York: Basic Books, 1973.
19. HENDIN, H.: *Black Suicide*. New York: Basic Books, 1969.
20. STOLLER, R.: Symbiosis anxiety and the development of masculinity. *Arch. Gen. Psychiat.*, 30:164-172, 1974.
21. WURMSER, L.: Psychoanalytic considerations of the etiology of compulsive drug use. *J. Amer. Psychoanal. Assn.*, 22:820-843, 1974.
22. LIDZ, T., LIDZ, R. W., and RUBENSTEIN, R.: An anaclitic syndrome in adolescent amphetamine addicts. *Psychoanal. Stud. Child*, 31:317-348, 1976.
23. LIDZ, T.: *The Family and Human Adaptation*. New York: International Universities Press, 1963.
24. LIDZ, T.: *The Person*, Rev. Ed. New York: Basic Books, 1976.
25. HARTMANN, H.: *Ego Psychology and the Problem of Adaptation*. New York: International Universities Press, 1958, (1939).
26. PARSONS, T. and BALES, R.: *Family, Socialization and Interaction Process*. Glencoe, Ill.: Free Press, 1955.
27. HAUSER, S.: *Black and White Identity Formation: Explorations in the Psychosocial Development of White and Negro Male Adolescents*. New York: Wiley-Interscience, 1971.
28. WHORF, B.: *Language, Thought, and Reality: Selected Writings of Benjamin Lee Whorf*, J. Carroll (Ed.). New York: M.I.T. and J. Wiley & Sons, 1956.
29. BROWN, R.: *Words and Things*. Glencoe, Ill.: Free Press, 1958.
30. SPIEGEL, J.: The resolution of role conflict within the family. *Psychiat.*, 20:1-6, 1957.
31. BERNSTEIN, B.: *Class, Codes and Control: Theoretical Studies Toward a Sociology of Language*. New York: Schocken Books, 1974.
32. LIDZ, T., CORNELISON, A., et al.: Intrafamilial environment of the

schizophrenic patient: VI. The transmission of irrationality. *Arch. Neurol. Psychiat.*, 79:305-316, 1958.

33. WYNNE, L. and SINGER, M.: Thought disorder and family relations of schizophrenics: I. A research strategy. *Arch. Gen. Psychiat.*, 9:191-198, 1963.
34. WYNNE, L. and SINGER, M.: Thought disorder and family relations of schizophrenics: II. A classification of forms of thinking. *Arch. Gen. Psychiat.*, 9:199-206, 1963.
35. SINGER, M. and WYNNE, L.: Thought disorder and family relations of schizophrenics, III. Methodology using projective techniques. *Arch. Gen. Psychiat.*, 12:187-200, 1965.
36. SINGER, M. and WYNNE, L.: Thought disorder and family relations of schizophrenics: IV. Results and implications. *Arch. Gen. Psychiat.*, 12:201-212, 1965.
37. JOHNSON, A. and SZUREK, S.: The genesis of antisocial acting out in children and adults. *Psychoanal. Quart.*, 21:323-343, 1952.

3

The Appraisal of the Individual in the Family: Criteria for Healthy Psychological Development in Childhood

Albert J. Solnit, M.D.

Introduction

The family has been repeatedly rediscovered and reaffirmed because it serves basic human needs at the same time that it expresses fundamental aspects of human motivation which surface in a variety of ways in different cultures throughout the ages. Appraising the individual in the family refers to observing and understanding the child, youth, or adult in a social context. The family as a basic social unit is inextricably associated with survival for infants and the fullest physical and psychological yearnings of adults for closeness and affirmation, as well as the universal search for an extension beyond the boundaries of one person's limitations.

The place of the child in his family has been changing as improved nutrition, preventive health, and the need for more education have resulted in more children surviving longer and living with their families for longer periods of time (1). However, these changes are episodic and uneven.

Recently, a distinguished social scientist reported, through the eyes of a Prime Minister of Sweden, some of these changes and the associated difficulties.

> A few months ago after giving a lecture in Stockholm, I was invited for a meeting with Prime Minister Olof Palme. He spent more than two hours discussing national policy on families and children. Much of our conversation dealt with two laws that had been introduced in the Swedish Parliament. The first, which passed by a wide margin, authorized sick leave for working parents whenever a child was ill, provided that half of the allotted leave time was taken by the father. The second law, which failed, would have permitted parents with a child under three to work a six-hour day instead of an eight-hour day, with the remaining two hours paid for out of Social Security, again provided that half of the released time was taken by the father.
>
> The Prime Minister had spent the whole day talking with representatives of the groups that had defeated the bill, trying to persuade them to change their position on it.
>
> "They do not," said the Prime Minister, "understand the crucial importance for the child's development of what you call 'irrational attachment.' "
>
> I replied that, nevertheless, his society had at least recognized the importance of the problem and was prepared to do something about it.
>
> "No," he responded, "you overestimate our progress. We still have a long way to go." He then recounted an incident that had occurred on the previous day. It had been his first evening off in many weeks, and he was just settling down to enjoy it when the doorbell rang. There stood a worker from the local day care center with two young children and a tale of woe. The parents had failed to pick up the children at the closing hour, so the worker had taken them to their home only to find that no one was present except a teenage son and his friends, all of them drunk.
>
> The Prime Minister then took his 18-year-old son to the home, got the teenagers out, cleaned and fed the children, and left his son there to wait until the parents arrived at home.
>
> "You see, our people still do not understand that when you are dealing with children, you cannot expect to work on a fixed time schedule" (2).

How can psychiatric education and research respond to some of the policy issues raised by these perspectives? Are there new challenges to mental health practices? How can the pyschiatrist view the changes in the family and the needs arising from these changes, e.g., the need for day-care for infants, the rising divorce rate, the increase of single-parent families, the increase of children born out of wedlock, the decrease in fertility?

The Appraisal of the Individual in the Family

Two basic ideas should be considered:

1) *There is considerable evidence that the structure and functions of the family have changed and are changing.* Many or most of the changes have strengthened family relationships and have affirmed the permanence of the family as a basic human institution. Other changes, such as the rising divorce rate, have been viewed as symptoms of instability or deficits in the family as a unit, also raising questions about the impact of such changes on children from generation to generation.

2) *The human infant's helplessness at birth and prolonged period of physical and social dependency evoke reactions from parents that lead to what we describe as family relationships.* The circumstance that all persons are helpless at birth and have a prolonged period of dependency becomes the basis for what is evoked in them as adults when they are responsible for infants and young children. These facts of life are acknowledged in custom and in law. The law, "without explicitly defining 'family' assumes that 'family' is an essential component of the 'good' society and that 'family,' like law, is one of the basic processes for the control of human behavior" (3)—a part, in Hartmann's (4) terms, of each person's "average expectable environment." As Anna Freud recently observed, "A privilege of childhood is to be sheltered from direct contact with the law and to have society's and the state's demands and prohibitions filtered by way of the parent's personalities. The parents thus not only represent the law to the child, but are also his representatives before the law."* "Indeed, the law of child placement may be perceived as a response to the success or failure of parents in fulfilling their task of nourishing in their children the internal mechanisms of control

* Verbal communication.

sufficient for each one, upon becoming an adult, to be a law unto himself, but not above the law" (3).

Recent statistical information from the Bureau of Census, the Bureau of Labor Statistics, and other agencies offers a shorthand account of how family structure and functions are changing in the U.S. and of other factors affecting family life. For example:

> Nearly half of the nation's 71.1 million households are now occupied by one or two persons.
>
> About one of every six children under the age of 18 now lives in a single-parent family.
>
> More than one million children were involved in the divorces that were decreed during 1978. The U.S. divorce rate, at five per 1000 population, is far above that of any other country and double the 1965 rate. The number of marriages likely to end in divorce is an estimated 38 percent of first marriages and 40 percent of all marriages among women now in their late twenties (5).
>
> In March 1975, more than half of the mothers with school-age children and nearly 40 percent of mothers with children under the age of six were either working or looking for work.
>
> It is estimated that at least one million children of working mothers take care of themsleves when they are not in school, including some who are under six.
>
> Estimates consistently demonstrate that at least one-third of our children do not receive adequate health care, including access to preventive services, adequate immunizations, early diagnosis of illness and adequate nutrition.
>
> In 1974, over 10 million children (15.5 percent) lived in families whose ability to rear children was severely handicapped by incomes below the poverty level. More than one-half of these children lived in families headed by a woman. An additional 3.6 million children lived in families whose incomes were between 100 and 125 percent of the poverty level.
>
> More than 400,000 children live in public and private residential institutions each year.

Our level of providing services is extremely uneven. Some experts wonder whether we are not really 50 loosely federated states, since standards of health and education services are so different that many of the states could be considered separate countries. For example, in 1974 the proportion of births where mothers received inadequate prenatal care (care starting as late as the third trimester of pregnancy, or no care at all during pregnancy) ranged from the low of 1.8 percent in Utah to 14.0 percent in Arizona. During the same year, the rate of infant mortality in the District of Columbia was 26.7 percent, more than double that of Utah, the state with the lowest rate (12.2 percent).

In California, according to *On the Capitol Doorstep,** "Two-thirds of the state's 1.4 million [recipients of] Aid to the Families of Dependent Children are children; 88 percent of AFDC families are female-headed, single-parent; 55 percent have preschool children. After Proposition 13, the cost-of-living increase for all welfare recipients was cut from the 1978-1979 budget. The cost-of-living index has risen 15.75 percent since the welfare grants were adjusted. One AFDC mother testifying on January 31 before the California Senate Health and Welfare Committee, she said she and her child receive $287.00 per month (the same for all welfare mothers with one child). After she pays rent and utilities she has $120.00 left for all other expenses. Her testimony echoed the desperation of other welfare mothers [concerned with] the critical need for more money to feed and clothe their children." Along that line, an American Friends Service Committee poster states, ironically, "It will be a great day when our schools get all the money they need and the Air Force has to hold a bake sale to buy a bomber."

Throughout the various census figures and related surveys, we see that young children, who are the most vulnerable, receive the least adequately supported care. A useful way to characterize the vulnerability of young children is to be aware of the empirical observation that at-risk environments tend to evoke and elaborate vulnerabilities more than strengths or healthy potentials. Similarly, there is a tendency for discontinuity to invite further disruptions in a child's life. Thus, our most vulnerable citizens are given propor-

* Vol. 9, No. 1, pp. 1 and 2.

tionately the least protection against the risks of family instability and the impact of social and economic deficits.

Indeed, there are substantial criteria for determining what relationships in the family are adequate to assure children of a sound development. However, criteria for what constitutes sound development for children in the family cannot be considered in a vacuum. The role of value preferences and the range of life-styles fostered by a pluralistic society should be taken into account in exploring the extent to which our knowledge permits us to conceptualize criteria for healthy development in childhood (6). Such criteria are based on the assumption that the parents as heads of the family can shelter children in their community as well as represent them in the society.

Developmental Perspectives

Children are born helpless and their survival depends on being protected, nourished, stimulated, guided, and loved by adults. The state of the infant was recognized in 1840 by Jeremy Bentham, who observed: "The feebleness of infancy demands a continued protection. Everything must be done for an imperfect being, which as yet does nothing for itself. The complete development of its physical powers takes many years; that of its intellectual faculties is still slower. At a certain age, it already has strength and passions, without experience enough to regulate them. Too sensitive to present impulses, too negligent of the future, such a being must be kept under an authority more immediate than that of the laws . . ." (7).

Freud recognized two basic dimensions in a psychological sense when he referred to "the long period of time during which the young of the human species is in a condition of helplessness and dependence" and commented that "in comparison with most animals, . . . it is sent into the world in a less finished state . . . [thus] the dangers of the external world have a greater importance for it" (8). In turn, the child with his unique makeup and temperament influences the unfolding personality and sense of fulfillment of his parents. The maturation and development of a child thus are a product of his biological and psychological heritage and of his experiences. Therefore, when we assess the development of any child, we must examine and understand the pattern and quality of interaction between the child and parent, as well as the nature of the family relationships at each stage of his growth and development (13).

The ultimate measure of the child's development is the extent to which the child is maturing, becoming a person who in adulthood is likely to be relatively free of internal conflict (4, 9). The healthy adult has a realistic self-regard that enables him to gauge and react with confidence to environmental demands, while at other times he criticizes and makes sustained efforts to change the society in order to improve or protect his preferred values. In this sense, developmental health or mental health is a relative concept in which the balance between individual expression and adaptation to the demands of family and community varies over time and from culture to culture.

However, observing behavior in itself is not enough for assessing a child's state of mental health. Evaluations of a child (or, for that matter, of an adult) which simply equate social compliance and conformity with mental health or which simply equate social deviance and noncompliance with mental illness ignore a fundamental finding of psychoanalysis. That is, what appears to be similar behavior, whether as a symptom of illness or a sign of health, may in different children be a reflection of and response to a wide range of different and even opposite pyschic factors (10).* Thus, the test of mental health is to be found not in any particular style of life, but rather in the sense of self—the sense of autonomy that provides one with a sense of authenticity as an individual who is unique and worthy and who adapts, criticizes, protests, and at all times has access to the self one is becoming.

To recapitulate, the human child is born helpless and perishes if he or she is not nourished, protected, soothed, and stimulated by an

---

* For example, a two-and-a-half-year-old child who is afraid of his mother because he has been abused by her may appear to behave the same as another two-and-a-half-year-old child who is afraid of his mother because he is afraid of his murderous feelings toward her. The behavior itself would not explain how different the motives, thoughts and feelings of each child are, nor what inferences can be drawn about the state of mental illness or health of each of these two children.

older person capable of providing such care on a continuing basis. What begins as biological helplessness leads to social and psychological attachment as a result of the interaction between the infant and maternal person or persons.

> What begins as the experience of physical contentment or pleasure that accompanies bodily care develops into a primary attachment to the person who provides it. This again changes into the wish for a parent's constant presence irrespective of physical wants. . . . Helplessness requires total care and over time is transformed into the need or wish for approval and love. It fosters the desire to please by compliance with a parent's wishes. It provides a developmental base upon which the child's responsiveness to educational efforts rests. Love for the parents leads to identification with them, a fact without which impulse control and socialization would be deficient. Finally, after years of childhood, comes the prolonged and in many ways painful adolescent struggle to attain a separate identity with physical, emotional, and moral self-reliance (11).

The infant progresses from biological dependency to psychological and social attachment in which the child craves affection, approval, and predictable, dependable responses from the caretaking adults. This craving, or social "addiction," is the stuff out of which social development emerges as a result of positive or negative identification. It is the vital "stuff" which leads to the need for a family and for the continuous replications of families. Through these close relationships, the child acquires and internalizes parental attitudes and expectations. These identifications are the core of the unique personality of each child, a derivative of the primary child-parent relationship, what we have termed the primary psychological child-parent relationship (12).

In a sense, we are endowed and plagued by this psychological and social "addiction" for the rest of our lives. The gradual transformation of the "addiction" leads to the need for social closeness, friendship, companionship, and eventually to the reestablishment of another family group. The privacy of the family, secure from intrusion by the community or the state, is the setting in which this socialization can take place, fostered by autonomous parents. Family privacy is an essential prerequisite for the establishment of a mutually intimate relationship, i.e., an essential and primary attachment (14). As with many of the lines of development, passive experiences, such as being fed or bathed, become the basis for actively taking care of oneself and later of others. Many of our neurotic and developmental deviations stem from the failure to turn passive experiences into active self-initiating capacities, unique to the individual, but influenced to a significant extent by how the child identifies with his or her parents and older siblings.

Identification with parents may entrap the child in conflict or may be the pathway to a unique and well-functioning personality. How the parents and other family members nurture and guide in regard to health care, schooling, and participation in the life of the community vitally influences the developing child's personality and sense of self. The content and style of child-rearing usually reflect the substance and style of the family's functioning, its own cultural legacy, as well as how the parents feel and function.

For example, when parents are depressed or suffer from the long-term effects of deprivation in their own childhood, they may lack the capacity to stimulate, nurture, protect, guide, and support their children. They transmit to their children what they themselves had suffered. In this way, certain deficits and deviations may be transmitted from one generation to the next through the dynamics of the family interactions.

On the other hand, in healthy development, these identification processes proceed from imitative behavior to the internalization of parental attitudes and expectations. This two-step process can be described in terms of the psychoanalytic theory of (love) object relations.

Object constancy is a state in which the child has the capacity to maintain his tie to parents and to feel their nurturing, guiding presence even when they are the source of frustration or disappointment or when they are absent. This is the second of two stages in the developing child-parent attachment, the first of which is a need-satisfying relationship of infant to mother, the first opportunity beyond the biological connection to begin reciprocal psychological ties. As the child becomes capable of recognizing those who care for him and later of differentiating himself from them, toward the end of the first year of life he enters into the second stage, that of object constancy. Now, knowing who the parents are, as distinguished from strangers, and gaining the independence conferred by walking and talking, he mentally becomes independent of the need-satisfying ties because in this second stage he has the capacity to feel the presence of and later remember the primary love object (psychological parent) as a reliable, nurturing, guiding psychological influence. Through the mental representations of the constant love object, neither dependent on their providing need satisfactions nor on their physical presence, the child holds on to his parents in ever more internalized and subtle ways. As the relationship extends into the toddler and school-age period, he becomes increasingly independent of his parents by internalizing and modifying their attitudes and expectations as part of his own unique personality.

Gradually, the capacity for object constancy enables the child to separate and individuate as the attachment to the dependable, guiding parental persons matures. The child learns to cope with short separations from the parents because these internalized mental and emotional resources enable him to have supporting parents available psychologically even when he feels frustrated by them or is physically apart. Children are now ready to go to a nursery school or play group. With the psychological presence of the parents, they are able to form attachments to teachers, peers, and others as their progressive development enables them to socialize, learn, play, and move along through the toddler, latency, and adolescent phases.

Styles of child-rearing offer many options. However, child-rearing starts with nurturance in the family and extends to services in the community when the child has needs (e.g., for education or health care) that the parent supplies from sources outside the home. These concepts should enable us to advise parents about standards and limitations of day-care and pre-kindergarten educational programs, especially when both parents work.

Throughout development, the need for continuity with the same primary love objects is crucial, as the children define themselves against parents, siblings, and later on peers, teachers, and others. Each young child attributes to the primary or psychological parents the omnipotence and omniscience that early on become the basis for feeling secure with and later awed by these parents in the family setting. As maturation and development proceed in the postoedipal (school-age, latency) period, these attributes and expectations undergo gradual change. The child's sense of himself becomes more clear and confident as he perceives reality more accurately and becomes capable of thinking logically.

Gradually, then, children undergo a disillusionment about their parents, who not only lose their mantle of omniscience and omnipotence but also reveal comfortingly as well as painfully their human imperfections. Normatively, as the disillusionment is worked through, children perceive their parents more realistically. This enables children and parents to move toward greater closeness as friends and companions, a family development emerging toward the end of adolescence (14). Throughout, the child and adolescent are storing up their future adult capacities to nurture, guide, rear, and become the founders of a new family. Then they can reexperience at a higher level of development the closeness, affection, and continuity that were crucial to their own survival and shaped their own personality. Thus, the craving for affection and approval is mastered anew as adults who are fulfilled by being active in creating, saving, and nurturing children who are born helpless.

In the healthy adult personality emerging from a family setting, the intellect, the emotions, and the capacity for personal relations and social awareness come into synchrony. This advance is accompanied by a realistic self-esteem and a sense of proportion between the need to adapt to the community and the need to change that community because of dissatisfactions with it, not with oneself. Such a level of functioning, inferred on empirical grounds, is usually given a chronological marker, for example, 18 or 21 years of age, for the legal presumption that a person has both the capacity and authority to exercise his rights fully, free of parental control and responsibility. Usually this is the same legal marker that qualifies a person to apply for a license to be married, i.e., to create a new family. The adult in law is presumed to have the capacity, for example, to make binding contracts, to acquire and dispose of property, to marry, to vote, to hold public office, to consent to or reject medical care, to commit crimes, to make wills—that is, to engage in any activity and to be held responsible for it (15).

According to this view, healthy child development emerges from an affectionate family unit. In our society, which purports to make children's interests paramount, parental autonomy and family privacy must be protected and supported. Such autonomy and privacy include the rights of parents to make decisions about their family in terms of who should help them care for their children.

No unit in our society other than the family has ever been able to provide the special qualities needed to nurture children to their fullest emotional and intellectual development. The human family with all its variations expresses the need for closeness, affection and approval that is derivative of the newborn infant's helplessness. The extension of this concept relates to the implications and insights of the human child's prolonged dependence on adults, parents, who supply those opportunities, restrictions, and stimuli that enable the young child to develop capacities for self-regulation, self-awareness, and self-directedness—capacities that we expect eventually from adults. Thus, the family, constituted by at least one child and usually two but at least one adult, represents a universal expression, with enormous variations, of how the infant's helplessness and prolonged dependency evoke the relationships between adults and children that we refer to as family relationships. Klaus and Kennell's (16) research requires us to attend to the beginning of this relationship. In this context, it is well to ask how the family has changed. If it has changed in its structure and functions, are these changes desirable from the point of view of children's needs, or are they changes that emphasize the adult point of view of children's needs, or are they changes that emphasize the adult point of view to the detriment of children?

The current state of knowledge about child development and families is sufficient—and there is a reliable and growing body of evidence—to justify the establishment of planned *opportunities,* as opposed to coercive interventions, for child health and care facilities and educational services that are likely to comport with healthy growth and development. The viability of such opportunities ultimately must rest on their usefulness and attractiveness to autonomous parents in furthering their own life-styles and value preferences. But the state of knowledge is not sufficiently advanced to justify the utilization of diagnostic or prognostic criteria of mental illness or mental health as a basis for threatening advice or coercive intervention into family preference or privacy. Recognizing the limitations of knowledge should caution against using the power of professionals or the state to intrude upon parental autonomy by advising or requiring that certain "preferred" child-rearing practices be followed or by imposing a monolithic educational curriculum.

In each culture, certain ethnic, political, and social patterns of a given historical period reflect the strengths of ambivalent parental attitudes in the priorities for assigning societal resources to meet the needs of children. However, the newborn helplessness remains a crucial, unchanging force that presses parents or some other caring adults to become child advocates.

Since the parents' right to be advocates of their children was also associated at times with absolute power over their children (17), starting in the early 1800s in this country, the state, acting in the role of *parens patriae,* began to limit parental power in certain areas in which the interests of children and society were believed to need protection or preference. As stated in a recent study at the Yale Child Study Center by Shelley Gaballe (18):

> For example, the enactment of compulsory education laws limited the parents' previously boundless power to determine the manner of their child's education by eliminating the option "no education." "The child is not the mere creature of the State; those who nurture him and direct his destiny have the right, coupled with the high duty, to recognize and prepare him for additional obligations." (Pierce v. Society of Sisters, 1925).* The parents' rights to the child's services and earnings was limited by the enactment of the child labor laws. [In Prince v. Massachusetts], [t]he Supreme Court stated: "But the family itself is not beyond regulation in the public interest . . . Acting to guard the general interest in youth's well-being, the state as *parens patriae may* restrict the parent's control by requiring school attendance, regulating or prohibiting the child's labor and

---

* Pierce v. Society of Sisters, 268, U.S. 510, 535 (1925).

> in many other ways."* "Child abuse legislation designed to punish offending parents and protect victimized children was enacted to try to curtail the more extreme methods of parental discipline punishment.** Courts ordered life-saving medical treatments over the religious objections of parents despite the traditional parental prerogative to determine what type of medical care children shall receive.†

Thus, the need for advocacy by parents has been associated with children living in their families for longer periods of time. At the same time, the autonomy of parents in regard to the care and control of children has been narrowed. Psychological roots for this are reflected not only in the parental ambivalence that has been described above, but also in the needs families have for support of community services to supplement the care and nurturance of their children. Thus, our concepts of mental health in childhood and adolescence imply certain parental obligations and authority. Parents are responsible for the dependent needs of their children in two ways: They nurture them, and they assume responsibility for guiding and planning for them. Nurture requires providing affectionate and stimulating continuity of care and being an adult with whom the child can identify and in relation to whom the child can be different and unique. Advocacy requires planning and making decisions that regulate the child's involvement in his community and society—for example, decisions concerning education, health care, discipline, and religious ethics.

Healthy child development rests, then, on an affectionate family unit. In a society which makes children's interests paramount, parental autonomy and family privacy must be protected and supported. Such autonomy and privacy include the rights of parents to make decisions about who should help them care for their children, including the utilization of close relatives, friends, and, of course, of professionals in child development. The aim of society ought to be to enable children to grow in a humane family setting dominated neither by their drives nor by environmental forces.

---

* 321 U.S., 1958, 166 (1944).

** See, e.g., Conn. Gen. Stat Rev. §§ 17-38, -38a *et seq.* (1975).

† See, Annot., 30 A.L.R. 2d 1138 (1953).

Therein lies the best available opportunity for the healthy growth and development of a child to adulthood (19), becoming an individual in his family.

REFERENCES

1. ARIES, P.: *Centuries of Childhood.* New York: Alfred A. Knopf, 1962.
2. BRONFENBRENNER, U.: Doing your own thing—Our undoing. *MD.* March, 1977, pp. 13-15.
3. GOLDSTEIN, J.: Psychoanalysis and a jurisprudence of child placement—with special emphasis on the role of legal counsel for children. *Inter. J. Law and Psychiat.*, 1:109-124, 1978.
4. HARTMANN, H.: Psychoanalysis and the concept of health. In: *Essays on Ego Psychology.* New York: International Universities Press, 1964, pp. 1-18. (Originally published in the *International Journal of Psycho-Analysis*, 20:308-321, 1939.)
5. TOTH, R. C.: Changes in family patterns forecast. *Los Angeles Times*, Part I, October 20, 1977, p. 22.
6. FREUD, A.: *Normality and Pathology in Childhood.* New York: International Universities Press, 1965.
7. BENTHAM, J.: *Theory of Legislation*, Vol. I. Boston: Weeks, Jordan, 1840, p. 248.
8. FREUD, S.: Symptoms, inhibitions and anxiety (1926). *Standard Edition*, 20:154-155. London: Hogarth Press, 1959.
9. HARTMANN, H.: Towards a concept of mental health. *Brit. J. Med. Psychol.*, 33, 1960.
10. GOLDSTEIN, J.: Psychoanalysis and jurisprudence. *The Psychoanalytic Study of the Child*, Vol. 23, 1968.
11. GOLDSTEIN, J., FREUD, A., and SOLNIT, A. J.: *Before the Best Interests of the Child.* New York: Free Press, 1979.
12. GOLDSTEIN, J., FREUD, A., and SOLNIT, A. J.: *Beyond the Best Interests of the Child.* New York: The Free Press, 1973.
13. SOLNIT, A. J. and SCHOWALTER, J.: Criteria for Healthy Psychological Development in Childhood. (Unpublished manuscript.)
14. ERICKSON, E. H.: *Childhood and Society.* New York: Norton, 1950.
15. GOLDSTEIN, J.: On being adult and being an adult in secular law. *Daedalus*, Fall, 1976, pp. 56-70.
16. KLAUS, M. H. and KENNELL, J. H.: *Maternal-Infant Bonding.* St. Louis: C. V. Mosby Co., 1976.
17. POLLOCK, F. and MAITLAND, F.: *The History of English Law* (2nd ed.), 1898.
18. GABALLE, S.: The evolution of children's legal rights. Unpublished research paper, Yale Child Study Center, New Haven, 1976.
19. SOLNIT, A. J.: Changing psychological perspectives about children and their families. *Children Today*, Vol. 5, No. 3, May-June, 1976, pp. 5-9, 44.

4

Pathways to Assessing the Family: Some Choice Points and a Sample Route

David Reiss, M.D.

During the 1970s, careful clinical research on the family is becoming firmly established. Among its primary concerns has been the systematic assessment of the family group. The first findings from this new area of research have been intriguing; however, as might be expected, there is no unanimity concerning the most productive theoretical analyses or the best methods to test the developing theories. Thus, a single most valuable approach to assessing the family has not emerged. Rather, it appears more useful to look at the current work in our field and describe "choice points": the options which are available now to both clinicians and researchers. Research has progressed far enough to describe with some specificity the kinds of choices now available to clinicians and clinical researchers who want to do effective evaluations of the family.

The co-investigator in the research reported in this chapter was Ronald Costell, M.D. Support of that research was provided by the Rehabilitation Research and Training Center (No. 9), George Washington University, which is funded by a grant (SRS DHEW, Project No. 16P56803-3-10) from the United States Public Health Service.

This paper has three aims: 1) to clarify the reasons for directly assessing the entire family group; 2) to describe the choices a clinician or clinical researcher now has in developing an approach to assessment; and 3) to describe briefly an approach to assessing families—a quantitative, laboratory-based method for assessing interaction patterns in families.

ASSESSING THE FAMILY UNIT

For most clinicians information about the family is important for the rational planning of a broad range of psychiatric treatment programs, including those that do not involve the patient's family directly. Family assessment is obviously critical for treatment plans which include family therapy. Accurate family assessment and diagnosis are important for precisely the same reasons that accurate individual assessment is important: 1) It must be determined whether family therapy is an appropriate treatment and, if it is, what special modifications the family may require. 2) It is important to develop a short-term and long-term prognosis: Is the family likely to improve or deteriorate (as perhaps 10 percent of families do) in family therapy, and are the gains, if any, likely to hold once therapy is completed? 3) It is important to know what strengths or resources the family has and is willing to commit to improve the chances of a good treatment outcome. 4) It is necessary to establish a baseline so that whether treatment has produced an improvement or deterioration can be determined. 5) Assessment is helpful in giving the family a clear picture (with due attention to the timing and method of the report of the clinical impression). 6) An economical and effective way to communicate our impression to clinical colleagues is needed. 7) A way is needed to communicate with the "third party": the agencies, peer review groups, and insurance companies who are a daily presence in clinical work.

The implication is not that a comprehensive diagnostic assessment of the family group is necessary before taking *any* clinical action, since many experienced family therapists will argue that they "learn by doing." They take some action on the basis of a partial assessment and learn more about the family by noting the outcome of their initial action.

As has been suggested, the family field cannot provide a uniform theoretical or methodologic approach. Nor is there an agreed-upon nosology or set of descriptive terms for characterizing family strengths and weaknesses. We are some distance away from a Diagnostic and Statistical Manual for families. Nonetheless, we have learned enough to state two general principles of family assessment. The first is that *the family must be considered as a unit;* it must be thought about as an integrated system and observed as one. Almost all students of the family seem to agree that it is very hard to learn about how the family operates from hearing the accounts of one or two members. Wherever possible, it is best to observe the whole family and to understand what is seen in each individual and dyad as related, in some fundamental way, to the functioning of the whole group.

The second basic principle is that *when observing the whole family, the richest and most useful source of data is the pattern of interaction between the members.* By "pattern" is meant two things: 1) the interplay of what is said and what is done during a period of observation; and 2) the temporal sequence of events: Who does what to whom and what response does that person have? By implication, I am suggesting that other important areas of inquiry are much more problematic. For example, it is difficult to reconstruct with a family a history of its past, as is often done for individual patients. In skillful hands, this reconstruction is possible, but in our field there is much dispute over the validity or importance of such data.

Workers in the family field probably do not agree on more than these two fundamental points about assessment, but there is good reason to believe that more agreement may soon occur and that such agreement will be based on objective, empirical evidence. There are several positive trends in clinical research in the family field that require more standardized and reliable assessment procedures. 1) There is a growing interest in careful scientific assessment of indications for family therapy itself. Family researchers now recognize that, among other areas, they must improve their objective assessments of the families being treated in order to generalize the results of their studies. Some very recent studies of family therapy have made serious attempts to do so. 2) There is a growing interest in comparing and synthesizing different approaches to family assessment. These efforts are attempting to derive a simple and straightforward set of concepts and terms which will embrace a number of disparate assessment schemes. 3) There has been a steady growth in the quality and precision of techniques for precisely measuring family interaction patterns. These techniques are being applied to clinical research programs to improve the systematic assessment of family groups. These trends have progressed far enough to map many of the options available to clinicians and researchers.

Choice Points in Assessing the Family

Substantive Choice Points

In all clinical settings, theory determines the phenomena we focus on to make assessments. Thus, a psychoanalytic clinician searches for developmental and transference phenomena to make a psychoanalytic diagnosis; the social psychiatrist examines the patient's interpersonal strategies and skills; and the biologic psychiatrist looks for indicators of neurological or drug-responsive disorders. Likewise, in the family field, differing theoretical perspectives direct our attention to different family phenomena. Many of these perspectives are not mutually exclusive; rather, each can be seen to offer a choice or an opportunity. In enumerating a few of these choice points, I have expressed them in terms of polarities to emphasize the contrast between different theoretical perspectives. The clinician need not choose between the two; he or she can consider both aspects of the polarity. However, if no choice is exercised at each choice point, the assessment approach will become extraordinarily complex and probably inefficient.

Developmental versus cross-sectional. One choice point concerns whether to focus on the family as it is currently functioning or to take a more longitudinal view of its development. Most diagnostic schemes choose the former. They attempt to characterize major family patterns or themes which distinguish a family at the time it presents itself for evaluation. In contrast, the developmental perspective sees the family as a group evolving over time and going through distinct developmental phases. Solomon, among others, sees the family as going through distinct developmental phases with each phase having its own task (1). For example, during Stage I (Marriage) each spouse faces the task of separating from his or her family of origin and investing in one another. In Stage II (Birth of the First Child and Subsequent Child-bearing), each spouse must transform his or her family role to include both spouse and parent. Stage III (Individuation of Family Members) has the primary task of encouraging, tolerating, and responding to the separate psychological growth of the children (and presumably all members). Stage IV (Departure of the Children) imposes a task of grieving, separation, and investing in new relationships. The final stage (The Integration of Loss) comes at the end of the developmental sequence, after the children have left, when issues of retirement and illness must be faced. The primary task for the family is working through these many losses and reinvesting in the marital relationship. According to this approach, a family's functioning is evaluated in terms of the requirements of the tasks of its stage of development and the success of the family in response to tasks of previous life phases.

The cross-sectional approach is the more familiar. It considers family process as it exists at the time of assessment. Developmental concepts are often used, but they are assessory: The primary assumption is that family patterns endure across developmental phases. Many of the approaches to family assessment which we will consider later on are cross-sectional; thus, no examples need to be given here.

Family direction versus environment direction. Both of these perspectives focus on the transaction of the family with its social environment and attempt to distinguish between families on the basis of the breadth and quality of their relationships with nonfamily members, extended family, and significant institutions such as schools and hospitals. However, the family-directed approach sees this pattern of transactions as determined by fundamental and shaping processes within the family itself. The environment-directed perspective focuses on process and properties of the social community and how they influence the family's behavior.

An example of the family direction perspective is the work of Richter (2). He has offered an intriguing classification scheme for families which focuses on subtle and persistent patterns of transactions between the family and its social community. However, these patterns are seen as a product of internal family dynamics. For example, one kind of paranoid family which he describes is called "the fortress family." Richter gives a subtle depiction of a closed, embattled group which must treat everyone outside the family as either trusted accomplice or dangerous enemy; the family feels itself to be besieged but infallible. Through careful clinical analysis, Richter attempts to demonstrate how this pattern is an outgrowth of enormous unacknowledged hostility and narcissistic relationships between members of the family. Their paranoid style of relating with the outside world is a last ditch effort to maintain some solidarity and to ward off awareness of the profound problems in their own relationships.

A different perspective is taken by the environment-directed approach. Here evaluation begins with an understanding of the fabric of external relationships in which a family is embedded and seeks to trace the impact of this broader net of relationship on internal patterns within the family. In some measure, this is the traditional social work approach—the exploration of resources in the community which have failed a family and must be restored. In the last two decades there has been a minor explosion in formal research on the network of relationships with kin and friends in which a family is embedded. This work was initiated by Elizabeth Bott (3), who observed that the relationship between two spouses was a result of the characteristics of the network of relationships in which that marriage was embedded. A critical property of the network was its "density": A dense network is one in which most of the people whom the couple knows also know one another. This kind of relationship structure is somewhat more typical in very small towns, but is also true of some networks in very large cities. What Bott observed (and her observations have been replicated several times) is that couples embedded in dense networks developed a very "segregated" relationship in which there was a clear distinction in role and responsibility between husband and wife. These distinctions followed very conventional gender-related prescriptions, the wife focusing on activities and values around domestic responsibilities and the husband focusing on job and activities outside the home. Where networks are less dense (the people whom the couples know do not know one another), the marital relationship is more egalitarian, with a higher degree of sharing of activities and interpenetration of roles.

One explanation for these findings focuses on the bond between the couple and its network. Loose networks are usually produced by considerable geographical mobility of all its members. Hence, all ties between nonmarried individuals tend to be weaker. They intrude less upon or compete less with the marital bond, which becomes primary and intense. In dense networks, strong, long-standing relationships engage each spouse; these relationships influence the spouses' attitudes and roles in many ways. Another explanation focuses on the power or control exerted by a dense network; a dense network functions like a very large group and can develop clear-cut norms with great influence on relationships within it. In this sense, dense networks give the couple less latitude to develop their "own relationship."

Speck and Attneave have carried the environment-directed perspective to extravagant clinical analyses and interventions (4). They consider psychopathology in individuals as arising, in part, from a breakdown in the network of relationships between the individual, his or her family, and their network. Speck and his associates' therapeutic approach, which involves reassembling this network, is called "retribalization." They bring together 40 to 50 people who have some connection to the troubled family and encourage the reestablishment of network ties.

Crisis versus character. This distinction is familiar to psychodiagnosis: The "crisis orientation" tends to focus on the more immediate difficulty, complaint, or disorder, whereas the "character orientation" focuses on enduring patterns of self-protection and adaptation. The evolving new Diagnostic and Statistical Manual (DSM III) now clearly recognizes distinctions of this kind. Axis I focuses on the current psychiatric syndromes, while axes II and V examine long-standing personality patterns and maximum levels of adaptive functioning respectively. DSM III encourages clinicians to integrate these two perspectives by making a multiaxial diagnosis. However, when we turn to assessment of the family unit, the distinction between crisis and character is less distinct, and a genuine integration between two perspectives is more difficult.

Clinical family research lacks a serviceable and empirically-based typology of family crises. Some clinicians, mostly in years past, typed family crises according to the diagnosis of the most conspicuously disturbed member. Thus, we had "schizophrenic families" or "depressed families." Some systems refined this approach by focusing on the interpersonal aspects of the individual's disorder rather than just on the overall diagnosis. Thus, Goldstein and colleagues divided families of troubled adolescents into four groups based on the adolescents' social behavior: 1) aggressive antisocial, 2) active conflict with family, 3) passive aggressive, and 4) socially withdrawn (5). Another approach has been to classify family crises according to the type of stress that appears to produce it. For example, Hansen and Hill distinguish three groups (6): "Dismemberment" includes death or prolonged separation; "accession" includes unwanted arrivals such as newborns and adopted children or elderly parents; and "demoralization" includes stigmatic events such as alcoholism and infidelity.

Assessments of family character have perhaps received more systematic attention. The basic task of all such approaches is to define stable or long-term patterns of interaction among family members and to use such patterns to group or type the family itself. Perhaps the most traditional approach to defining the character of a family is to examine the role relationships within it. Most clinicians approach families with analyses aimed at understanding how, for example, the leadership role in families is defined, who occupies it, and how effectively it is carried out. Another concept relating to family character is that of family rules. Rules are defined as stable, underlying, and shared conceptions of what is permissible in family life—what sorts of relationships, interaction patterns, and goals or objectives are acceptable. Of particular importance are the very general rules of family life that shape almost all the family members' life together. Ford and Herrick have attempted to delineate such overarching rules in family life and have typed families according to the character of these superordinate rules (7). As they describe it, the superordinate rule often has an overt component which is superficially healthy, acceptable, and conventional. However, on a more covert level, the rule actually operates to restrict relationships and limits the psychological growth and adaptive capacities of each member. For example, Ford and Herrick define a rule that organizes life in one group of families, a rule they call "children come first." On an overt level, the family supports the principle "the children's needs are always given first priority." On a more covert level, the rule is equivalent to "in this family, in order to get what you need you must behave like a child." Thus, no one takes an effective parenting role.

Pathology versus competence. Most clinical approaches to assessing the family focus on a search for disorder, whether chronic, as in assessment of family "character," or acute, as in assessments of family "crisis." Several examples have already been given, and others will be offered; thus, no further examples are needed here. What is less familiar to clinicians are approaches which focus on family competence.

One concept which has been useful for organizing observations is the notion of *family resources.* Howells' volume on family therapy focuses on the financial and material resources of families (8). However, more pertinent to our concerns are the psychological and social resources which the family can utilize to meet crises and conduct its daily life. Hill provides one approach in his study of separation and reunion of soldiers from their families during World War II (9). He was concerned with the resources families could use to deal with the stresses of both separation and reunion. Among those isolated were the capacity of families to make decisions which took account of everyone's views, called the "consultive process," the family's previous experience with similar stresses (such as other losses), and the breadth of the wife's experience outside the home (giving her a wider range of skills to fill in for the absent husband). From quite a different perspective, the "cognitive and perceptual resources" in family groups have been analyzed in an effort to understand how the family could use the intellectual capacities of its members (10). These include their capacities to organize stimuli, develop hypotheses, and make generalizations. It appears that such individual skills are an important resource for a family when it is faced with complex situations and decisions.

Another concept is the notion of *adaptive style*. Here the primary focus in assessment is on understanding the family's major goals, objectives, or values. Differences between families—in role relations, rules, and interaction patterns—are not judged as more or less pathologic. Rather, they are understood as organized or shaped by a prevailing sense of values or objectives which the family has elaborated over time. Spiegel has shown how overarching subcultural values play a role in shaping these family value systems (11). Using Florence Kluckhohn's scheme of analysis (32), Spiegel showed that families differ in their orientation to time, to the basic principles of forming and maintaining loyalties, to the value of work, and to the relationship of man to nature. For example, Spiegel compared Puerto Rican working-class families with those from the mainstream of the American middle class. The Puerto Rican family is oriented to the present, whereas the American middle-class family plans for the future; the Puerto Rican family supports intense loyalties among peers, while the American middle-class family encourages self-sufficient individuality; Puerto Rican working-class families value activity for what it expresses about a person's immediate experience and mood, whereas the American middle-class family looks at activity for what it can produce. The Puerto Rican family experiences man as subject to the forces of nature; the American middle-class family views man as capable of mastery of natural forces. Even within a given subculture, there are radical differences between basic value orientations and consequent adaptive styles of families. For example, Fallding distinguished between the "adaptation type" of family with a primary emphasis on individual achievement in the world outside the family and the "identification type" where members' primary concern was the maintenance of family welfare and continuity (12).

A third approach to studying competence in families has involved an effort to define the *healthy family system*. Lewis and his collaborators used systems theory to define a healthy family as an open, growing system capable of responding in innovative ways to outside challenges (13).* The families of this kind can be recognized by

---

* See Chapter 1 in this volume for a more detailed description of this approach.

observing 1) their power structure, 2) the individuation of each member, 3) their capacity to deal with separation and loss, 4) their perception of reality, and 5) the quality of their affective expression. The healthy family has a clear-cut power structure with opportunity for negotiation and cooperation; individual uniqueness is encouraged and respected; separation and death can be recognized and grieved with major changes in family functioning ensuing if necessary; reality can be confronted directly without the need for myths or distortion; and warmth and optimism are freely expressed, while negative feelings are expressed with supportive awareness of their impact on others. The Lewis group has developed reliable scaling procedures to assess their aspects of family functioning.

Thematic versus behavioral. Of the various choice points facing the family clinician, this is perhaps the starkest and most mutually exclusive. It is shaped or structured by a deep and abiding contrast in how human life is to be analyzed and understood. From one perspective, human behavior—including behavior in families—is a surface phenomenon giving only a hint of underlying experience and motive, much of which is inaccessible to the actor himself and is discovered only with difficulty by the observer. Psychoanalytic theory remains as the shaping paradigm of this perspective. From a contrasting perspective, human behavior is the primary objective of assessment: The task is to determine those events—immediately preceding or following—which influence the frequency or force of that behavior.

This distinction has a major impact on the approach to family assessment. The psychoanalytic paradigm—implicitly or explicitly—continues to encourage many family clinicians to search for underlying (and often unconscious) structures that give family life its meaning and shapes the pattern of its interaction. Thus, Wolin and his colleagues assess a family by determining its largely unconscious "family identity"(14). This term refers to a shared concept the family has of itself vis-à-vis other families and the outside world. This concept of "who we are" or "what kind of a group we are" cannot be easily verbalized, and the family members are unconscious of some of the feelings, fantasies, and myths about one another which color and shape this identity. Using concepts originally developed by Bossard and Boll (15), Wolin has shown how the family identity is symbolically expressed in certain repetitive behaviors of family life such as the family's behavior at the dinner table. For example, a lawyer's family was observed to have an unvarying ritual for answering the telephone calls of clients that came during dinner time. One of the sons in the family could be counted on to take the call and, feigning a woman's voice, would say that the lawyer was not in. As soon as he hung up, the family would burst into laughter. This ritual served to maintain the family's sense of being a unique and exalted group as well as its sense of contempt for people asking for help. Although this family identity played a powerful role in shaping the lives of the family, none of its members was aware of most of its most crucial aspects, particularly the narcissism and contempt.

In sharp contrast to the thematic approach is the behavioral approach to assessment. Perhaps the best example is the work of the Patterson and Weiss' group in Oregon (16). They have been concerned, for example, with analyzing what is the behavioral basis of a couple's reports of marital dissatisfaction. Their interest focuses on frequencies of certain classes of behavior, which are directly measured by trained observers in the laboratory and home setting, and by the spouses themselves, who observe and count their own behaviors as well as those of the marital partner. A major objective is to determine what classes of behaviors are most frequent in couples who report they are dissatisfied with their marriages. This assessment is the major objective of this approach, for then the behaviorally-oriented therapist begins a program to reduce the frequencies of those behaviors associated with distress in a relationship. For the "thematic" clinician, the discovery of critical behavioral patterns (i.e., rituals) is only the start of the investigation.

Technical Choice Points

To some extent, the diagnostician's perspective establishes what he or she wants to learn about the family; this, in turn, determines the methods used to make the assessment. However, there is some independence between perspective and method so that even after the diagnostician has made the decision about which perspective or perspectives to adopt, there remain a number of choices to be made about methods of observation. Five of these are: 1) the pacing of the assessment, 2) the primary site where the assessment is accomplished, 3) the principal approach to measurement employed, 4) the basic approach to aggregating or accumulating the data, and 5) the fundamental stance the diagnostician takes towards interpreting the data.

Pacing the assessment: Initial versus sequential. The primary aspect of pacing to be specified refers to the relationship between assessment and intervention. Some clinicians and clinical researchers advocate making a thorough assessment of the family before beginning treatment or intervention; for example, Olson and Cromwell (17, 18) have argued that careful assessment is required in order to tailor a specific treatment to a specific family. Behaviorally-oriented therapists must complete their assessments in order to select the target behaviors whose frequencies they wish to alter and to clearly measure the baseline or pretreatment frequencies of such behaviors.

Other clinicians argue that assessment and intervention go hand in hand. In some cases, what is learned about a family is revealed only when the clinician gets to know and understand it quite well. This is true, for example, when the search is for the superordinate hidden rules of family life or the deep-seated family identity. It is difficult to recognize these underlying structures and their role in the life of the family until the clinician has worked with the family for some time. At times, a family may not open itself up to the observations required until a firm therapeutic relationship has been structured. In other cases, it is the family's response to the initial interventions which is diagnostically informative. Finally, it is the family's use of its relationship with the therapist that provides critical data. For example, Minuchin deliberately allies himself with one individual or a subgroup within the family (19). He does so in order to probe internal alliances and boundaries in the family and to learn how flexible and open to change these are.

The site of assessment: Home versus institution. In virtually all areas of psychiatry (and the behavioral sciences more broadly), assessment goes on in the institution or office of the diagnostician. This is such an established practice that we rarely reflect on the enormous influence that the site of assessment has on the individuals or families we are attempting to assess. In work with families, this becomes a central concern. For almost every family, the primary locus of operation is in the home. When family members come as a group to an institution to review some serious problem in their lives, they are doing something unusual. There are two vantage points which are useful in comparing and contrasting the home and the institutions as a site of assessment; 1) the contrast in the meaning of the institution and the home to the family, and 2) the contrast in the nature of the social task confronting the family in each location.

The home and the institution mean something quite different to the family. The institution is part of an outer world, less well known and filled with convention, external expectations, and strangers. In such a setting, some vigilance, deference, conventionality, and anxiety are quite probable. The home, by contrast, is a more familiar setting, where conventional social prescriptions ordinarily exert less influence. In an early study, O'Rourke examined part of this problem by comparing family interaction patterns in an interaction laboratory and in their own home (20). He reasoned that the laboratory, being a more business-like setting, would be viewed by most families as the "men's turf." It was the men's perogative, if not responsibility, to exert leadership and define the main parameters for action. Quite the reverse was true for the home, the "women's turf." O'Rourke predicted that there would, as a consequence, be more conflict between father and son in the laboratory and more conflict between mother and daughter at home. Careful measurements confirmed these hypotheses.

A primary task of the family in an institution is to negotiate a useful and relatively safe set of relationships with one or more strangers. In a clinical setting, the family is often asked to dwell on a problem or a crisis in its midst. The focus is on relatively short-term negotiations, arrangements, and immediate problems and events in family life. Peter Steinglass has argued persuasively that when we look at the family in its home we can see family members approach a fundamentally different task (21). He calls this family task "pattern maintenance." For the most part, family interaction in the home is not geared to manage crises or even moderately severe problems. Indeed, Steinglass's quantitative, reliable, and comprehensive observations of family behavior in the home support the notion that problematic events are relatively rare in the life of the family. Rather, most of family life involves managing more routine events of its daily life: answering the telephone, preparing meals, fending off salesmen, dispatching children to school, paying bills, sorting the mail, etc. Although these activities are commonplace and undramatic, they may reveal the most fundamental principles or structures which regulate family life. Further, observations of these routines of daily living may be the most sensitive and powerful means to distinguish between families. Kantor and Lehr studied 19 families in depth by having their research staff live with each family for an extended period (22). By examining the routines of family life—the "pattern maintenance"—they detected major differences between families in their management of space in the home, their use of time, and their investment of energy. Kantor and Lehr argue persuasively that these domains of family routine represent the family's fundamental style in achieving its objectives.

Approach to measurement: Individualized versus standardized. In general, the usual approach to clinical assessment of families attempts to incorporate both of these elements. The clinician attempts to define the uniqueness of the family's present difficulties and its particular strengths. He or she uses this individualized assessment to develop treatment strategies which are tailored to the particular family. At the same time, the clinician is implicitly comparing the family to all others he or she has seen. The consulting room and the clinician's own presence are regarded as relatively constant, and major differences between families are attributed to differences in *them* rather than in the assessment setting or procedure. These two perspectives can now be made more explicit, as clinical family research is developing techniques to pursue both individualized and standardized assessments in which the attempt is to keep all aspects of the measurement situation as unvarying as possible.

One example of a quantitative and systematic approach to individualized assessment is the use of goal attainment scaling by

Woodward and his colleagues (23). This technique is designed for use by the therapist and is based on individual observation of each family. In this technique the therapist establishes early in treatment a set of reasonable objectives for work with the family. Most important, he or she specifies how attainment of these objectives can be recognized at the conclusion of therapy. Each of these objectives is converted into a five-point scale so that the therapist can give a quantitative estimate of the family's progress towards (or regression from) the explicit goals of treatment. The Woodward group reports that these ratings can be done reliably, and the scores are sensitive indicators of significant clinical changes in families.

At the same time, a number of standardized assessment procedures have been developed and recently reviewed by Cromwell (18). Of particular interest are those techniques that allow direct measurement of interaction patterns in the whole family. In general, these procedures present the family members with some standardized challenge and measure their reaction to it. The challenge can be a logical puzzle, the task of discussing a family problem, a requirement to resolve a disagreement, or the challenge to interpret an ambiguous situation such as a TAT card or a Rorschach blot. The family's reaction to the challenge is measured by coding or scaling their discussion, or measuring their nonverbal behavior, or some combination of the two. The challenging situation and the measurement procedures are held constant for all families assessed. Equally important, the relationship between the tester and the family is held relatively constant by keeping the tester a routinized stranger. Contact with and prior knowledge of the family are kept to an absolute minimum. In the next section one approach to a standardized assessment of family interaction will be described.

The individualized and standardized approaches each have their unique advantages, and one can imagine that in future years both might become explicit and routine approaches on the clinical family scene. The individualized approach is most sensitive to the special crises or difficulties the family brings to treatment. Thus, it is an essential component in any comprehensive evaluation of the success or failure of a treatment program. It is also particularly useful for building a relationship with a family since it takes the family's own views into account; further, the results of such an evaluation are easier to feed back to a family. The standardized approach is superior in comparing a particular family with a large number of others. Thus, it is particularly valuable in making predictions and in generalizing findings from one setting to another. It may also clarify areas of strength or difficulty which the individualized approach may overlook. However, the findings from standardized assessment may be difficult to feed back to the family. Moreover, they may be distorted by the more formal and distant quality of the assessment setting.

*Aggregation of data: Dimensions versus typology.** Data from evaluation can be used to place a family somewhere along one or more continuous dimensions. Clinicians and clinical researchers have often turned to another form of aggregating data: the use of types. A type or class is often defined by an aggregate of dimensions. The distinguishing feature of a type is that some central concept or property is assigned to the type or class, making it an easier fulcrum for dealing with large amounts of data. An example of the use of types has been cited in Richter's work—recall the "fortress family." This class or type can be identified by many features (implicitly, some of them are continuous dimensions). In general, the construction of an adequate typology constitutes a synthesis of many observations. It provides us with a modal idea, concept, or feature of family life and explains how it underlies many observations. For example, the "fortress family" can be readily distinguished from another of Richter's types, the "theater family." In the latter, the fundamental family property is the artificiality and dramatic qualities of interaction. The typing approach, however, also has limitations. For example, this approach breaks down when there are too many types, too many gray zone cases, or too many mid-range families.

Interpretive stance: Inside or outside the family. The clinician's theoretical perspective determines what is looked for in families and how the data are interpreted. However, there are two contrasting approaches to interpreting family data which cut across specific

---

* Strauss (24) has considered this distinction as it applies to the assessment of individuals.

theoretical perspectives and measurement techniques. One approach, which can be called the "inside" one, interprets the data for what it discloses about feeling states within the family. More specifically, the diagnostician tries to answer these questions: What does it feel like to be a member of this family; how does this family view itself in relationship to the world; and how does it perceive or experience that world? The contrasting interpretive stance views the family from the outside. Data are examined to answer questions like this one: How competent is the family in managing its fundamental tasks in relationship to other families?

One interesting example is the study of how families work as a group to solve standard problems. A frequently used approach is to give the family members a logical puzzle or have them participate in some game. Their task is to figure out the best solution or the most effective strategies in the game to maximize wins. One technique is the problem-solving task of Straus and his colleagues (29, 30). They ask families to play a game in which the rules are not clear. The families must learn the rules for themselves by observing which of their moves increase their score and which do not. Specifically, each member is given a pusher and puck similar to shuffleboard. Each member pushes the puck to hit a board some distance away. They learn the basic rule that only a certain color combination of pusher, puck, and board is a "correct" move. Straus makes careful measurements of what the family members say or do as they work on this problem and also of how quickly they reach the right answer.

The two interpretive stances can be applied to these data. The "outside" perspective will examine the data for what they imply about the efficiency and effectiveness of the family's problem-solving. Data will be interpreted for what they reveal about how effectively each member attends to the others' suggestions; whether the family remains cohesive and talks supportively to one another; whether the solution is accurate; and how quickly it is reached. The perspective that begins inside the family is also concerned about these aspects of the family, but subordinates them to a question with a different emphasis: What does family communication, support, and effectiveness reveal about how the family perceives the testing situation? In other words, what can we learn from the family's performance about how it perceives the tester and the testing situation, and about its own competence?

An Example Route to Assessment

Clinical family research has progressed far enough so that both the theoretical and technical options available for assessing the whole family can be defined. We are now at a point where careful, theory-based assessments can be made and where such assessments can be tested for their usefulness in clinical work. Costell and I have been investigating one particular approach, which can be summarized as a way of illustrating some of the points raised earlier. With respect to some of the choice points previously considered, this is a cross-sectional (rather than developmental) analysis which focuses on family character (rather than crisis) and attempts to define underlying themes of family life. Most specifically, this assessment approach focuses on the family's adaptive style, particularly its capacity to explore, understand and adjust to novel situations. From a technical point of view, the assessment uses a standard laboratory problem-solving situation; families are compared according to how they respond to this setting. Thus, our method is an example of the standardized approach. This approach was designed exclusively for research purposes, although it is possible that it could be used as a component of the clinical assessment of families seeking treatment.

A family comes to our research laboratory for assessment. We have tested parents with one child, although more children could be tested (27, 28, 29). Each family member is seated in a separate booth as shown in Figure 1. Each booth has a signal system and a sorting system with seven ruled columns. Family members can talk to one another on a microphone-earphone apparatus. Each member is given a deck of cards (Figure 2), and the family is told they can sort these cards in any way they wish into as many groups (up to seven) as they wish. They can use any method for sorting the cards that seems reasonable to them.

At this point, the family is faced with an ambiguous situation. They are being asked to engage in a task that has no obvious relevance to them or obvious similarity to the tasks of their daily life.

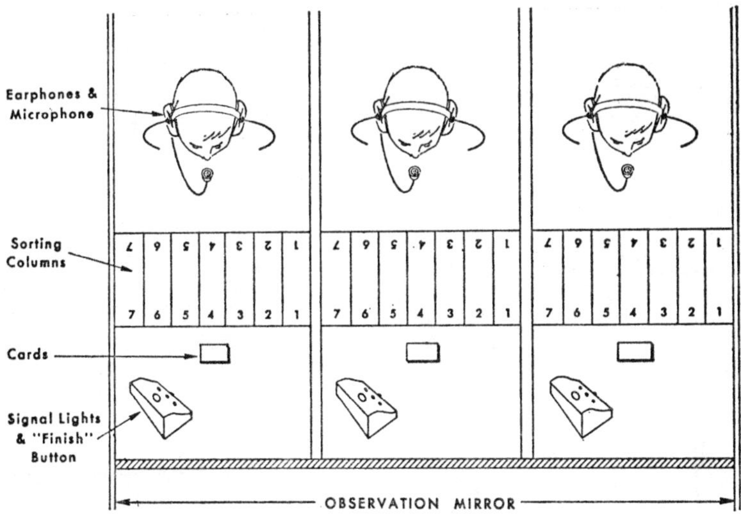

FIGURE 1. A bird's-eye view of the apparatus for the card sorting procedure.

To some extent they must interpret for themselves what the research staff is up to. It is this shared interpretative activity that is of primary interest to us. Thus, we take an "inside" perspective in interpreting our data. We have found that families differ a great deal in how they perceive us and the research setting. Furthermore, how they construe the research setting seems to be an indication of how they view a broad range of novel and ambiguous situations.

There are two principal qualities of interpretation which distinguish the hundreds of families we have seen. One concerns the degree to which they trust us. Some families take us on our word: If we give them a problem to solve we must really be interested in how they solve problems and, more important, we have given them a problem that is genuinely solvable. By contrast, some families are suspicious from the start; they think we are holding back or concealing an ulterior motive; often these families feel there is no genuine solution to these puzzles. The second important quality of interpretation which differs among families is their sense of being assessed as a group. Some families, whether they trust us or not, feel that they are

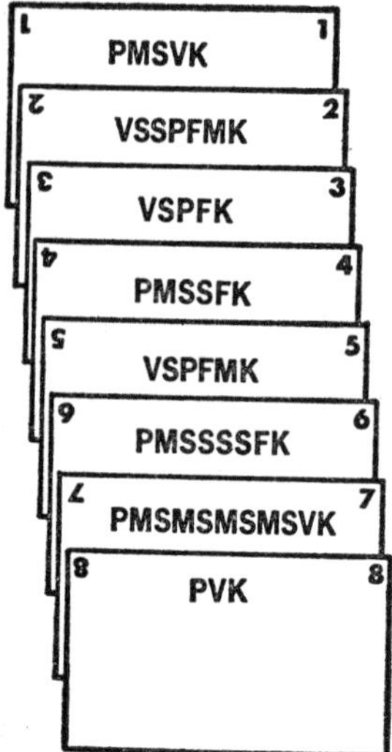

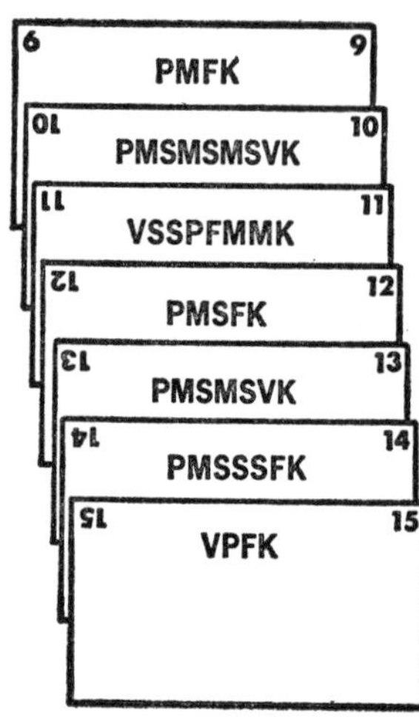

FIGURE 2. The deck of cards given to the family during the second or family phase of the card-sorting task. The cards are shown in the order of presentation to the family. Similar but not identical decks of cards are given to the families in the initial and final phases of this task in which the individuals work alone.

being examined or challenged as a group. In other words, whether they see the task as interesting and solvable or diabolical and insolvable, they perceive the situation as a group test: Whatever one member does somehow will have an impact on the others. Other families see our test as some kind of individual intelligence or stress test. Thus, the best approach, as they see it, is for each person to strike out on his own. Often, members in these families don't even talk to one another.

I want to review two important features or aspects of these shared interpretations which are relevant to the main topic of family assessment. The first is that they can be clearly and objectively measured by quantitative analysis of family interaction patterns. The second is that they form a basis for a classification system of families that has been useful in predicting the family's response to psychiatric treatment (30).

The Measurement of Shared Interpretations in Families

Two more things about the card sorting procedure are necessary to understand how we use it to measure shared interpretations. First, the procedure has three parts. In the initial, individual phase, each member works alone on a set of cards similar but not identical to those in Figure 2. Then those cards are collected and in the second (family phase) the family is encouraged to discuss the sorting of a new deck of cards among themselves. Some families leap at this opportunity; they avidly discuss every aspect of the task and often improve their understanding of it. Other families maintain a stony silence; each member works in almost perfect isolation. In the final phase, they work alone on a third deck, similar but not identical to the first two. In this phase we get a chance to see what each has learned from work with his or her family.

A second point about the card sorting procedure is that almost every subject, at some point in his or her work, uses a variant of either a pattern or a length system for sorting. The perfect pattern system is illustrated in Figure 3. Here, the subject recognizes three

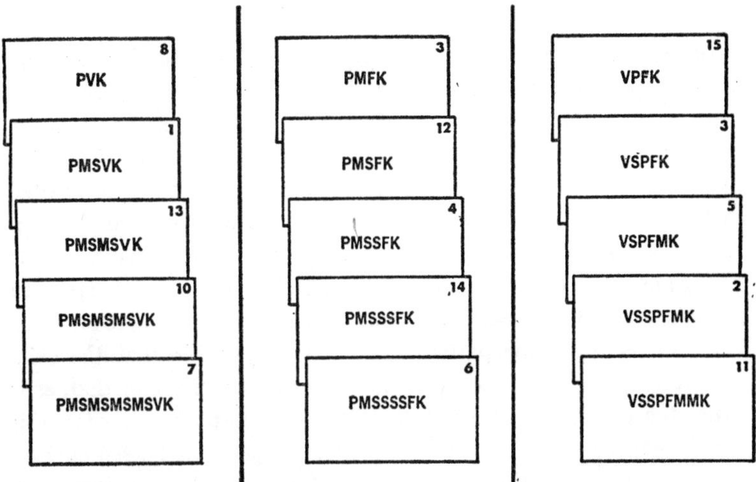

FIGURE 3. The deck of cards, shown in Figure 2, is rearranged into a perfect "pattern sort." Many families use a variant of this approach; some discover the groupings precisely as shown. This array makes most effective use of the pattern information on the cards themselves.

nuclear or stem sequences from which all the others can be derived through repeating certain letters. The much simpler and more superficial length system is illustrated in Figure 4.

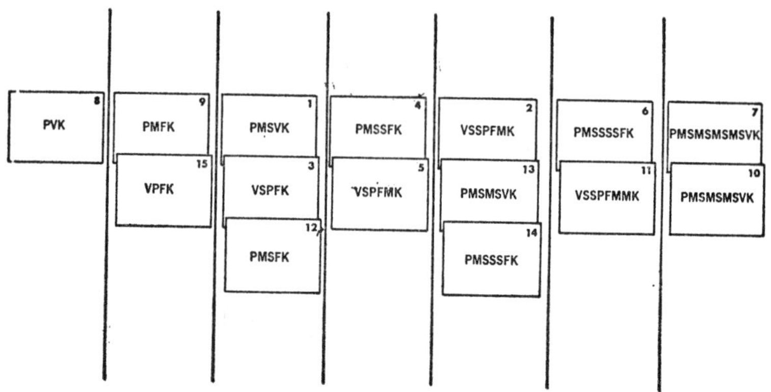

FIGURE 4. The deck of cards rearranged in a perfect "length sort." This is a more superficial solution to the task. It uses only one feature of the sequences, their length, and fails to capitalize on the rich pattern information inherent in the sequences.

In exploring how the family interprets our test situation, we look at two aspects of their behavior in the card spot. The first aspect we call configuration. It refers to the family's growth or deterioration in their ability to recognize the underlying patterns or configuration in the deck of cards. A family high on configuration is illustrated in the schematic representations in Figures 5 and 6. Figure 5 represents an initial, individual phase where the parents have trouble seeing any underlying system, but the child has recognized the pattern system. Figure 6 represents the family phase and shows that everyone came to recognize the pattern system. It is possible that the child taught his parents the system he had already perceived, or that, as is often the case, he let them learn for themselves. In any case, this family improves as they work together. They would be scored high on configuration if they continued to use the pattern system when they worked alone, again, in the final individual phase.

A family very low on configuration can be illustrated by the

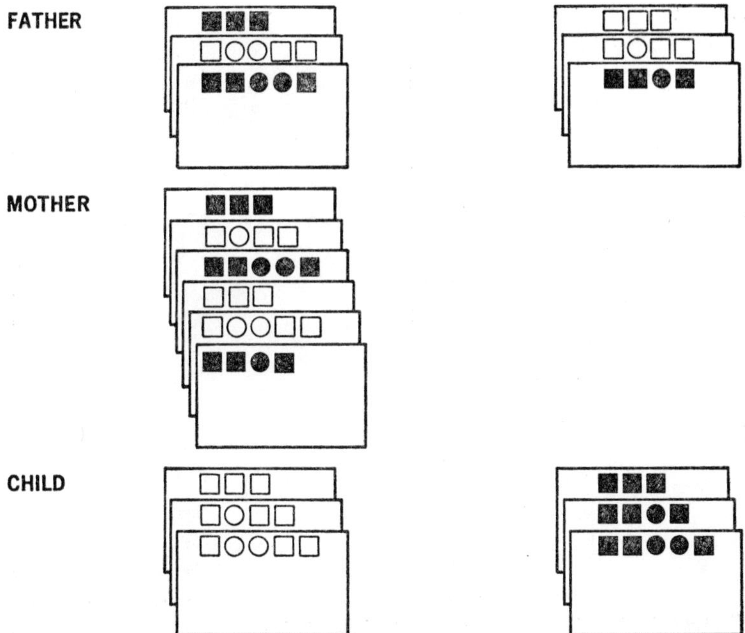

Figure 5. This is a schematic representation of one particular form of family performance. The child has recognized the pattern sort; the father has a more ungainly mix of pattern and length systems, whereas mother's sort is chaotic and without system. Standard algebraic formulae are used to develop scores expressing the closeness of any sort to either the best length or best pattern solution.

sequence of Figures 6, 7, and 8. In some families all individuals recognize some form of the pattern system (although they almost never work it out as completely as the schematic illustration in Figure 6 implies). However, when they work together they give no evidence to one another that anyone has accomplished the pattern system. Instead, they accept a much more superficial length system as shown in Figure 7. Quite often, members in these families, when working alone in the final phase, sort the cards in a haphazard and chaotic manner as shown in Figure 8. Any observer is struck by the profound impact of family process on these individuals: They clearly

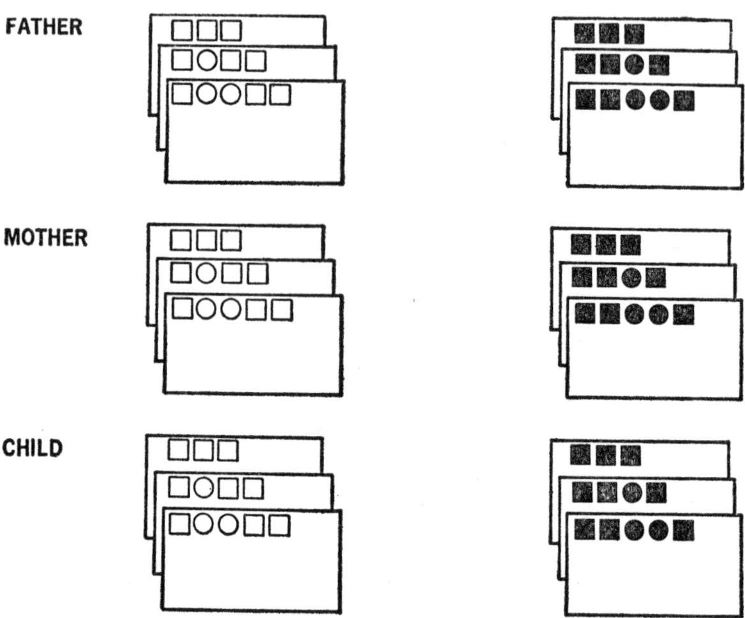

FIGURE 6. A schematic representation of family performance where all members recognize the pattern solution.

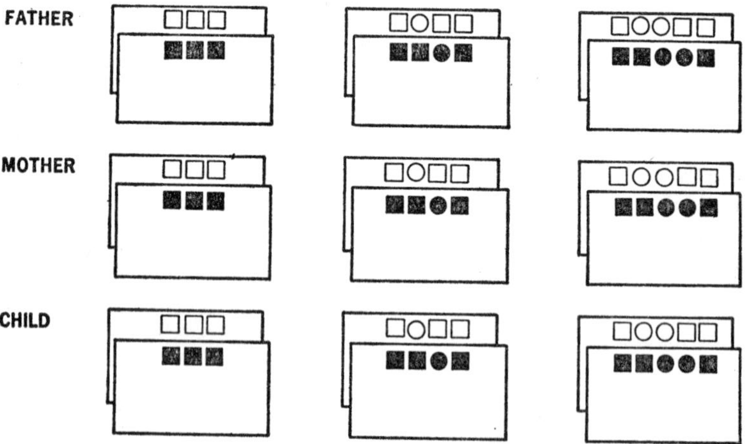

FIGURE 7. A schematic representation of length sorts by the whole family.

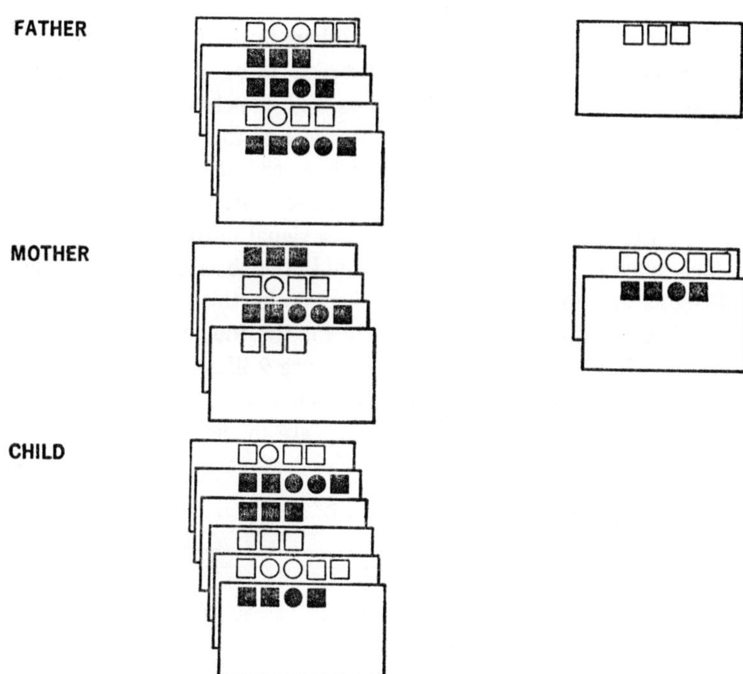

FIGURE 8. A schematic representation of chaotic or disorganzed sorts, without discernible system, by all family members.

become disorganized and dispirited through the course of a family task. A long series of studies in our laboratory suggests that whether a family is high or low on configuration depends on whether it believes or does not believe we have given them a solvable puzzle. In other words, the behavioral dimension of configuration (improvement or deterioration of the quality of the problem solutions) reflects an underlying experience of trust and mastery or mistrust and pessimism. Interestingly, this dimension of family behavior is unrelated to the intelligence, education, or problem-solving skills of its individual members.

A second important behavior dimension we call coordination. It refers to how well members of the family dovetail their work (whether they improve or not) with others in the family. Of particular importance is whether they proceed through the task at the same rate, checking each hypothesis and hunch with one another before proceeding. To measure this aspect of their behavior, we ask families, in the family phase, to sort one card at a time. They begin with two cards and place them as they see best. When each is ready to go on to the third card, they press a signal button (see Figure 1) which lights up in the other booths and in the observation area. When all lights are on, each member picks up the third card, sorts, and presses the button when he is ready for the fourth card. This goes on until all 15 cards are sorted. As Figure 9 illustrates, highly coordinated families are careful to press their buttons at the same time. This clearly reflects the fact that they are in the task together: No

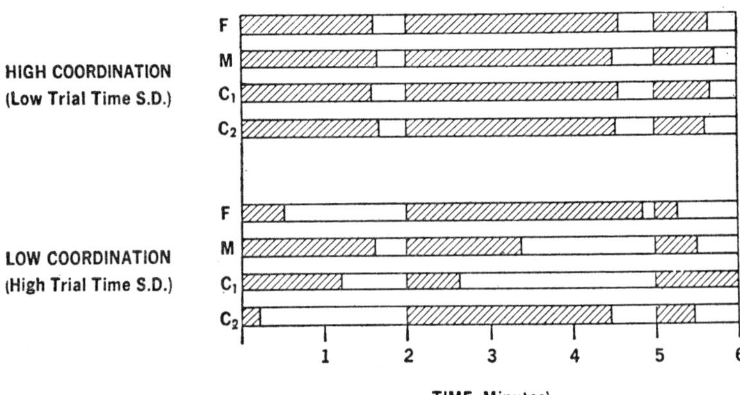

FIGURE 9. Representation of trial times, for three trials, in the family phase of the card sort. All trials begin at the same time following a "go" signal from the tester. However, family members are free to signal when they have completed a trial and are ready for the next one. In the upper portion of the figure, family members are giving their trial-ending signal at virtually the same time. This implies they are coordinating precisely their pacing or exploration of the task. In the lower portion of the figure, members are ending the trials at very different times. This implies little coordination of pacing and exploration. The card sorting procedure is suitable for testing three to four members of the same family at the same time. The text refers to testing three members. The figure illustrates behavior when four people are tested simultaneously.

one gets ahead of the rest, but everyone keeps in close touch with the others throughout the task. Members in poorly coordinated families press their buttons whenever they wish without reference to how the others are proceeding in their work. Again, a lengthy series of studies suggest that a major determinant of coordinated behavior is whether the family perceives the test situation as a challenge to the whole group or a challenge to each individual.

I can point out that our approach illustrates another choice point: dimensional versus typological. Here we take both alternatives. Configuration and coordination are independent and continuous dimensions. Families can be located on either extreme or at any intermediate point. We have also found it useful to combine these dimensions to create four family types, as illustrated in Table 1.

Families that are high on configuration and coordination work cooperatively to master the problem-solving situation. Since their dominant orientation is to explore effectively the laboratory environment, we call this type "environment-sensitive." Clinicians working with these families and blind to the laboratory data have described these families as "gregarious, honest with one another, willing to discuss grievances with one another, and hopeful."

Families that are low on configuration and yet high on coordination work cooperatively, but deteriorate nonetheless. It appears as if family members, as a group, fear the test situation; their cooperation is really a form of mutual protection. Since the thirst for consensus dominates their interaction, we call this type "consensus-sensitive." Clinicians working with these families describe them in these terms: "Parents had many unacknowledged differences; parents will not separate no matter what the condition of the parental unit; the family denies their circumstances."

Families high on configuration but low on coordination can be seen as highly competitive. Each member wants to do well to outshine the others. Thus, we call them "achievement-sensitive." Clinicians have used these terms: "They have a nasty view of people and the world; parents are angry at kids; anger puts them at a distance; the parents are often bitter."

Finally, families low on both configuration and coordination put a premium on maintaining isolation of members from one another at

TABLE 1

Four Types of Families as Defined by the Two Dimensions of Shared Experience: Coordination and Configuration. Each Cell of the Table Shows Name of the Family Type, Its Pattern of Problem Solving, Its Presumed Perception of the Testing Situation and Clinician's Description of Prominent Characteristics of the Family

		CONFIGURATION	
		Low	High
COORDINATION	High	CONSENSUS-SENSITIVE. Work cooperatively but deteriorate. Testing situation seems menacing. Clinical description: "will not separate no matter what . . . unacknowledged differences."	ENVIRONMENT-SENSITIVE. Work cooperatively to master problem. Feel optimistic about work with confidence in the group. Clinical description: "gregarious . . . honest with one another . . . hopeful."
	Low	DISTANCE-SENSITIVE. Work separately and deteriorate. Feel defeated by a test situation perceived as a challenge to isolated individuals. Clinical description: "perplexed . . . not psychologically minded . . . mothers not coping or entirely absent."	ACHIEVEMENT-SENSITIVE. Work competitively to master problem. Optimistic towards task they see as a test of individual ability and superiority. Clinical description: "nasty view of people . . . parents angry at kids . . . anger puts them at a distance . . . parents bitter."

the expense of effective problem-solving. We call this type "distance-sensitive." Clinicians have used these descriptive terms: "Parents not with it, not pyschologically minded; the family is perplexed and doesn't seem to know what's going on in the unit; the mothers are not coping or are absent entirely." Quite often these are "reconstituted" families with a stepparent or an adopted child.

The Clinical Utility of Family Classification

Costell and I are just completing the analysis of an extended series of studies exploring the clinical utility of this classification of families. Our fundamental interest has been in the inpatient treatment of seriously disturbed adolescents; the treatment program uses a family-oriented approach. One question has been whether this classification system would help predict which families would become effectively engaged in treatment and which would not. Further, it is important to know what mechanism might account for successful and unsuccessful engagement and just what kinds of difficulties the unsuccessful families might present.

First, it is important to determine if classifying a family into one of our four types could predict its actual adjustment to and engagement with the inpatient treatment program. The first step was to classify each family soon after admission according to its performance on the laboratory problem-solving task. The family's engagement in the treatment program was measured directly by observing its behavior in the multiple-family therapy group which met weekly on the ward. In order to measure the adjustment and engagement of each family, one must look not only at its own performance in the group, but also at the response the family elicited in others. Computer-assisted methods are helpful for monitoring who spoke to whom in the group, who sat where, who chose whom on a standard sociometric questionnaire, and who attended which meetings. Figure 10 is a computer rendering of seating position in one multiple family group we studied and gives a feel for the size and spatial configuration of these groups (31).

Table 2 summarizes some of the results. As was predicted, the environment-sensitive families were most fully engaged, and the distance-sensitive families were least. The other two groups fell in between but each presented different patterns (28). It is important to ask what might account for these differences in patterns of engagement. In other words, what could account for the successful predictions? What aspects of family life are being tapped in the laboratory which enable one to make these predictions? As has already been indicated, this approach to family assessment focuses on how families explore and interpret new social settings. Thus, a plausible explanation was that a family's pattern of engagement with the treatment program followed from its shared perception or interpretation of the objectives, procedures, and people in that program. In other words,

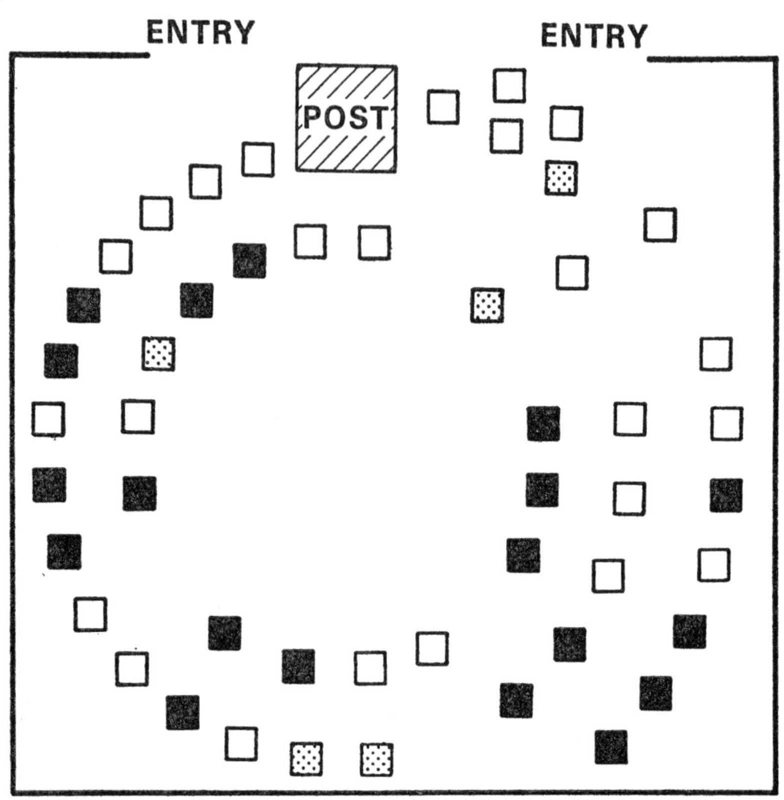

FIGURE 10. A computer rendering of seating location in a multiple-family group. The artist has darkened outlines and added labels. Computer-assisted representations such as these permit the detailed tracking of a family's seating locations over many weeks and months of meeting in a multiple family group. These seating locations, in turn, provide critical data on boundary formation and maintenance in families. For example, some families stay clumped together whereas others disperse. The clumped families appear to have relatively impermeable boundaries.

TABLE 2

Summary of Research Findings on the Patterns of Adjustment of the Four Groups of Families to an Inpatient Treatment Program. The Summaries in the Table Show Patterns of Adaptation to One Major Component of that Program: The Multiple Family Group

		CONFIGURATION	
		Low	High
COORDINATION	High	CONSENSUS-SENSITIVE. *Restricted engagement*—Participated actively and known by other families but more preoccupied with themselves than with people outside the family.	ENVIRONMENT-SENSITIVE. *Fully engaged*—Participated actively and known by other families, engaged with themselves and others.
	Low	DISTANCE-SENSITIVE. *Disengaged*—Low participation, not known by other families, attendance sporadic and members isolated from one another.	ACHIEVEMENT-SENSITIVE. *Restricted engagement*—Low participation rates but regular attendance. Relatively unknown by other families and preoccupied more with each other than with people outside the family.

as the family is being assessed, it is also assessing. Family members come to their own conclusions about the motives, reliability, and effectiveness of the researchers. One hypothesis is that such assessments, on the family's part, might be made very early and play a fundamental role in shaping attitudes towards and adjustment to the program. To continue the hypothesis, the laboratory successfully predicts the family's adjustment to a new setting because it predicts the fundamental assessments and interpretations which the family as a group is making.

One way to examine this hypothesis is to see if the four different groups of families do, indeed, perceive the treatment program in different ways, and whether these differences could explain the actual adjustment patterns observed. Costell and I developed a procedure to learn how families view clinicians. What quality or atmosphere do they think is provided in the inpatient program? What do they think motivates the behavior towards them? What facts and information have they learned about us? Environment-sensitive families learn a good deal about clinicians, often see them as altruistically motivated, and see the ward as an orderly and safe place. By contrast, the distance-sensitive families learn less about clinicians, see the ward as more chaotic, and perceive staff as selfishly motivated. The consensus-sensitive and achievement-sensitive groups fall in between these two views or assessments of staff and the program. Thus, the early findings are, at the least, consistent with a view that the laboratory problem-solving procedure taps an enduring style or disposition in families to construe novel environments in certain ways. The data suggest one can take advantage of this in assessing and classifying families and in using such a classification to make useful clinical predictions.

There are probably many practical advantages of performing assessments like the one just described. For illustration, two can be noted. First, it helps to identify very early those families which may not become engaged in the treatment programs. These families may try to pull the identified patient out of the program: They may do so overtly by signing the patient out against medical advice or covertly by undermining the program in various ways. Second, it gives staff some sense of special and early interventions which some families may require. For example, for distance-sensitive families, their pessimism about themselves as a worthwhile or effective group might be the earliest issue addressed in the treatment program.

Summary

This paper reviews the current approaches to assessing the whole family. While there is still much disagreement in the field on this fundamental matter, it is possible to clearly define several choice points or options available to the clinician as he or she fashions a personal approach. Two fundamental principles of family assessment can be recommended: 1) Try to observe the whole family together, and 2) pay special attention to both what it says and what it does in the sequences of interaction it displays over time. Beyond that, attend to some options or choices one has in formulating an approach. These options concern the theoretical perspectives the clinician may assume and the techniques available for gathering and interpreting data on family process. The approach to assessing families presented illustrates some of the choice points described and demonstrates an approach that has been more systematically developed and tested than most.

REFERENCES

1. Solomon, M. A.: A developmental, conceptual premise for family therapy. *Family Process*, 12:179-188, 1973.
2. Richter, H. E.: *The Family as Patient*. New York: Farrar, Straus, & Giroux, 1974.
3. Bott, E.: *Family and Social Network*. New York: The Free Press, 1971.
4. Speck, R. V. and Attneave, C. L.: *Family Networks*. New York: Pantheon Books, Random House, 1973.
5. Goldstein, M. J., Judd, L. L., Rodnick, E. H., Alkire, A., and Gould, E.: A method for studying social influence and coping patterns within families of disturbed adolescents. *J. Nerv. and Ment. Dis.*, 147:233-251.
6. Hansen, D. A. and Hill, R.: Families under stress. In : H. T. Christensen (Ed.), *Handbook of Marriage and the Family*. Chicago: Rand McNally, pp. 782-822, 1964.
7. Ford, F. R. and Herrick, J.: *Family Rules, Family Life Styles*. Paper presented at the Southwestern Regional Meeting, American Orthopsychiatric Association, Galveston, Texas, November 6-18, 1972.
8. Howells, J. G.: *Theory and Practice of Family Psychiatry*. New York: Brunner/Mazel, 1971.
9. Hill, R.: *Families Under Stress*. New York: Harper, 1949.
10. Reiss, D. and Elstein, A. S.: Perceptual and cognitive resources of family members: Contrasts between families of paranoid and non-paranoid schizophrenics and non-schizophrenic psychiatric patients. *Arch. Gen. Psychiat.*, 24:442-455, 1971.
11. Group for the Advancement of Psychiatry. *Treatment of Families in Conflict: The Clinical Study of Family Process*. New York: Science House, 1970.
12. Fallding, H.: *The Family and the Idea of a Cardinal Role.* Human Relations, 14:329-350, 1961.

13. Lewis, J. M., Beavers, W. R., Gossett, J. T., and Philips, V. A.: *No Single Thread: Psychological Health in Family Systems.* New York: Brunner/Mazel, 1976.
14. Wolin, S. J., Bennett, L., and Noonan, D. L.: Family rituals and the recurrence of alcoholism over generations. *Am. J. Psychiat.*, 136, No. 4B, April 1979, 589-593.
15. Bossard, J. and Boll, E.: *Rituals on Family Living.* Philadelphia: University of Pennsylvania Press, 1950.
16. Weiss, R. L. and Margolin, G.: Assessment of marital conflict and accord. In: A. R. Ciminero, K. S. Calhoun, and H. E. Adams (Eds.), *Handbook of Behavioral Assessment.* New York: John Wiley, 1977, pp. 555-602.
17. Olson, D. H.: Circumplex model of marital and family systems I: Cohesion and adaptability dimensions, family types and clinical applications. *Family Process,* 1979, in press.
18. Cromwell, R. E. and Olson, D. H.: Tools and techniques for diagnosis and evaluation in marital and family therapy. *Family Process,* 15:1-49, March, 1976.
19. Minuchin, S.: *Families and Family Therapy.* Cambridge, Mass.: Harvard University Press, 1974.
20. O'Rourke, J.: Field and laboratory: The decision-making behavior of family groups in two experimental conditions. *Sociometry,* 26:422-534, 1963.
21. Steinglass, P. J.: The home observation assessment method (HOAM): Real-time observations of families in their homes. *Family Process,* in press.
22. Kantor, D. and Lehr, W.: *Inside the Family.* San Francisco: Jossey-Bass, 1975.
23. Woodward, C. A., et al.: The role of goal attainment scaling in evaluating family therapy outcomes. *Am. J. of Orthopsychiatry,* in press.
24. Strauss, J. S.: Diagnostic models and the nature of psychiatric disorder. *Arch. Gen. Psychiat.*, 29:445-449, 1973.
25. Reiss, D.: Individual thinking and family interaction III. An experimental study of categorization performance in families of normals, character disorders and schizophrenics. *J. Nerv. and Ment. Dis.*, 146:384-403, 1968.
26. Reiss, D.: Variations of consensual experience III. Contrast between families of normals, delinquents and schizophrenics. *J. Nerv. and Ment. Dis.*, 152:73-95, 1971.
27. Reiss, D. and Salzman, C.: The resilience of family process: Effect of secobarbital. *Arch. Gen. Psychiat.*, 28:425-433, 1973.
28. Reiss, D. and Costell, R. M.: The family meets the hospital: A laboratory forecast of the encounter. *Arch. of Gen. Psychiat.*, in press.
29. Reiss, D., et al.: The multiple family group as a small society: Family regulation of interaction between its members and nonmembers. *Am. J. of Psychiat.*, January, 1977.

30. STRAUS, M. A. and TALLMAN, I.: SIMFAM: A technique for observational measurement and experimental study of families. In: J. Aldous, et al. (Eds.), *Family Problem Solving*. Hinsdale, Ill.: Dryden Press, 1971.
31. TALLMAN, I. and MILLER, G.: Class differences in the family problem solving: The effects of verbal ability hierarchial structure and role expectations. *Sociometry,* 37:13-37, 1974.
32. KLUCKHOHN, F.: Variations in the Basic Values of Family Systems. In: N. W. Bell and E. F. Vogel (Eds.), *A Modern Introduction to the Family.* Glencoe, Ill.: The Free Press, 1960.

5

Family Interviewing as a Basis for Clinical Management

Saul L. Brown, M.D.

Family Interviewing Versus Family Therapy

I find it important to differentiate the process of family interviewing from that of family therapy. By separating one from the other, differing objectives can be conceptualized. Once having recognized that several family interviews are not the same thing as therapy of a family, clinicians become freer to use such interviews for planning appropriate clinical management without feeling constrained to do family therapy. The result is increased clinical flexibility and a broader basis upon which to make decisions about the modalities to be used. Moreover, when family interviews are introduced early, their intercurrent use during subsequent treatment feels natural and relatively uncomplicated.

Family therapy, on the other hand, implies a clinical process which includes the expectation that transactional subsystems of the family will be modified. It is anticipated that, as a part of that process, psychodynamic changes will also occur. While full-scale family therapy inevitably includes family interviews as the basic procedure, it usually also includes significant variations from that procedure. Sub-units of the family may be seen for one or more interviews; family members may be seen individually for a series of sessions or intermittently; the parental dyad may be seen for conjoint therapy, while family interviews may be interposed only from time to time, and so on. In some instances, one or several of the members of the family may be referred to a colleague for therapy which may be concurrent with, but still independent of, family interviews. Thus family therapy, as I am defining it, may be a large-scale project far more complex than family interviewing. As an ideal model it is an extension of Nathan Ackerman's early views, in which he repeatedly emphasized the theme of flexibility (1). It is a model that, in my opinion, conflicts with neither the systems and communication theory model for family therapy nor the psychodynamic model for psychotherapy. Both have their place in a flexible approach to family therapy. However, as in all clinical process, the model challenges the clinician with decisions about appropriate sequence (2). What is to be done immediately? What later? And what can occur concurrently?

These questions introduce the next theme, that of "clinical reality." In formulating the rationale for the use of family interviews on the one hand, and for the decision to attempt a more elaborate therapy with a whole family on the other, I believe there may be value in offering a basic review of how, when, and under what circumstances clinical process begins, at least as it is viewed by a family therapist. I offer the following ideas in order to define a common point of departure.

Clinical Reality

For those who live with or are attached to a family, or who have some kind of intimate relationships with others, clinical reality has its beginning when psychological dysfunction discomforts a person and those who are closely related to that person enough so that need for professional help is recognized. What happens then depends upon a variety of factors. Viewed from a family system frame of reference, some of the factors that shape the emerging clinical reality are:

1) The degree of organization (or disorganization) of the person's family system (or intimate interpersonal support system).

2) Each family member's level of sophistication about psychological problems and openness to using a mental health resource.
3) The availability of appropriate mental health resources and the nature of those resources, e.g., private practitioners, well-endowed clinics and mental health centers, poorly endowed ones, sophisticated and well-trained therapists, novices or trainees, etc.
4) The attitudes—both encouraging and discouraging—present in the school in the case of children, or in the person's social group or in his or her extended family, with respect to the use of psychiatric help.
5) The definitiveness and persistence of the dysfunction in the troubled family member.
6) The emotional pain and the interpersonal disruption engendered in others by his or her dysfunction.
7) When the dysfunctional person is a child, the degree of consensus between the parents that professional help is needed.
8) When the patient is an adult, the degree of cooperation from the spouse or mate or, in the case of a much older person, the children.

All of these factors together determine not only whether clinical help is sought, but also what kind of help is expected. What each person in a family expects from a clinical resource will affect the subsequent flow of events. Expectations therefore need to be addressed and clarified repeatedly during the clinical process in order to keep the clinical reality in focus.

Clinical Reality and the Inner Life of the Family

Factors more specific to the inner life of a family than those just mentioned also shape the clinical reality. These are:

1) The level of ego development of each of the family members—in the case of parents, whether strong regressive tendencies or fixations at early childhood levels are dominant in their ego functions and whether split-off or dissociated ego dynamisms of a relatively infantile or immature nature are actively present in their behavior.
2) The major ego defenses and the psychodynamics of the patient and of each family member, especially the parents.

3) The presence of obtrusive psychopathology in any of the family members, e.g., recurring depressions, thinking disorders, alcoholism, chronic or recurring psychotic states, impulse disorders, and chronic sociopathic behavior.
4) The existence of major somatic disorders of a chronic or recurring type in any of the family members.
5) The current status of the marriage and the dynamics of the marital dyad.
6) The nature of the family communication systems, the modes of affect expression, the role designations and behavior, the family myths, the family secrets, the family image of itself.
7) Traumatic events that have affected the family in the recent or remote past.
8) Recent or current crises in the life of one of the family members.

This listing is a reminder of the existential complexity that may underlie any clinical problem. Emphasis placed upon clinical reality as I have defined it introduces a significant difference from the traditional psychiatric diagnostic orientation, which, if limited to arriving at formal diagnostic phrases about a patient, oversimplifies understanding of clinical process in psychiatric practice and fails to take sufficiently into account the potent field factors affecting an individual patient's status.

Although most well-trained clinicians are certainly to some degree cognizant of the many factors I have reviewed, their diagnostic-clinical procedure may or may not take them into account. It is only in this complex context that the value of family diagnosis and family interviewing will be understood. Decisions about whether to do family interviewing or family therapy and how clinical management should occur evolve from such understanding.

The clinical setting, an additional and central contributor to clinical reality, requires specific mention. The ways in which a therapeutic system functions and the degree of ease a patient or a family feels in using it are its core elements. In some instances the fit between the clinical resource and the patient or family may be a poor one. Sometimes ethnic or cultural factors may be of such force that they overwhelm narrower psychological issues. Every clinical resource, whether private or public, eventually sets some limit to the range of factors it will work with both in diagnosis and in therapy. Such a limit evolves out of the history peculiar to a given clinical setting, the theoretical frame of reference that is dominant there, the training backgrounds of the professionals working in it, the socioeconomic surroundings, and the nature of the social pressures playing upon it. Socioeconomic or ethnic differences, though perhaps conspicuous, may be only surface problems. Actual clinical engagement with a family group allows the clinician, in effect, to feel out the significance any of these factors holds for the clinical management that is to follow (3). This theme will be discussed again in a later section, where resistance to change in family systems will be reviewed.

A Case Illustrating Family Interviewing

A case illustration may serve to illustrate how a series of family interviews were used as a part of the clinical management of a case in which a young adult woman had become psychotic.

> Marjorie was a college graduate, with considerable artistic talent, working as a salesgirl and living in an apartment. She began to decompensate when her relationship with her boyfriend deteriorated. She moved back to her parents' house and became obsessed with her "badness." She felt compelled to confess to her parents about what she viewed as her "promiscuity" over the preceding years, became anguished over the idea that her parents might die, and slipped into a depressed obsessive state, in which she ruminated about her love for her parents. She verbalized vague premonitions about a political group's plan to poison her. When outpatient therapy failed to reverse her depression, she was hospitalized. She responded to psychotropic medication with only modest change, and developed some signs of extrapyramidal reactions, accompanied by an immobile facial expression and retarded body movement. The staff interactions with her, as well as her psychiatrist's sessions, were largely limited to eliciting a repetition of her relentless self-accusations, alternating with her fears of being poisoned and fears of something happening to her parents. She insisted that she must return home because she loved her parents so much. Her mother made repeated phone calls to the staff nurses and to the psychiatrist, seeking reassurance but also expressing doubt about whether the treatment was progressing as it should.

The nursing staff observed that after each visit from her mother, Marjorie seemed even more anguished. The mother complied with a limitation placed on her visits, but her phone calls to the psychiatrist and to the unit social worker increased. The father's visits aroused less distress, but he was frequently out of town. The patient seemed all the more in pain when contacts with her mother were reduced. The family internist called me to inquire whether something more could be done, and a visiting relative, a physician, raised the same question. After an initial family meeting, both parents and the patient responded with gratitude to my suggestion of family meetings, scheduled on an every-other-week basis. (This matched the father's travel schedule.) The patient's psychiatrist was in full accord. In the first two of these family meetings, the patient again repeated her confessions about what she regarded as promiscuity. The parents tried to reassure her. Mother's style was one of providing excessive, infantilizing, comforting to Marjorie, almost a patronization. Father's style was that of a stiff, poker-faced, controlled but kindly executive—deliberately logical and careful. Each parent repeatedly emphasized that they did not want Marjorie to come home until she was "well."

My approach was slowly and very cautiously to interpret to each of them what I believed was happening. At several junctures I emphasized to the parents that Marjorie loved them but feared that her occasional anger at them would destroy the family; that mother loved Marjorie, but that she sometimes talked to her as if she were a tiny child; that father loved Marjorie, but, because of his formality, was often perceived by Marjorie as judgmental. In effect, I gently mirrored their characteristic behaviors and commentary back to them, and added additional clarifications calculated to ensure their ties to each other. I carefully avoided any focal discussion of Marjorie's need to separate from them, but I often noted that she was somewhat fearful of adulthood, of being hurt in relationships with men, and of going out into the world on her own. On the several occasions when Marjorie began verbalizing ideas about being poisoned, I talked past these and commented to the parents that I thought Marjorie was feeling frightened about certain inner feelings. Her mother expressed relief that she could now understand what set off Marjorie's strange talk, and could see that it was futile to argue with her.

Concurrently with the series of family meetings, Marjorie's psychiatrist continued to meet with her two or three times weekly. Marjorie slowly became able to acknowledge to him some of her deeply angry feelings and to tolerate the associated affect. On the inpatient unit she became ever freer with her affect, communicated more openly in group meetings, and began to reveal an excellent, even buoyant, sense of humor. When I ran into her in the hallways, she greeted me with great warmth, and on one occasion she told me how safe it felt when she and her parents came to my office for the family talks.

As discharge time approached, after about three to four months, one major issue in the family meetings involved medication. The parents expressed fears that Marjorie would not take it, once she returned home. The parents and Marjorie asked if their two other daughters and one son-in-law could come for the final session. In that session the important supportive role provided by Marjorie's brother-in-law was revealed, as he spoke of how often he had lent an ear to her. This provided an opportunity for me to reinforce his role. The difficult competitive position of Marjorie with her very attractive (married) younger sister also became evident. I touched on this only with a light comment, but Marjorie seemed to understand. Using the son-in-law for leverage, I amplified on the dangers of the mother's slipping into too much babying of Marjorie through her preoccupation with the medications. I cautiously explained how the mother's frequent checking up evoked in Marjorie a feeling of being controlled, thus creating great anger, which she feared showing because of her love for her parents. Marjorie listened closely.

In this case the series of eight family interviews were, I believe, crucial in facilitating a fairly successful individual treatment which continued after hospitalization. Until we began the family meetings, the treatment situation was on a plateau. The parents had begun to panic and were searching for a new psychiatrist and a change of treatment, a move which would probably not have been constructive. As I perceived it, the immediate clinical reality required that the parents and the patient be helped to retain cohesion while they experienced the profoundly disintegrative event of the daughter's psychotic decompensation.

Viewed from a combined developmental and systems frame of reference, Marjorie and her family were not able to master her transition into young adulthood and an age-appropriate emancipation from the family (4). This is, of course, a summary statement. It does not suggest what the individual psychodynamic contributions to this failure of developmental transition in the family system may have been. My goal was to keep the family system relatively functional in spite of Marjorie's psychosis and thereby to provide her opportunity and time to achieve some mastery of her internal conflicts about anger and sexuality. The hospitalization, on the one hand, and the family sessions, on the other hand, made the world somewhat safer for her, as she was guided through her process of individuation by her own psychiatrist (4).

A serious danger that I perceive in the conventional management of cases such as this one lies in the clinician's frequent decision to use the therapy or hospitalization to disconnect the young adult patient from the parents and the parents from the patient. Emotional surgery of this kind is often viewed as the way to foster the patient's emancipation. My belief is that it is likely to create more separation panic on all sides, with a consequent rigidification of individual defenses and an intensification of the psychotic anxiety in the young patient. I believe that, not infrequently, a result of the forced separation evoked by the clinical procedure is an intensification of the pathological intrafamilial transactions. On the other hand, by holding the family together through the use of family interviews, there is opportunity for a certain kind of constructive reorganization to occur. This is especially true if the clinical reality is one which allows the decompensated person to be in a concurrent dynamic psychotherapy and, when indicated, in a benign and supportive inpatient setting.

In accordance with my earlier theme, namely, the differentiation of family interviewing from family therapy, the family interviews in the case described aimed at only a minimal change in the transactional subsystems of the family. While I made comments to the mother about her style of communication, my basic intention was to help Marjorie, who was within listening distance of them. It is true that I also hoped to make the mother just a little more self-aware, but I had no expectation of effecting a major change in her character style (of projection and reaction formation), nor did I expect to create much discussion about the confusion evoked in Marjorie because of this style. Furthermore, I saw no value in getting into the dynamics of the marriage, the equilibrium of which appeared to rest upon a rather stylized denial system, which had supported father's immersion in his work, including extensive travel on sales trips every other week for 20 years. Nor was it my intention to unveil issues related to sexuality or sensuousness in the family system, which may have underlain Marjorie's alleged promiscuity. I avoided intensive confrontation of the ways in which the family faced and settled interpersonal conflicts, since I saw that their equilibrium had been maintained through careful avoidance of issues. In short, I did not see this family as one open to or able to handle full-scale family therapy, in which focal attention might be paid to various transactional subsystems operant among the members (5). This brings me to the notion of resistance to change, and how I see its usefulness in clinical work with families. ("Resistance to change," as used here, is a field concept, not to be equated with individual psychodynamic resistance.)

Resistance to Change

When immersed in clinical work, it is of some value to remind oneself that change is an inevitable and inexorable accompaniment of family experience. It becomes most evident at times of developmental transitions, but it is also perceptible as reactions to events occur. Since changes of both kinds evoke shifts in interpersonal equilibrium, they frequently evoke resistance in the family system. Loosely analogous are mechanical systems, where a part that has become changed through long-term wear, or a worn part that has been replaced, causes misalignment of the remaining parts, and a mechanical resistance or a jamming of total function occurs. While both the developmental and the experiential changes that occur in families are well-known to clinicians, my observation has been that clinical management is too often planned and carried out as if these phenomena were not operating. One explanation for this circumstance is that the changes are so multivaried and occur on so many levels that a clinician, confronted with the formidable task of responding constructively to a troubled individual, feels inclined to narrow his field and simplify his work by focusing on the single patient. It is here that the field concept of resistance to change becomes helpful. It offers a framework for understanding clinical process in a total family system, even as one attends to the sub-units or the individual persons in the system (2).

The notion of resistance to change may be applied to developmental phenomena, i.e., to transitional shifts and changes in a family, or it may be applied to current events affecting the family. Inevitably the two dimensions, the here-and-now and the developmental, overlap and intersect. Developmental transitions—the birth of a new baby, an adolescent's leaving for college, a marriage, a grandparent's becoming aged and incapacitated, a death—also affect the family as here-and-now events. Events that are not specifically developmental in nature but which may be significant in family experience are a severe or chronic illness, a psychological decompensation, a career or business failure, and a divorce. A particular kind of here-and-now event that affects a family is the seeking of psychiatric help by one of its members. Another is when a family enters family therapy. A family member's being placed on a psychotropic medication is certainly a family event. Clearly, the range of possibilities which may lead to shifts of interpersonal equilibrium in family systems is almost infinite. How a family system adapts to any of these changes is a result of the intrapsychic dynamics of each individual, the current developmental level of each, the quality and nature of the transactional subsystems operant in the family, ethnic traditions, current social milieu, economic viability of the family, and environmental options open to it (6).

My thesis, then, is that one or a few family interviews provide initial insight into what may be possible and provide the early sounding for where field resistance to change may lie. From a family therapist's view the following questions become pertinent:

1) Is the clinical syndrome in the designated patient a reaction to a developmental transition in the family?
2) Are there structural deficits in the family? (Unclear intergenerational boundaries? Confusion of role functions? Schisms? Misalliances?)
3) Are there developmental faults in the family system? (An early failure of basic commitment between the spouses; or

an inadequate system for providing mutual nurturance and protective empathic concern for one another; or a failure to have established viable mechanisms for coping with daily life—planning, organizing, goal completion, socializing.)

4) Are the mechanisms for encouraging individuation and age-appropriate autonomy faulty?
5) Are there relative failures of function of the transactional subsystems in the family for communicating clearly, for resolving conflicts, for planning together, for expressing feelings to each other, for touching each other, etc.?
6) Does any of the family members have major or profound psychic disorders that affect the family life and relationships in a massive way?

By assessing the family system according to the preceding kinds of questions, one ascertains the degree of rigidity of the system and the locus or loci of resistance to change. What I have just reviewed is, of course, very general. As one gets to know a family, one learns the details. For example, resistance to a transitional developmental change, such as to the arrival of a new baby, may manifest itself as a lingering depression in a young mother and at the same time as sexual acting-out in the young father. Standard clinical interest is in the individual diagnosis and in the dynamics provoking these reactions. One asks, is the young woman still emotionally tied to her own mother? Is the young man unable to tolerate a competitive rival in his newborn? Does each require psychotherapy? What kind? Would crisis type therapy be of help? Does the mother need supportive therapy? Is each parent a candidate for intensive psychotherapy? Answers to such questions are traditionally formulated in psychodynamic terms. In contrast to—not in contradiction of—these kinds of formulations, a family systems approach to the problem begins with hypothesizing about the nature of the resistance to developmental or transitional change that is occurring. A logical first clinical step evolving from this approach would be one or several family interviews in order to explore the hypotheses and to form a notion about what the next clinical interventions ought to be. This procedure becomes a parsimonious clinical process. A series of conjoint sessions with the couple—possibly with the baby present—may enlighten everyone and might even settle the problem. It might become desirable for the young woman's mother to join in a session or two with the young couple in order to facilitate the developmental transition that is meeting resistance. These are only possibilities. Engaging the family system provides understanding of where resistance to change lies and what measures might be useful both for immediate and later implementation. Psychodynamic understanding is essential for this process.

Viewing the family system from the framework of resistance to change opens opportunities for creating hypotheses and hunches which can then be tested in clinical action with the family. This may be a recurring or an ongoing process. That is, as clinical contact proceeds, whether with individual or family, field resistance to change may form in new ways or in different places. If this occurs, decisions about clinical interventions that might reduce field resistance can be made. This does not mean an automatic commitment to family therapy or even family interviews, but merely that an overall orientation to the family system keeps those possibilities available. In the case of the young couple, for example, two family meetings might have been enough to clarify that the most imposing source for the resistance to developmental change in their new family system was their total ignorance of how to take care of a baby. The answer might then simply have been to put them in contact with an appropriately chosen child development specialist. Complex arrangements and referrals for individual therapy would have been avoided.

A Case for Family Therapy

The following example illustrates aspects of my earlier comments about the workings of a clinical decision made according to clinical reality, using resistance to change as a guide, and resulting in the use of a broad scale family therapy to bring about psychodynamic and transactional systems change.

> Marlene, the eldest child in the Kent family, became pregnant in the first year of high school. An abortion was arranged for her through a local clinic and her parents stood by her, in spite of their intense dismay and anger. For a brief period they were accusatory toward her, but a counselor at the abortion clinic

helped them see that this would be of no help to anyone. However, in the weeks following the abortion, Marlene withdrew very markedly from the family life. She avoided eating dinners with them, was moody and unapproachable, and would not bring friends to the house. Mother became alternately depressed and exhortative toward her. Father tried a couple of times to "have a talk with her" but met a stone wall of silence. On the telephone before a first family session, the mother told me that the younger brothers, 13 and 10 years of age respectively, did not know of the abortion, though they knew Marlene had needed treatment at a clinic.

In the first family meeting the formality and emotional distance between the parents were notable. Marlene was aloof although superficially polite. The older brother was open about his dislike of the meeting, but the younger brother said he did not mind it. He sat close to his mother. The parents agreed with each other that the problem was Marlene's. They recounted the fact that she had become difficult and alienated from the family. The abortion was not raised as an issue. Marlene was defensive, and in due course made several tart comments about how stupid her parents were and how she could hardly wait to leave the family. Each parent tried to remind her of how happy a child she used to be, but she seemed to be amnesic for this.

Here, then, was a family system failing to master the transition of their eldest child into and through adolescence. How might the resistance to change in this family be most effectively addressed? Marlene showed no interest in individual therapy and resented being singled out. Both parents attributed their emotional distress to Marlene's behavior. A marked relationship problem could, however, be discerned in the parents. Communication between them appeared limited and superficial. Thus, a first clinical task from a family systems viewpoint was to find a way to address the problem in the marital dyad.

For the second session, I arranged the participation of an art therapist, explaining to the family that this would provide everyone with a way of communicating and that everyone might learn something from the experience. In that session, a jointly done family drawing graphically depicted the emotional distance between the parents that I had observed the week before. The drawing was really a replica of that first session, with the younger boy placing a connective line between his part of the drawing and the mother. In looking at the drawing together, comments were made about the separateness between the parents, and the mother began to cry. In the third meeting the parents told of how difficult the week had been because they had realized how angry each had been at the other and how long a time this state had been going on. They could see that they were as much alienated from one another as Marlene was from them.

As the session moved along, the subject of the mother's tie to the younger brother came up. Marlene expressed a feeling of having been pushed aside by her brothers, expecially the younger one. The mother could see that she had turned to the youngest child some years earlier, at a time when her husband became preoccupied with a complex new business and was away for extended periods. (The brother was a cute little six-year-old at that time.) Marlene's amnesia began to lift, and she remembered that her mother was often irritable and unapproachable in those years when she was about nine or ten, and that it was then that she decided her mother loved her little brother more than her. We all agreed that a few sessions for the parents were in order and that the three children would not come in for a while.

The parents made good use of the next three sessions, reviewing the cumulative angers and disappointments each had felt with the other and facing the fact that each had lost interest in the other's feelings and needs. By the third week, Marlene called independently and said she was feeling sad and thought perhaps she could gain from talking to someone, though she preferred that it would not be I. She thought a woman would be better. We arranged this. (Still farther down the road, she was enrolled in an adolescent group). A family meeting about three weeks after Marlene's call to me led to a review of the youngest brother's hurt feelings. He became a little tearful and said his mother was not as nice to him anymore. We discussed the facts that she was now working on being closer to his father and that this was making him feel left out. The mother shared her guilt about this situation, but was able to speak clearly and directly to the children about some of the problems between her and their father. Every child expressed anxiety about a potential divorce. The parents reassured them that they were trying to work things out. As it turned out, the parents continued in a conjoint therapy for about six months, and there were two more family meetings during that time.

The early basic commitment in the marriage turned out to be sufficiently strong to restore the good feeling between the parents. The mother became aware of her tendency to avoid direct statements of her angry feelings and joined dynamic therapy group to which I referred her with the idea of overcoming that problem. The father was not inclined to go on with therapy, but he had become remarkably more accessible and open to expressing feelings.

Compared to many others, this case was fairly uncomplicated. However, it demonstrates how the initial approach to the family system made it possible for Marlene to progress through adolescence without further self-destructive behavior and for the family to regain integrated function through a therapeutic effort with the whole family rather than an individualistic clinical approach to the named patient.

Summary

I have attempted to show how family interviewing differs from family therapy and how family interviews provide a basis for organizing clinical management in general psychiatry. By differentiating family interviewing from family therapy, I hope to reduce what I consider an unfortunate deterrent to the use of family interviews, namely the belief that interviews with a family lock the therapist into full scale family therapy. I have reviewed the factors that make up clinical reality and demonstrated how family interviewing helps to clarify this reality. Finally, I have discussed how an understanding of resistance to change, viewed as a field or systems phenomenon, provides pragmatic guidelines for decisions about clinical interventions and deepens insight about the developmental as well as the here-and-now factors affecting family experience.

REFERENCES

1. Ackerman, N. W.: *The Psychodynamics of Family Life*. New York: Basic Books, 1958.
2. Brown, S. L.: Diagnosis, clinical management, and family interviewing. In: J. Masserman (Ed.), *Science and Psychoanalysis*, Vol. XIV. New York: Grune & Stratton, 1969.
3. Beels, C.: Family therapy and schizophrenia. In: P. J. Guerin (Ed.), *Family Therapy: Theory and Practice*. New York: Gardner Press Inc., 1976.

4. BOWEN, M.: Theory in the practice of psychotherapy. In: P. J. Guerin (Ed.), *Family Therapy: Theory and Practice.* New York: Gardner Press Inc., 1976.
5. ANTHONY, E. J. and MCGINNIS, M.: Counseling very disturbed parents. In: L. E. Arnold (Ed.), *Helping Parents Help Their Children.* New York: Brunner/Mazel, 1978.
6. BROWN, S. L.: Concepts of family development in the training of family therapists. In: K. Flomenhaft and A. Christ (Eds.), *Family Therapy Training.* New York: Plenum, 1979.

Part II

6

The Family as a System

James Grier Miller, M.D., Ph.D., F.A.C.P.

and

Jessie L. Miller, M.S.

Most medical specialties benefit from the fact that they are based on advanced and sophisticated fundamental sciences such as biochemistry and physiology, whose fundamental concepts are logically integrated and generally accepted. This fortunate circumstance is not nearly so true of psychiatry (or of the other mental health professions), although cultural anthropology, experimental psychology, endocrinology, psychopharmacology, and neurophysiology are adding new insights. Many investigators believe that American psychiatry has moved beyond the point at which classical psychoanalysis can provide its principal conceptual integration—yet the need for such integration is pressing. The present writers believe that general living systems theory may well provide it.

An analysis of human families from the point of view of such theory relates a particular kind of living system, the family, to the other social, environmental, and biological systems in which it is included and with which it interacts (1). While it does not offer a new system of therapy, the theory offers a novel conceptual context in which all the factors affecting a particular patient or group of patients can be interrelated and brought to bear on the problems for which therapy is sought.

Many theories of personality have asserted the importance of relationships within the family to personality development and mental health, and some (e.g., in Soviet psychiatry) have explicitly required that the relationship of patients to society be central to the therapeutic process. General living systems theory considers these aspects of families and many others in order to determine the characteristics specific to each unique family system and discover the adjustments that will improve its internal and external steady states.

Basic Concepts of General Living Systems Theory

General living systems theory is the part of general systems theory that is concerned with living systems. It regards the phenomena of life as parts of a continuity that includes the entire physical universe. General systems theory employs concepts from cybernetics, communications theory, information theory, thermodynamics, and computer science. A further set of concepts applies particularly to living systems. (A *system* is defined as a set of units with interrelationships. The state of each unit is constrained by the state of other units. There is at least one measure of the sum of the units which is larger than the sum of that measure of all the individual units.) General living systems theory conceptualizes living systems as a subset of the class of concrete (real) systems.* It provides a context in which all forms of life are studied in their relationships to each other and to nonliving natural phenomena. A concrete system is a nonrandom accumulation of matter-energy in a region of space-time, organized into interacting, interrelated components. Such systems include atoms, molecules, all the living systems, and the larger systems, such as planets, solar systems, and the universe itself. Living systems may, of course, include nonliving components, such as a person's false teeth or other prostheses, as well as the automobiles, buses, and airplanes that transport persons.

* All systems are not concrete. There may be systems of ideas, for example, expressed in words or mathematical or logical symbols.

Living systems occur in a hierarchy in which each more advanced *level* is made up of systems at lower levels. Seven such levels may be readily conceptualized: 1) Cells, for example, are composed of nonliving systems, such as atoms, molecules, and multimolecular organelles. 2) Organs are composed of cells aggregated into tissues. 3) Organisms are composed of organs. 4) Groups typically have organisms and smaller groups as components. 5) Organizations are usually made up of groups or smaller organizations, although relatively small ones may be composed of individual organisms. 6) Societies are made up of organizations, groups, and individuals. 7) Supranational systems have societies and organizations as their components. Although systems at a given level may differ as greatly as do petunias and elephants, they have certain similarities. Their units are alike in many ways. Thus both petunias and elephants are organisms with organ components. The levels of living systems are not, however, sharply distinct, but grade into each other, so that some systems are hard to classify. This is true, for example, of slime molds, which live part of their lives as separate cells and part as organism-like multicellular aggregates. It is also true of some organizations, which closely resemble face-to-face groups.

The *structure* of a system is the arrangement of its parts in space at a given moment in time. The words "subsystem" and "component," both of which refer to parts of systems, are not used interchangeably. Components are discrete, separate organizations of matter. They may or may not be systems. (A man's heart is a system, the motor subsystem of his distributor subsystem. His leg is a component but not a system in itself.)

Process is change over time. It includes the ongoing *function* of a system, with actions, often reversible, succeeding one another from moment to moment. It also includes *history,* which is change less readily reversed or irreversible, such as mutations, birth, growth, development, aging, and death. (Processes may occur within a single subsystem or may involve interactions among several or all subsystems.)

A *subsystem* is a component or group of components that carries out a particular process in a system. Each subsystem keeps particular, important system variables within their steady-state ranges. The process of extruding products or wastes from a human organism, for example, involves lungs, breathing passages, excretory organs, breasts, mouth, and birth canal. These components together comprise the extruder subsystem. (One important variable among many in which the extruder plays a critical role is body water balance.)

All systems, living and nonliving, are subject to entropy, but living systems, unlike nonliving, have the capacity to combat entropy. They can grow instead of decline and also repair damage to their parts. This is possible because they are relatively more open than nonliving systems. They take in, process, and put out matter-energy and information.

Information is used to mean order, formal patterning, or complexity. It is equivalent to negative entropy. (It is not the same thing as *meaning,* which is the significance of information to a system which processes it.) Matter-energy and information always flow together. Information is carried on matter-energy *markers* such as electromagnetic waves, marks on paper, or the arrangement of atoms in a molecule which makes cellular "recognition" processes possible. Some flows into and out of systems are important primarily for their matter-energy content, others are important for their information, while still others are almost equally important for both.

All living systems, at whichever level of the seven described on page 143 they may be, must perform (or have performed for them) certain essential subsystem processes in order to remain alive and to continue from generation to generation. These subsystems may be conceptualized in various ways. We have chosen to delineate 19 of them, and these are presented in tabular form in the Appendix. Two of these subsystems, the *reproducer* and the *boundary,* process both matter-energy and information. The others process primarily either matter-energy or information.

The Human Family as a System

Human families are systems at the level of the group. This level also includes mammalian and insect families and social groupings such as flocks, herds, and ant and bee "societies," as well as the many sorts of human groups that are formed for work, social activity, therapy, or laboratory experiments.

A group is defined as a set of organisms, commonly called *members,* which, over a period of time or multiple interrupted periods, relate to one another face-to-face. The distinction between a group and a single organism, which is the next lower level, is rarely difficult to make. The distinction between groups and organizations, the level above, is that groups lack echelons in their decider subsystems, while organizations, even very small ones, have echelons. Ordinarily, also, each group member can communicate directly with every other one over two-way communication channels, although some channels may not always be open.

Cooperation in nurturance of young, control of territories, protection from predators, and securing of food led to independent evolution of complex social behavior in several phyla. Among insects, evolutionary sequences from solitary life to simple groups to elaborately organized groups may be inferred from the existence of these different social structures in closely related species. Cooperation and division of labor among organisms evidently conferred selective advantage upon those species in which they occurred.

As the evolution of groups proceeded, a number of characteristics emerged. Groups of animals or men were able to control larger territories in which to live and hunt than single organisms. They could mobilize a greater amount of physical energy and manipulative capacity to alter the environment and manufacture artifacts. They could command more effective adjustment processes against stress. By replacing lost members, groups can survive over longer time spans than their members, and therefore group activities often continue over much longer periods than organism activities. Symbolic language is an emergent at the level of the group, although the capacity for such language evolved at the organism level in the higher primates. Symbolic communication brings about integration and coordination of human groups even when members are dispersed. The capacity to create new sorts of living systems by devising and implementing an implicit or explicit *charter* is also dependent upon human communication. The charter establishes the relationships among the human components of the new system, which are the result of biological reproduction of systems at the organism level. The variety of complex human social systems in the world exemplifies such charters.

Human beings have lived in groups from the beginning, as do their primate relatives. The structure of these earliest groups is a matter of conjecture. They were, however constituted, the evolutionary precursors of all other types of groups and of the levels of living systems above the group. These groups were necessarily totipotential; that is, they carried out all the critical subsystem processes essential for the life of the system and for its continuation into succeeding generations.

A study of any living system from a general living systems point of view involves an empirical examination to determine, first, its level and species or type and, then, its individual characteristics, such as its subsystem structure, its role in the processes of its suprasystem, its interactions within its environment, its relationship to the other, higher level systems of which it is a component, and the nature of its adjustment processes. Appropriate tests, measurements, and indicators of change over time can be used to determine whether the system conforms to norms for its species or type and whether deviation from these norms constitutes pathology.

It is difficult to define the word "family" precisely, since it is used to refer to many different sorts of systems. Sexual and genetic relationships among members and/or simply living together are defining characteristics in dictionary definitions. A *nuclear family* can be clearly defined as a man, a woman, and their children living together.

In this discussion the word *family* will be used to refer to a variety of different types of systems, usually composed of people who are genetically related or of people living together as if they were related. Kinship systems will not be considered to be families, since they are not concrete systems but conceptual systems that specify the relationships among members of a society for the purposes of regulating marriages and prescribing appropriate interpersonal behavior. (Families are to be distinguished from family organizations, in which all descendants of a particular ancestral line are recognized as members.)

Families are clearly systems, whose organism components interact in carrying out matter-energy and information subsystem processes. Members can ordinarily relate to one another face-to-face, at least some of the time, and communicate with each of the other members over two-way channels. Their decider subsystems do not have formal echelon structures. Families, therefore, satisfy the criteria for inclusion at the level of the group. Sociologists consider families as *primary groups,* in which the relationships among members are based upon affective rather than conscious collective interest and formal associations.

Anthropologists recognize a bewildering variety of family structures in societies throughout the world. In many of these the nuclear family is the basic unit. This is true of extended families, in which a couple and their married children and grandchildren live together. Other patterns also exist, however, such as those in which men live separately from women and children.

The nuclear family is the basic unit in Western cultures, although a family may sometimes be constituted of a man and woman with no children, with adopted children, or with children from previous marriages, and it may be made up of a single parent with children. (In 1976, 7,482,000 families in the United States [13.2 percent] were headed by a woman. Moreover, increasing numbers of families have only a father.) The nuclear family unit, however, has proved to be quite resistant to various organized attempts to disrupt it. Social experiments, like those in some communist countries, which have attempted to destroy these basic relationships, have had only limited success.

The *suprasystems* of groups are either larger groups or organizations. In the case of families, a nuclear group may be a part of a larger, extended family group in which it lives or with which it comes together from time to time. A family group is often also part of one or more organizations, such as a church, neighborhood organization, city, or town. As individual organisms, family members may also be components of other groups and of organizations.

The *subsystems* of groups are single organisms or smaller groups. Like living systems at other levels, groups must perform or have performed for them all of the 19 subsystem processes. Many groups lack a complete set of subsystems, and consequently they must be symbiotic with or parasitic on some other system or systems. Such other system or systems may be nonliving or living, at the level of the group or at some other level. A psychotherapeutic group which comes together for relatively brief periods of an hour or so has little need for its own matter-energy processing subsystems. It may, however, have most or all of the information-processing subsystems. On the other hand, for an isolated, rural family to survive, it must be totipotential, or nearly so. It must have a complete, or nearly complete, set of subsystems.

Obviously, a group that has fewer than 19 members cannot assign one person to each subsystem. Consequently, members of small groups are components of several or all of the group's subsystems.

A systems analysis of a family, or any other group, may include a review of the normal structure and process, as well as the pathology, of each of the subsystems, just as a physical examination of an organism does. It is necessary to know which members constitute each subsystem and which subsystems are dispersed to other living systems. In addition, the nonliving artifacts or prostheses employed in each subsystem process and the inclusions within the system which are not a part of the structure of the system itself must be identified. Each subsystem process is performed at some cost, in matter, energy, information, money (a form of information), or time. These costs must also be identified.

Most societies have recognized norms or expectations with which the behavior of persons, groups, and organizations are compared. Deviation is regarded as an indication of pathology, although what is normal for one society may be grossly pathological for another. Though this fact causes difficulty in dealing with families of the world's many cultures, pathology is ordinarily distinguishable in any of them. Pathology may be within a single subsystem or in the system-wide processes which will be discussed in a later section. Often pathology in one subsystem affects some or all of the others.

Subsystems of Family Groups

Examples of structure, process, and possible pathologies of each of the 19 subsystems of families are presented below. The names given to the subsystems have been chosen to be as appropriate as possible for all seven levels of living systems—from cells to supranational systems. It is impossible to find such general terms that are in ordinary use by all the disciplines that study these seven levels. Consequently, we must use a few words that are not in common use in psychiatry or in the other relevant specialties. Nevertheless, our terms are all ordinary English words, easily understood by all scientific and professional specialists.

Subsystems Which Process Both Matter-Energy and Information

> 1) *Reproducer.* The subsystem which is capable of giving rise to other families similar to the one it is in.

Structure. Groups are reproduced by those individual persons, groups, or higher level systems that produce an implicit or explicit charter for a new group and select or recruit its members. A single person, for example, may sometimes invite others to play a bridge game or make up a golf foursome. Organizations, societies, or supranational systems may establish new work groups.

Components that create new families include the bride and groom who come together as a mating dyad; other groups such as the wedding party and matchmakers who arrange marriages or family members who negotiate marriage contracts; and organizations such as a marriage license bureau. Artifacts employed by this subsystem include wedding rings, marriage canopies, and wedding costumes.

Process. Groups and systems at levels above them do not reproduce themselves as cells and organisms do. When parents procreate children they are not reproducing groups but rather are producing organisms which are components of groups (see *Producer* subsystem below). These new members in the family group also may become components or subcomponents to carry out processes of other groups, organizations, societies, and supranational systems. Groups may reproduce or form new groups by dividing or by acting as organizers for other groups. In any case, the group or higher level system that acts as reproducer for the new group provides a charter or template. This may be a formal document or set of directions that prescribes the purposes, structures, and processes in the new group. Or it may be a simple statement or an implicit understanding that, for example, the group is being formed for purely social reasons.

The creation of new families in even the most primitive human society is regulated by law, religion, and custom. Many societies limit the choice of marriage partners. Contractual obligations of the marriage partners are matters of social custom or of formal negotiation, sometimes involving gifts of goods or payments of money. In some current Western societies, less conventional family groups may form without the usual legal and religious formalities. In some of these, structures and processes are specified in written contracts, enforceable in courts of law. In others, the biological father or fathers of a woman's children do not interact with others of the family.

Pathology. All societies consider incestuous matings illegal and pathological, although they define incest differently. The majority of people in Western societies probably consider the various experiments in group marriages or other unusual arrangements pathological, and in many places these are also illegal. Matings considered unsuitable by the society, such as those between persons of widely different ages or of different races, even if legal, may be taken as evidence of pathology, although in fact such families may be as normal as pressures from the society permit them to be.

> 2) *Boundary.* The subsystem at the perimeter of a family that holds together the persons which make up the family, protects them from environmental stresses, and excludes or permits entry to various forms of matter-energy and information.

The boundaries of living systems are regions of increased density which can inhibit matter-energy or information transmissions. There may be an empty zone or region of decreased density surrounding the system and separating it from other systems. Since all living systems are open systems, there must be regions in their boundaries through which matter-energy and information can pass.

Because of the physical separateness and independent mobility of the component organisms, boundaries of groups and of systems at higher levels, which are the human beings and associated artifacts at the periphery, often lack the physical continuity of the membranes, capsules, skins, and exoskeletons that form the boundaries of systems at levels below the group. For the same reason, boundaries of these systems may change rapidly in shape. The boundaries of separate groups often also interpenetrate each other as the members of the groups move about. The boundary components that process matter and energy in some families may not be the same as those that process information.

Structure. It is important to distinguish between the boundary of a living system and the borders of the territory which it occupies. The limits of a family's property do not exactly coincide with the family's boundary. The latter is composed of those group members who maintain boundary artifacts, take special responsibility for protecting the group's periphery, or carry out other boundary processes. The arrangement of the bodies of members in space may form a physical barrier to the passage of either matter-energy or information. Or the perimeters of a group's territory may be protected by doors, walls, fences, or other nonliving structures. Use and maintenance of boundary artifacts in homes are the responsibility of living boundary components, such as parents, guards, or doormen, as well as fathers, other family members, or workmen who repair roofs and fences or take responsibility for locking doors. Because the father and other adult males traditionally take the primary responsibility for protecting family members within and outside the home, families without fathers often are particularly vulnerable.

Upwardly dispersed components of the matter-energy boundary of a family or other group are members of police and fire departments and of organizations that repair and maintain buildings.

The boundary to flows of information in a group is continuous in space-time, because group members must use continuous channels to process the messages that keep them coordinated as a system.

Artifacts such as telephones and letters are used to keep components within the group boundary, even when they are separated from other members by long distances. All members of families, except perhaps infants or mentally retarded members, may serve as components of the information boundary.

Process. Boundaries carry out three separate but related processes: (a) They are barriers to flows of matter-energy and information into and out of systems. More work must be expended to move matter-energy and the markers which bear information across a boundary than on either side of it, except at components of the boundary that are specifically adapted to carry out such transmissions. (b) They filter certain sorts of matter-energy and information, permitting some sorts to cross into or out of the system but not others. The amounts of either sort of flow vary from time to time. (c) They maintain a steady-state differential between the interior of the system and its environment, making it more likely that a given sort of matter-energy or information will be on one side or the other of the boundary.

In general, inputs not needed or wanted by the system, harmful or excessive inputs, or inputs of inappropriate size, shape, chemical structure, or information content are excluded from entering, while their opposites are admitted.

In some sorts of living systems at the level of group or above, these boundary processes are complicated by the special characteristics of the living components. A football team in a huddle is bounded by a wall of sturdy bodies. On the field, the boundary of the team loses its close continuity, as components of the two teams mingle in complex patterns. The offensive team attempts to find vulnerable places in its opponent's line through which a man or a ball can be forced. The defending team maneuvers to form an impenetrable barrier to these forms of matter-energy.

Families ordinarily have houses or apartments which prevent certain harmful kinds or excessive amounts of matter-energy from impinging on the living system within. Doors are opened only to people who are known or appear to be harmless. Weapons may be kept to protect family members.

Two sorts of information flow cross family boundaries. The first consists of patterned inputs carried in speech, writing, and other sorts of communications. The second is monetary information. Money is information, because a marker of metal or paper carries the message that in a particular society it can be exchanged by the holder for a certain amount of goods or services, as determined by current prices.

The boundary to interpersonal communications surrounds everyone in the family, even when they are widely separated in space. Certain private communications are made only within the family, and all members are aware that these are not to pass beyond the boundary, so that people outside the family cannot learn of them. When a child is away at college, she or he continues to be included inside this boundary, using letters and telephone calls to exchange information and remain coordinated with the rest of the group.

Incoming information of various sorts is also filtered out at many family information boundaries. Parents censor television programs and other entertainment considered inappropriate for children. A father may read *Penthouse* in the barber shop, but take care to keep it out of the house.

Monetary information flowing out of the family is also usually controlled. A budget has various functions. One of these is to restrict the rate of output of money from the family.

Pathology. Families that fail to exclude visitors at times when they need privacy, peace, or quiet are failing in boundary maintenance. Poor protection of children, whether on or off the family's property, represents abnormal boundary processing. Carelessness in locking windows and doors or in using protective devices may decrease the effectiveness of family boundaries so much that family property may be damaged or stolen, or family members may be harmed.

Some parents so fear impacts from the communications media and the secular society that they arrange for the boundary of the family to filter out impinging information which they fear might corrupt their children or damage the family structure. They may refuse to send their children to school, forbid them to have contact with children they consider unsuitable, or limit their access to books and other media. When carried to extremes, this is a pathology of the boundary process.

Subsystems Which Process Matter-Energy

The matter-energy processing subsystems of families have not traditionally been of as much concern to psychiatrists as the other subsystems. Their activities are, however, essential to families, and perhaps psychiatrists should pay more attention to them than they have.

> 3) *Ingestor.* The subsystem which brings matter-energy across the family boundary from the environment.

Structure. The subgroups or single members that bring into a family whatever matter and energy are required for its processes are ingestor components. Refreshment committees of social groups belong to this subsystem, as do members of a work group who carry in materials needed for a job or members of families who buy and bring home food and all the great varieties of things needed for family members and their home. Components are lacking in some groups, like committees, which chiefly process information and meet for short or interrupted periods. Their members are dependent upon other systems for their ingesting. Upwardly dispersed components are common in this subsystem. Groups that are parts of organizations or that meet in buildings maintained by organizations receive heat, cool air, and illumination as services provided by the organization. Delivery of purchases by stores and provision of energy by gas and electric companies to a family's home are other examples.

Process. Division of the labor of the ingesting process according to sex is traditional in human families. In many primitive societies women and children gather food and firewood, and men hunt.

The expectation that women will be responsible for grocery shopping and for buying clothing and household items continues in Western urban society. Men are expected to concern themselves more with outdoor equipment and the larger and more expensive forms of matter-energy like automobiles. These traditional assignments can no longer be taken for granted, however. Traditional sex roles in recent years are increasingly reversed. It is important when observing families to discover how the essential ingesting processes are carried out in any particular family.

Pathology. Abnormalities of ingesting include bringing into the family foods lacking in nutrition instead of more healthful foods, and obtaining of clothing that is unsuitable for each family member or is uncomfortable in their climate.

> 4) *Distributor.* The subsystem which carries inputs from outside the family or outputs from its subsystems around the family to each member.

Structure. A family subgroup or single member may be the component responsible for assuring that matter-energy of various sorts is appropriately distributed to family members in accordance with their needs and the subsystem processes they perform. This subsystem is often dispersed to all members of a family, each of whom helps himself.

Family members who are separated in space or interacting in other systems may receive matter-energy distributions from their own family (for example, from parents who visit them in a hospital), or the matter-energy may flow through the distribution subsystem of the organization or society in which they are located (for example, the food services of a university, an express company, or the national mail).

Artifacts such as cars, delivery trucks, express vans, or airplanes are used in this subsystem.

Process. In most families the parents are responsible for distribution among family members of the matter-energy appropriate for them and necessary for their health and comfort. The process of food distribution in some families is very informal, each person helping himself from the refrigerator.

Pathologies of this subsystem can include giving alcoholic drinks to young children, or inequitable distribution of clothing, toys, or food, favoring one child above others.

> 5) *Converter.* The subsystem which changes certain inputs to the family into forms more useful for the special processes of that particular group.

Structure. Families ordinarily have a converter subsystem, although it is less fully developed in modern urban families than in primitive and rural families.

All members of families except small children can be part of this subsystem. Choppers of wood, grinders of corn, butchers of animals for food and leather, and seamstresses who cut cloth for clothing are all components. Upwardly dispersed components are the many organizations that prepare matter-energy for use.

Artifacts range from stone axes to sophisticated food processors and machine tools.

Process. Modern urban families receive their matter-energy in more immediately usable forms than most rural families. Wood is delivered by the cord, many kinds of food are prepared in advance by manufacturers, and clothing is bought at stores. In contrast, rural families start with intact trees, corn in the shock, large dead animals complete with fur or feathers, and yards of material for clothing.

The division of labor by sex found in primitive groups, by which women grind corn and men chop wood and kill animals, continues into modern life in probably the majority of families, where women are in charge of preparing food and providing clothing materials.

Pathologies of this subsystem concern improper cooking of food or incompetent preparation of other necessities.

> 6) *Producer.* The subsystem which forms stable associations that endure for significant periods among matter-energy inputs to the family or outputs from its converter, the materials created being for nutrition or health care or comfort of members of the family, for repairing damage to or replacing property of the family, or for providing energy for moving or constituting the family's outputs of products or information markers to its suprasystem.

Structure. Parents who, by procreating, add new members to the family group are components of this subsystem. The family member who cooks food, builds furniture or other objects for the family's use, sews or mends their clothing, or creates art objects for the home is also a component. Whoever takes care of the health of family members, heals their wounds, and treats their illnesses is a producer component. Many of these processes are upwardly dispersed to organizations that provide health care to the community.

Artifacts of this subsystem are all the implements and tools used in the many processes represented.

Process. As in the two previous subsystems, processes of this subsystem are often allocated on the basis of sex. Depending upon how totipotential the family is, it may carry out many producing functions or few. Some urban families do little more than mix instant coffee.

Pathology. Failure to care properly for the health of family members can be a pathology of this subsystem. Perhaps some would say that producing more children than the parents can care for is also a pathology.

7) *Matter-energy storage.* The subsystem which retains in the family, for different periods of time, deposits of various sorts of matter-energy.

Structure. Components of this subsystem in human families are the members responsible for placing and keeping foods and other useful items in storage areas in the family's territory.

Process. Almost all families store some foods, and the more totipotential ones may store over a summer almost everything they expect to eat in the next winter. Out-of-season clothing is usually stored. Outgrown clothes and shoes may be saved until the next younger child is big enough for them. In addition, all sorts of valued and useful objects are tucked away in closets and storage areas. In urban families, many processes of this subsystem are upwardly dispersed. Grocery, department, and other types of stores keep large supplies so the family need not store more than are needed for a few days or weeks.

Artifacts of this subsystem include containers and storage places such as closets, dressers, chests, cupboards, freezer, and refrigerators.

Pathology. Storage areas arranged like Fibber McGee's closet, out of which half the contents tumbled every time he opened the door, represent one sort of pathology of this subsystem. So does storage so careless that potentially useful things are misplaced, damaged, or destroyed.

8) *Extruder.* The subsystem which transmits matter-energy out of the family in the form of products or wastes.

Structure. Usually this subsystem includes most or all of a family's members. A child who carries out the garbage, an adult who orders intruders off the property, any member who disposes of things she or he no longer wants—all are extruder components. A housekeeper employed by the family is an inclusion in the system, who carries out some functions of this and several other subsystems. If the family grows or makes a product for sale, the person who takes it to market is a component of the extruder subsystem.

Artifacts used by this subsystem include garbage cans, wastebaskets, and cleaning equipment. Upwardly dispersed components include the garbage men of the community in which the family lives, a private company paid to remove wastes, or the municipal civil servants that operate the community's sewer system.

Process. Persons and animals on a family's property are input-output systems constantly putting out products or wastes in their individual or group matter-energy processing activities. The total rate of these activities determines how rapidly wastes or other unwanted materials pile up on the family's land or in the home.

Pathology. One abnormality of this subsystem and of the matter-energy storage subsystem is permitting wastes to pile up in the home. This can be a fairly simple evidence of poor housekeeping or, in some publicized cases, of severe emotional pathology on the part of the people involved.

> 9) ***Motor.*** The subsystem which moves the family or parts of it in relation to part or all of its environment or moves components of its environment in relation to each other.

Structure. Systems at the group level and above, composed as they are of relatively autonomous separate organisms, lack the sort of motor subsystem that is found in systems whose components are held together within skins or membranes. Movement of a family is either dispersed laterally to each separate family member, or artifacts are used. Infants that cannot crawl or walk are parasitic upon older members of the family for moving from place to place.

A member of a family driving a car or boat in which the group rides is a part of this subsystem. A member who takes responsibility for the care of the car is another. A member responsible for organizing and carrying out a family move is another. Upwardly dispersed components of this subsystem are transportation companies of various sorts, moving companies, and automobile maintenance companies.

Artifacts used by the subsystem include cars, boats, wheelbarrows, shopping carts, and baby carriages.

Process. Families move as groups when they change their place of residence, when they travel together on vacations, or when they carry out coordinated tasks that require moving parts of the environment in relation to each other—for instance, if they all help to clear a fallen tree from their driveway. Some gypsy families live in motorized vans and have no home territory.

Pathologies of this subsystem include situations in which family moves are not well coordinated, as when one member is late and they all miss a plane or when one child gets separated from the others on a trip.

> 10) *Supporter.* The subsystem which maintains the proper spatial relationships among members of the family so that they can interact without weighing each other down or crowding each other.

Structure. Living systems at the level of the group and above lack skeletons or other internal supporters. Primitive human families make use of natural objects such as logs, rocks, caves, and trees to maintain comfortable spatial relationships among their members. Modern families use houses and furniture for the same purpose. Automobiles and other means of transportation are designed to carry out support as well as moving functions.

Process. This subsystem provides rigid support and so there is little action to describe. If a house collapses or an automobile is damaged, the family members within it are disorganized and may be injured.

Pathologies of this subsystem occur when supporting artifacts are not properly constructed to carry out subsystem processes.

Subsystems Which Process Information

Information-processing, especially emotional and cognitive communication by gestures, symbols, and languages, is particularly characteristic of the human species and human families. Consequently, the subsystems of families which process information are of special interest to psychiatrists.

> 11) *Input transducer.* The sensory subsystem which brings markers bearing information into the family, changing them to other matter-energy forms suitable for transmission within it.

Structure. All members of families, except those who cannot communicate, at one time or another are components of the input transducer, since they go out into their environment and bring back accounts of their experience. Input transducer components of families are almost always components of the decoder subsystem as well. The input transducer of a family may be upwardly dispersed, as when a messenger, perhaps from Western Union, enters the home to deliver a message. It can be downwardly dispersed if every member transduces (and decodes) input for himself. This happens when a sound from outside, such as a television tornado warning, is heard and understood by all the family.

Artifacts transduce a great deal of information input into modern families. Radio, television, and telephone are all mechanical transducers which bring into a home news of the world, music, entertainment, and information about the latest washday miracles.

Process. Like input transducers at the levels of the cell, the organ, and the organism, the input transducers of groups can be described in the terms used for mechanical and electronic transducers, although no great degree of precision of description has yet been achieved at levels above the organism.

The memory and coding capabilities of the person who brings information to the family can affect the completeness and accuracy of the transmission if he is not able to remember part of what he observed in the environment or is unable to decode it properly, like the child who reported "a big worm" in the yard when what he had seen was a big rattlesnake. Parts of a message may be left out as unimportant because the person reporting was unable to recognize their importance. Distortions occur because of personal bias or because of "noise" in the system, which obscures part of the information. Families come to recognize which members cannot be considered entirely reliable reporters and take their stories with a grain of salt. The channel capacity of the input transducer can be raised by having more than one member act as transducer components and comparing their reports. An older member, who may be a more competent observer, can be used instead of a child. This procedure can also reduce lags in transducing.

Pathologies of input transducing can include deliberate distortion of reported messages or occurrences. Parents sometimes shield children from learning of events in the outside world which they consider potentially damaging to them. This is sometimes helpful, but under some circumstances such shielding can be harmful to the children.

> 12) *Internal transducer.* The sensory subsystem which receives, from subsystems or components within the family, markers bearing information about significant alterations in these subsystems or components, changing them to other matter-energy forms of a sort which can be transmitted within it.

Structure. Families usually do not have designated members who carry out this subsystem process, although some have a family council in which exchanges take place, among all members who can communicate, about their feelings and attitudes. Ordinarily, all family members are part of the internal transducer.

Process. Communications transduced by this subsystem may be about tasks to be carried out by group members or about feelings and attitudes of family members. Members also report information from their memories. Communications may be verbal, or they may be transmitted over other communications bands—by gesture, behavior, or expressive sounds, such as the cries of an infant. These two sorts of information are called "work" and "emotionality" by Thelen (2), "internal" and "external" systems of the group by Homans (3), and "task-related" or "socioemotional" acts by Bales (4).

In a family, the first sort could be exemplified by a parent's assigning chores to each child and discussing their performances with them. The second could be the emotional exchanges among members of the family who express their feelings toward one another. The two types of communications have been experimentally separated in studies of laboratory groups in various artificially constrained networks. These group members communicate by means of written messages and do not see each other.

Results of such researches show that the more "central" members—those more easily accessible for communication—were more satisfied, more likely to become leaders, and more able to solve group problems correctly. This may be true of family groups interacting under normal surroundings, but this has not yet been demonstrated.

Members of families often become so sensitive to the feelings and attitudes of other members that much of their communication is nonverbal. A mother interprets the sounds her baby makes to know whether he is hungry, wet, in some kind of trouble, or simply enjoying himself. When a child is cross or out of sorts, he often need not communicate his feelings verbally. The rest of the family knows.

Pathologies of the input transducer subsystem are common and serious. Parents who are, for whatever reason, insensitive to the feelings of their children or unwilling to listen to their problems, children who cannot communicate their feelings and withdraw from interactions with others in the family, children who express very negative feelings toward one or more other family members—all contribute to group pathology, damaging the group and its individual members.

> 13) *Channel and net.* The subsystem composed of a single route in physical space, or multiple interconnected routes, by which markers bearing information are transmitted to all parts of the family.

Structure. Each group member is a part of the group channel and net subsystem, although when members are absent the direct face-to-face channels to them are not open. Information that is transduced into the system from the input and internal transducers of the group travels over communication channels to one or more group members. Several communication bands are used for these exchanges. The most usual is speech, carried over the auditory band, which carries also expressive sounds and music. Gestures, facial expressions, and postural changes are carried on the visual band. (Aside from perfumes, the use of odors, which constitutes an important communications band for many species of animals, is uncommon among humans.) Bodily contact is another communication channel, very important in families. Another part of the channel and net subsystem is that over which monetary information flows.

Artifacts of this subsystem include telephones and other media through which distant members can communicate with the family. These are upwardly dispersed components, since they are parts of the communications network of the society.

Process. Although all family members are part of the group channel and net, communication does not flow equally over all channels. The form of the net that is actually used may be different from the totally connected networks which are one of the experimental variations in the artificially constrained network researches (1, pp. 533-550). Some channels are one-way, at least much of the time. A father's relation with his son is sometimes of this sort—he speaks and gives orders, but the son makes little response. Subgroups in the family form coalitions within which confidences are exchanged and secrets are whispered. Other members are excluded from these exchanges. (For example, mother and daughter sometimes exclude father.) In studying a particular family it is important to learn how its channel and net subsystem operates.

Pathology of the channel and net is common in families. Parents may send messages of rejection over nonverbal channels while simultaneously verbalizing affection and normal parental feelings. Channels may be closed between parents and one or more children. Channels may operate ineffectively between the parents, so that little undistorted communication between them takes place. Some of the most seriously disturbed family groups have problems in this subsystem.

> 14) *Decoder.* The subsystem which alters the code of information input to it through the input transducer or the internal transducer into a private code that can be used internally by the family.

Structure. Any member or members of a family, who explain to other members the meaning of any sort of input, putting it in terms that the others can understand, is/are a decoder component. The decoder function includes translation into the language spoken by the family if it is not the usual language of the place in which they live.

This subsytem can be upwardly dispersed if the needed translation or explaining is done by representatives of the school system, the police department, or other organizations.

Process. An important form of decoding, needed by all children at an early stage of their lives, is telling the name of objects that they perceive. A toddler will ask "What's that?" hundreds of times a day, eventually building a vocabulary.

The decoder in some families who speak a language unlike that of the people around them may be a school-age child who can help his mother with translation, since in many such families the mother is the last to learn a new language. Such parents need help with reading also.

Even families which have no language problem may have special words and expressions that outsiders do not understand but which explain some event very accurately to the members who understand the family's private language.

Pathologies related to this subsystem include the failure of parents to talk to their children and do the perceptual decoding that children need. A family group surrounded by an alien culture which they do not understand can become withdrawn and distrustful, refusing education and health care which their children need.

> 15) *Associator.* The subsystem which carries out the first stage of the learning process, forming enduring associations among items of information in the family.

Structure. At the levels of the group and above, the association of items of information must be done by one or more organism components, since learning takes place within the nervous systems of individual persons. Group associating or learning occurs, however, since the behavior of a group, including a family, can be significantly changed as a result of such associations made by one or more of the members. If one member makes a critical association and directs the others in such a way that the entire behavior of the family is altered, or if every member makes the association separately, group associating occurs.

Process. Families, as their members interact over time, associate in ways that are reinforced by feedbacks from past group actions that reduce strains within the system. For instance, a family may find that solutions arise more rapidly and with less bickering if problems of importance are not discussed until after dinner.

Each family has the equivalent of its own personality, what Cattell calls "syntality" (5). As a group it may be hostile or paranoid or withdrawn from social interactions. Rewards and punishments from the suprasystem can alter these attitudes to some extent, and family therapy can have such change as a goal.

Pathology in this subsystem is failure of families to associate information that might lead to improved group attitudes and happiness.

> 16) *Memory.* The subsystem which carries out the second stage of the learning process, storing various sorts of information in the family for different periods of time.

Structure. This subsystem usually includes all group members who store information in their own nervous systems. In addition, specialized components also exist. These include members of the family who keep records, genealogies, or photograph albums. In some families, certain older members are storehouses of information about the past of the family.

In preliterate groups, crucial aspects of the culture, such as its language, songs, dances, and art forms, as well as its history, are stored in the nervous systems of members who have learned them and can pass them down to the next generation.

Artifacts in this subsystem include correspondence files, financial records, diaries, and birth and marriage records. Upwardly dispersed to the control of banks at the organization level are safe deposit boxes and computers which keep financial records of many families.

Process. Information storage, or memory, has four separate functions: (a) reading into storage, (b) maintaining information in storage, (c) loss and alteration during storage, and (d) retrieval from storage. Families are usually very informal about most of these processes, although they are ordinarily more careful of important financial records and such things as marriage licenses and birth certificates. As a result, retrieval from storage can involve frantic searches and much frustration.

Monetary information in modern families is usually stored in safes or banks. In earlier times it was often stored in mattresses, in a well, or under the floor.

Pathologies include losing records and failing to store enough money to meet family needs.

> 17) *Decider.* The executive subsystem which receives information inputs from all other subsystems and transmits to them information outputs that control the entire family.

Structure. A single authoritarian figure may be the decider for a family group, or particular sorts of decisions may be the province of particular family members, while others control other decisions. A few modern families try to have a democratic decider structure in which important matters are put to a vote, and the majority opinion of all members, including the children, is taken as the decision.

Different cultures designate the father, the mother's brother, or the oldest male as head of the family. The scope of issues over which he decides, and over which the wife and husband decide, may also be culturally prescribed. Usually the wife makes decisions in matters concerning the household and young children. One cross-cultural study of domestic problem-solving situations found that the spouse whose prestige was bolstered by the society's kinship system tended to dominate the deciding (6). Among Navahos, who inherit through the mother's line, family decisions were made in the wife's favor 46 times to the husband's 34. Among Mormons the paternal line is dominant, and the ratio was reversed—husbands 42, wives 29.

Present-day culture in the United States has no monolithic doctrine on who shall decide in a family, but the expectation lingers that the man will "wear the pants." Present social customs developed from religious and legal traditions that gave the man all rights to children, property, and his wife's person. Wife and children were expected to obey the husband or father. Even at the height of this tradition, however, there were "hen-pecked" husbands.

Process. Family decision-making is frequently irrational. Outcomes are often the result of power struggles in which one family member, perhaps a determined young child, manages to overcome opposition of the others. Nevertheless, in at least some decisions of some families, the deciding process follows the four stages found at other levels of living systems. They are:

(a) *Establishing purposes or goals.* Each family member as an individual has his own purposes, as well as steady states he would prefer to maintain. They are not necessarily the same as those of other family members. In addition, families often have group goals toward which they all strive. They may want to save money to buy a car, or have a vacation, or improve their house. Longer-term goals may include saving for advanced education for the children or for setting them up in housekeeping when they marry.

Purposes and goals of family groups, as of other levels of living systems, are set with reference to the family's *values.* Explicitly or implicitly, each family has a hierarchy of values which are fundamental to its decisions. One family puts its religious beliefs first and shapes the family life in accordance with them. Another may put acquisition of money and property first. When faced with a particular decision, the family is ruled by these values, whether or not they are fully explicit. The values of a family are not necessarily always acceptable to others in their society. They may even be antisocial, as in the cases of some robber, brigand, or Mafia families.

(b) *Analysis.* When a family must solve a problem or make a decision, the second stage of deciding is to determine what alternative actions are feasible and what must be done to achieve each. Every alternative has a cost in money, matter, energy, time, or other resource. If a family is buying a car, it has the choice of a new or used vehicle, and of many makes and models. Decisions range from simple binary choices to situations in which many factors must be taken into consideration.

(c) *Synthesis.* This stage involves the actual determination of a strategy for problem-solving or a choice among alternatives. In the first case, an order in which strategies will be tried may be determined. If we want more library books in the children's school, first we go to the principal. If he doesn't decide in our favor, we go to the superintendent. Then we try to find other families to join our campaign. Finally, we may employ a lawyer and go to court.

If the choice is among automobiles, the costs, sacrifices, and expected gains and preferences of family members are weighed and the decision made. During the stage of synthesis, family members exert influence on others to sway them toward some particular choice. The hierarchy of values of the family is often referred to in this process.

(c) *Implementing*. In this stage group members agree upon who is to carry out particular parts of any action they have decided on. Perhaps the mother will ask the principal for his help. The children may at the same time speak to their teachers. And the father will exert his influence on friends within the community, but only if the initial attempts fail.

Pathology. Failure to carry out any stage of deciding cost-effectiveness is pathological.

> 18) *Encoder*. The subsystem which alters the code of information input to it from other information-processing subsystems, from a private code used internally by the family into a public code which can be interpreted by other groups in its environment.

Structure. Juries, committees, investigating commissions, and some other sorts of work or experimental groups have formally designated components of this subsystem that put into suitable language the decisions or opinions of the group. It is not common for families to have such formally designated components. A family member capable of encoding family business into a language not used within the family—say the language of accountants—is such a component. A family member who writes a letter on behalf of the family is another.

This subsystem may be upwardly dispersed, as when a social worker fills out forms requesting aid for the family or a lawyer puts family business into legal language.

Process. The encoding process involves a change in codes from that used within the family to one suitable for transmission to systems outside the family. It is obviously an important process for families who do not speak the dominant language of the community they live or are staying in. It may be equally important for people of poor education or retarded mental ability. Someone must put their needs or requests into terms comprehensible to their suprasystem.

Pathology. If the encoded message from the family does not accurately represent the family's view, there is pathology. An incompetent lawyer may not understand the desires of a family he defends and so may not be a valid spokesman for them in court.

> 19) *Output transducer.* The subsystem which puts out markers bearing information from the family, changing markers within the family into other matter-energy forms that can be transmitted over channels in the family's environment.

Structure. This subsystem, like the encoder, is less likely to have formally designated components in families than in other types of groups. In any case, the member who does the encoding is frequently the same one who transduces the information from the group into the environment. Perhaps this is even more frequently the case in families. A parent often both writes the family's opinion in a letter and sends the letter to the person to whom it is addressed.

Artifacts such as telephones, pens, and paper are frequently used in this subsystem.

Process. Examples of transduction from one sort of marker to another in this subsystem include summarizing a verbal discussion within a family in a letter to friends or representing the consensus of a family by casting a vote in a local election.

Pathology related to this subsystem process may include writing a check or letter and not mailing it, or giving a message to the wrong person, or abbreviating it so much that the receiver misunderstands it. Omissions of important facts occur. Lags also occur in the transmission so that the message arrives at its intended receiver too late for the best effect.

Adjustment Processes

The subsystem and components of a family, like those of other types of living systems, maintain the steady states of the group by continual interactions among themselves. When any of the innumerable variables of matter-energy or information flows within the family or between the family and its environment move out of steady-state range, the family acts to correct the resultant strain by making use of one or more of its available adjustment processes. Whenever the deviation from the steady state continues for long or is so extreme that the costs of adjustment processes are significantly increased, family pathology exists. Pathological steady states can continue over extended time periods—a condition often observed in families—producing individual pathology in one or more family members. Ultimately, the family system may terminate, as a result of the continued strain. Such pathological steady states, in spite of their threats to family members and the integrity of the family as a whole, are often remarkably stable, because, at high cost, they correct personal and family disequilibria that are even more threatening.

Feedback. Many of the adjustment processes available to systems are guided by feedbacks. Both negative and positive feedbacks are present in living systems. ("Feedback" is a term taken from control theory.)

Negative feedback is the process by which system components use information about their own past outputs as inputs to change their future outputs. Thermostats do this. When the temperature in a room rises above an established point, they transmit a signal which turns off the heat until the temperature drops below the established point. Then they send another signal to turn the heat back on again. Many other mechanical and electronic control and guidance systems also employ negative feedback.

Positive feedback also uses information about past outputs of a system to change future outputs. Positive feedbacks, however, do not maintain steady states in systems. Instead, the initial output is continually amplified, unless the process is self-limiting. Positive feedbacks can diminish the control of a system and finally lead to its destruction.

Families continually make adjustments, with the guidance of multiple feedbacks. Some feedbacks are internal, that is, among the subsystems and components of the system itself. Others are external, flowing back into the system from the outside environment.

Family members respond to reactions of other members to their own behavior. Depending upon their own dynamics and the dynamics of the total family system, they either change or continue their previous behavior. Such responsiveness in some families can be exceedingly acute. Minimal signs are correctly interpreted, even when the responding member may not be entirely aware of his own feelings. Such sensitivity can produce harmony in the family if the members' adjustments to signals serve to reduce interpersonal strains. If they serve to increase them, the sensitivity can be destructive.

The importance of feedback in maintaining steady states in families was emphasized by Jackson (7). His clinical observations led him to view family interactions as information flow with corrective feedback. For example, in one family a boy won a popularity contest, but he found that this displeased his mother. The son then used various adjustment processes in order to restore her favor, including efforts to keep from being so popular. Psychotherapy received by one member of a family can change her or his interactions with the others, thus altering interpersonal steady states of the whole family.

As a family interacts in its neighborhood and in other parts of its suprasystem, such as the school system, the church, the city, and larger governmental units, negative feedbacks guide its behavior. Report cards to parents from the school system usually are signals to them to do something to help their child if she or he is performing poorly, or to continue their past behavior if the child is doing well.

Neighbors are often all too quick to provide vociferous negative feedback if children encroach on their property or misbehave outside the home—unsubtle hints to the parents to mend their ways. But when the property is neat, parents and children well-behaved, and relations with the neighbors friendly, the family basks in supportive and encouraging negative feedback. Social agencies, law enforcement agencies, and courts may also provide a family with negative feedback on its behavior in the suprasystem.

A family's political activities also are influenced by feedback. If the economy deteriorates after they have voted for one candidate, they may switch to another at the next election.

Positive feedbacks also occur, particularly in neighborhoods in which there are racial tensions, extreme poverty, or widespread unemployment. These can lead to quarrels within and among families which may well escalate to delinquency, crime, and violence.

An amusing example of positive feedback in a husband-wife dyad occurs when the dual controls of their electric blanket are reversed. In the normal, negative feedback situation, either can turn the heat up or down on her or his side as she or he wishes. In the positive feedback situation, however, if the husband is cold, he turns up the heat on his wife's side of the bed, and she, becoming too warm, turns his control down. As he gets colder, he turns her control up more, and so on.

Family quarrels can have similar positive feedback effects. Beginning with a small, even trivial disagreement, they may become more and more bitter, involving more and more issues, sometimes leading to escape of the children from the home, to breakdown of the family system by separation or divorce, or, in extreme cases, even to murder.

Other sorts of adjustment processes. Adjustments of various kinds occur in families to lacks or excesses of matter-energy or information inputs, internal processes, or outputs. Lacks of essential matter-energy inputs, such as food, result in a variety of behaviors, including applying for welfare and stealing from the grocery store. Excess matter-energy inputs, such as lightning, blizzards, or floods, can cause damage to a family and its property. Consequently, each of these stresses ordinarily elicits appropriate adjustments within the family's capabilities.

An important set of internal adjustment processes results from loss or addition of a family member. Either death or divorce causes profound adjustments on the part of each member individually and on the part of the group. Remaining members must find some way in which essential services that the lost member had previously carried out can be performed. When a child goes away to college or leaves home for any reason, similar adjustments occur. Loss of the child's contribution to the family's information exchange—the conversations, emotional interactions, teaching or learning situations—must be adjusted to in some way.

The adjustments may be pathological: A widow may become overly dependent on her children, to their detriment. A child may be forced into a maternal or paternal role unsuited to his age. A previously satisfactory steady-state may become unstable, as when a couple whose children have left the home discover they have nothing to say to each other.

Addition of a member to a family also requires adjustments on the part of all the others. Relations among the parents and other children are changed. A new baby, even though eagerly desired, may disrupt what had appeared to be a successful marriage. In general, anything that disturbs the personal steady state of one family member can affect each of the others and alter in some way the system interrelationships.

Research has been done on interaction rates among group members. According to Chapple and Coon, each participant in a group has a characteristic interaction rate (8, p. 47). One is talkative, another is notably quiet—"You would never know he was in the house." When a member leaves the group, some or all the others increase their rates of interaction to allow for the change. If a new person is added, increasing the number in the group, the average interaction rates of the others will be decreased. Interaction rates of families have not been studied, but it seems probable that the research findings apply to face-to-face interactions of families.

Integration. Families are integrated when their multiple, simultaneous, separate processes are under control of centralized decision-making and work toward common purposes or goals. Over time a family may become progressively more integrated or more segregated. Segregation may in some cases become so extreme that the family's system characteristics disappear. Members drift apart, and centralized decision processes no longer control or coordinate them.

Families obviously vary in their degree of integration. Particularly when the children are young, parents may maintain discipline, control the behavior of their offspring, and coordinate family processes. As the children grow older, an integrated family permits them to have a part in decisions, and many decisions are based on family consensus. Inevitably, integration weakens as the children mature and leave the family home, either living alone and making their own decisions, or forming new family groups. Some families, even when the children are young, are not very integrated. A minimum of attention is paid to the children, and little control is exercised over their behavior. Parents may go their separate ways, each making her or his decisions with little regard to the other. In some cases such disintegration of the family becomes pathological. Then the children are not properly cared for and may even be abandoned, so that components of the suprasystem—neighbors, social agencies, or the police and courts—must intervene to protect the children.

Some of the factors that produce integration in groups have been studied (1, pp. 577-578). They include liking to be together, sharing common goals, and accepting common values.

Conclusion

We have now outlined general living systems theory and shown how it can be applied to an understanding of the human family. In doing so, we have introduced terms which are not currently in the usual clinical vocabulary of psychiatrists, even though they are ordinary English words. Some may ask if this new terminology is necessary or if it is just another jargon which can easily be dispensed with. Our answer is that the new terms are essential to our attempt to find the most neutral and acceptable words to fit all types and levels of systems and reveal whatever cross-level identities may exist among them. Each scientific and clinical specialty develops its own terminology, and there often appears to be no Rosetta stone to make it possible to translate one into another. As a result, the various scientific and professional disciplines appear to be unrelated islands that do not intercommunicate. A major purpose of general living systems theory is to bridge these islands by using systems concepts expressed in the new terms which are designed exactly for that purpose.

General living systems theory will not be of optimal value unless it is accurately understood and applied. Of course, this theory is relatively new, and it has not often been applied in ways that use its full potential to psychiatry. The systems approach frequently is approved of by psychiatrists, but commonly they refer only to such vague principles as that a system's capabilities are greater than the sum of the capabilities of all its parts, or that a single person or other component of a living system must be studied in relationship to all of the other components with which she or he interacts, or that systems are maintained in steady states by negative feedbacks. All these statements are relevant, but until specific attention is paid to all of the levels of living systems, to each of the 19 matter-energy and information-processing subsystems, to the variables of each one of them, and to their steady states, the full capability of systems theory to contribute to psychiatry will not be realized. An uncritical and enthusiastic acceptance of a few general principles is not enough.

In the field of family psychiatry we have shown general living systems theory to be relevant not only to human families but potentially, because of its evolutionary nature, to infrahuman families as well. It deals with families both in health and in disease, examining human development in families and the relation of the individual member to the total family. Such theory can be applied to a range of issues in family psychiatry—to diagnosis, therapy, and prevention.

At all levels of living systems, including the individual human organism and human families, the diagnostic strategy of general living systems theory involves the following steps: (a) Identify each of the 19 subsystems in the system under consideration. (b) Identify a number of variables which are worthy of being measured in each of the subsystems. (c) Find meters, measuring sticks, or indicators with which to make quantitative readings of these variables over time. (d) After making such measurements, determine what the normal steady-state range is for each of the variables and how they interrelate. (e) Make a systematic examination of each of the subsystems, as, for instance, a physician does in a physical examination, to discover which variables are within normal ranges and which are abnormal. (f) Examine all the abnormal variables together in order to identify a syndrome of pathology which these abnormalities reveal.

After this diagnosis, therapy should follow. The goals of family therapy—when the interactions of the various components and subsystems of the family are understood and when its pathologies have been discovered—are to attempt to change the structures or processes in the family or in the environment around it, so as to relieve the strains that exist. If this can be done, all the variables should return to their normal ranges.

In the therapeutic process, new insights are obtained from viewing a family not simply as a set of individual persons but as a system in itself made up of interacting human beings. Our cross-level approach makes it possible to look at the persons in a family as living systems at the same time that we view the family which they compose as a system, with comparable subsystems. It is thus possible to determine whether pathology lies in the family as a whole, in one or more individual members, or in the suprasystem, such as an economically stressed neighborhood where theft, drunkenness, and violence surround the family on all sides.

General living systems theory is not only a descriptive conceptual approach. It also provides a means for explaining and predicting interpersonal and family processes. This is done by testing relationships among various subsystem variables in one or more subsystems. It is essential that research be carried out to extend the present limited contributions of systems science to the study of families and other psychiatric problems. This can be done by case studies, by laboratory experiments, particularly by cross-level systems researches comparing similar processes at various levels of living systems, and also by analysis of the complexity of living systems at all levels using models and simulations. These methods can be employed by psychiatrists much more than they have been to advance our comprehension of the behavior not only of individual human beings but also of families and higher levels of living systems.

Such research, persevered in methodically by committed scientists and clinicians, may well provide a better conceptual integration than we have today of all that is known about human behavior. Then perhaps there will be a sounder foundation not only for family psychiatry but for all psychiatry.

Appendix

TABLE 1

The 19 Critical Subsystems of a Living System

SUBSYSTEMS WHICH PROCESS BOTH MATTER-ENERGY AND INFORMATION

1. *Reproducer*, the subsystem which is capable of giving rise to other systems similar to the one it is in.

---

2. *Boundary*, the subsystem at the perimeter of a system that holds together the components which make up the system, protects them from environmental stresses, and excludes or permits entry to various sorts of matter-energy and information.

SUBSYSTEMS WHICH PROCESS MATTER-ENERGY

3. *Ingestor*, the subsystem which brings matter-energy across the system boundary from the environment.

SUBSYSTEMS WHICH PROCESS INFORMATION

11. *Input transducer*, the sensory subsystem which brings markers bearing information into the system, changing them to other matter-energy forms suitable for transmission within it.

12. *Internal transducer*, the sensory subsystem which receives, from subsystems or components within the system, markers bearing information about significant alterations in those subsystems or components, changing them to other matter-energy forms of a sort which can be transmitted within it.

SUBSYSTEMS WHICH PROCESS MATTER-ENERGY

4. *Distributor,* the subsystem which carries inputs from outside the system or outputs from its subsystems around the system to each component.

5. *Converter,* the subsystem which changes certain inputs to the system into forms more useful for the special processes of that particular system.

6. *Producer,* the subsystem which forms stable associations that endure for significant periods among matter-energy inputs to the system or outputs from its converter, the materials synthesized being for growth, damage repair, or replacement of components of the system, or for providing energy for moving or constituting the system's outputs of products or information markers to its suprasystem.

7. *Matter-energy storage,* the subsystem which retains in the system, for different periods of time, deposits of various sorts of matter-energy.

SUBSYSTEMS WHICH PROCESS INFORMATION

13. *Channel and net,* the subsystem composed of a single route in physical space, or multiple interconnected routes, by which markers bearing information are transmitted to all parts of the system.

14. *Decoder,* the subsystem which alters the code of information input to it through the input transducer or internal transducer into a "private" code that can be used internally by the system.

15. *Associator,* the subsystem which carries out the first stage of the learning process, forming enduring associations among items of information in the system.

16. *Memory,* the subsystem which carries out the second stage of the learning process, storing various sorts of information in the system for different periods of time.

17. *Decider,* the executive subsystem which receives information inputs from all other subsystems and transmits to them information outputs that control the entire system.

18. *Encoder,* the subsystem which alters the code of information input to it from other information processing subsystems, from a "private" code used in-

8. *Extruder,* the subsystem which transmits matter-energy out of the system in the form of products or wastes.

9. *Motor,* the subsystem which moves the system or parts of it in relation to part or all of its environment or moves components of its environment in relation to each other.

10. *Supporter,* the subsystem which maintains the proper spatial relationships among components of the system, so that they can interact without weighting each other down or crowding each other.

ternally by the system into a "public" code which can be interpreted by other systems in its environment.

19. *Output transducer,* the subsystem which puts out markers bearing information from the system, changing markers within the system into other matter-energy forms which can be transmitted over channels in the system's environment.

(From J. G. Miller. *Living Systems.* New York: McGraw-Hill, 1978, 3. © McGraw-Hill Book Company, 1978. *Reprinted by permission.*)

TABLE 2

Subsystems at Each of the Seven Levels of Living Systems

Selected Major Components of Each of the 19 Critical Subsystems at Each of the Seven Levels of Living Systems

SUBSYSTEM / LEVEL	Cell	Organ	Organism	Group	Organization	Society	Supranational System
Reproducer 3.1.1	Chromosome	*None;* downwardly dispersed to cell level	Genitalia	Mating dyad	Group that produces a charter for an organization	Constitutional convention	Supranational system which creates another supranational system
Boundary 3.1.2	Cell membrane	Capsule of viscus	Skin	Sergeant at arms	Guard of an organization's property	Organization of border guards	Supranational organization of border guards
Ingestor 3.2.1	Gap in cell membrane	Input artery of organ	Mouth	Refreshment chairman	Receiving department	Import company	Supranational system officials who operate international ports
Distributor 3.2.2	Endoplasmic reticulum	Blood vessels of organ	Vascular system	Mother who passes out food to family	Driver	Transportation company	United Nations Childrens Fund (UNICEF), which distributes food to needy children

Converter 3.2.3	Enzyme in mitochondrion	Parenchymal cell	Upper gastrointestinal tract	Butcher	Oil refinery operating group	Oil refinery	European Atomic Energy Community (EURATOM), concerned with conversion of atomic energy
Producer 3.2.4	Enzyme in mitochondrion	Parenchymal cell	*Unknown**	Cook	Factory production unit	Factory	World Health Organization (WHO)
Matter-energy storage 3.2.5	Adenosine triphosphate (ATP)	Intercellular fluid	Fatty tissues	Family member who stores food	Stock-room operating group	Warehouse company	International Red Cross, which stores materials for disaster relief
Extruder 3.2.6	Gap in cell membrane	Output vein of organ	Urethra	Cleaning woman	Delivery department	Export company	Component of the International Atomic Energy Agency (IAEA) concerned with waste extrusion
Motor 3.2.7	Microtubule	Muscle tissue of organ	Muscle of legs	*None;* laterally dispersed to all members of group who move jointly	Crew of machine that moves organization personnel	Trucking company	Transport component of the North Atlantic Treaty Organization (NATO)
Supporter 3.2.8	Microtubule	Stroma	Skeleton	Person who physically supports others in group	Group that operates organization's building	National officials who operate public buildings and land	Supranational officials who operate United Nations buildings and land

TABLE 2 (*continued*)

Selected Major Components of Each of the 19 Critical Subsystems at Each of the Seven Levels of Living Systems (Cont.)

SUBSYSTEM \ LEVEL	Cell	Organ	Organism	Group	Organization	Society	Supranational System
Input transducer 3.3.1	Specialized receptor site of cell membrane	Receptor cell of sense organ	Exteroceptive sense organ	Lookout	Telephone operator group	Foreign news service	News service that brings information into supranational system
Internal transducer 3.3.2	Repressor molecule	Specialized cell of sinoatrial node of heart	Receptor cell that responds to changes in blood states	Group member who reports group states to decider	Inspection unit	Public opinion polling agency	Supranational inspection organization
Channel and net 3.3.3	Cell membrane	Nerve net of organ	Components of neural network	Group member who communicates by signals through the air to other members	Private telephone exchange	National telephone network	Universal Postal Union (UPU)
Decoder 3.3.4	Molecular binding site	Receptor or second-echelon cell of sense organ	Cells in sensory nuclei	Interpreter	Foreign-language translation group	Language-translation unit	Supranational language translation unit

Associator 3.3.5	*Unknown**	*Unknown**	*Unknown**	*None:* laterally dispersed to members who associate for group	*None:* downwardly dispersed to individual persons, organism level	Teaching institution	Supranational university
Memory 3.3.6	*Unknown**	*Unknown**	*Unknown**	Adult in a family	Filing department	Library	United Nations library
Decider 3.3.7	Regulator gene	Sympathetic fiber of sinoatrial node of heart	Part of cerebral cortex	Head of a family	Executive office	Government	Council of Ministers of the European Communities
Encoder 3.3.8	Component producing hormone	Presynaptic region of output neuron of organ	Temporoparietal area of dominant hemisphere of human brain	Person who composes a group statement	Speech-writing department	Press secretary	United Nations Office of Public Information
Output transducer 3.3.9	Presynaptic membrane	Presynaptic region of output neuron of organ	Larynx	Spokesman	Public relations department	Office of national spokesman	Official spokesman of the Warsaw Treaty Organization

NOTE: The components of seven subsystems, identified by an asterisk (*), are as yet unknown.

Animal components are selected in preference to plants, although many components of plants are comparable. If possible, human components are mentioned in preference to components of other types of living systems, although comparable components exist for many other types. When a choice must be made at the level of the group, the family is selected in preference to committees or other sorts of groups because the mating dyad and then the family were the original groups and are still of prime importance. When a selection must be made at the level of the group and above, examples from the United States are given, although there are usually comparable examples in other societies. At the level of the group and above, communication information flows are selected in preference to monetary information flows, since the former sort of flow is found in all types of living systems including human systems; while the latter are limited to only some higher-level systems of human beings.

(From J. G. Miller. *Living Systems.* New York: McGraw-Hill, 1978, 1028-1029. © McGraw-Hill Book Company, 1978. *Reprinted by permission.*)

REFERENCES

1. Miller, J. G.: *Living Systems*. New York: McGraw-Hill, 1978.
2. Thelen, H. A.: *Methods for Studying Work and Emotionality in Group Operation*. Chicago: Human Dynamics Laboratory, University of Chicago, 1954.
3. Homans, G. C.: *The Human Group*. New York: Harcourt, Brace, 1950.
4. Bales, R. F.: *Interaction Process Analysis: A Method for the Study of Small Groups*. Cambridge, Mass.: Addison-Wesley, 1950.
5. Cattell, R. B.: On the theory of group learning. *J. Soc. Psychol.*, 37:27-52, 1953.
6. Strodtbeck, F. L.: Husband-wife interaction over revealed differences. *Amer. Sociol. Rev.*, 16:468-473, 1951.
7. Jackson, D. D.: The question of family homeostasis. *Psychiat. Quart. Suppl.*, 31:79-90, 1957.
8. Chapple, E. D. and Coon, C. S.: *Principles of Anthropology*. New York: Holt, 1942.

7

Evolutionary Aspects of the Family

David P. Barash, Ph.D.

Human beings are animals. We are all at least that. Of course, we are also rather special animals—symbolizing, self-conscious, and to a large extent products of the culture into which we are born. The great biologist Sir Julian Huxley warned against what he called "nothing butism," the notion that because we are animals, we are nothing but animals. His warning is well-taken.

However, it could equally well be turned around: Just because we are strongly influenced by our experiences, it does not necessarily follow that we are nothing but our learning and our customs. Our human nature, whatever it may be, comes ultimately from our biology, and this biology we share with other animals.

In considering infrahuman families, my approach will be to emphasize the biological continuities that make a look at animal families of interest to those whose primary concern is the understanding of human families. First, however, two brief caveats: 1) As a zoologist, I am firmly committed to the proposition that all animals are well worth knowing and understanding in their own right, as an important and interesting part of the natural world and without regard to their relevance to human beings. 2) There is no clear natural progression discernible among infrahuman families, which could then be traced through animals, culminating in the families found in *Homo sapiens*. A hard look at any taxonomic group of animals, provided it is of sufficient size, reveals enormous diversity, with no simple message for human beings. Thus, among birds alone, we find monogamy, harem polygyny, sequential polygyny, polyandry, and even a degree of promiscuity. In some cases, males court females; in others (admittedly, much rarer), females court the males. In some species, both parents help care for the young; in others, the female only; in still others, the male only; and in a very small minority, care is dispensed by a variety of parental figures, most of whom are not biological parents.

This diversity of animal behavior derives from the fact that each species is a unique population of individuals, each of which brings a unique evolutionary background to bear on the ecological problems that it must face. Accordingly, the solutions to these problems tend to be unique and idiosyncratic. This is not to say that they are uninstructive. A simple phylogenetic cataloging of animal families provides virtually no useful information concerning human families. However, if we step back from the trees, it is possible to appreciate the forest as a whole. In other words, by examining the factors that have combined to produce monogamy in some cases, polygyny in others, polyandry in yet others, and so on, it should be possible to gain considerable insight into how the structure of family systems results from the action of natural selection, a basic biological process to which all living things are subject. A comparable approach can also illuminate issues concerning courtship and mate attraction, the production and care of offspring, and so on.

In short, I am proposing an evolutionary rather than a phylogenetic treatment of infrahuman families. My approach will be to use our understanding of evolution as a mechanism rather than as a dead, historical fact, to suggest a new way of viewing all living families, human as well as infrahuman. In particular, I shall emphasize that underlying—and in fact, unifying—the apparently kaleidoscopic diversity of animal family arrangements is one remarkably consistent trend: Such families are the result of most individuals' behaving in a way that maximizes the probability that a maximum number of their genes will be projected into future generations. In other words, each individual tends to behave in a manner that maximizes his or her *inclusive fitness* (1). Depending on the species and the issue at hand, this may be accomplished in different ways, but the underlying principle of fitness maximization provides a valuable way of viewing animal (and human) families and, in fact, suggests an overall theory of why families form in the first place.

Before directly considering families in this evolutionary perspective, a bit more groundwork is in order. What I am proposing is a gene's-eye view of evolution (2), an approach that looms large in the new discipline known as sociobiology (3, 4, 5, 6). The basic premise here is that natural selection will operate upon behavior so as to maximize fitness. Thus, if we imagine two alternative alleles, A and a, competing with each other for space at a given chromosomal locus, such that allele A inclines its bearer to behave in a way that results in its being more successfully projected into future generations, then eventually allele A, and its behavior, will tend to predominate over its alternative, allele a, and its behavior. These behaviors could involve such things as mate selection, the nature of the reproductive unit, and the kind and duration of parental care. Obviously, any genetically-influenced tendency to make a behavioral "decision" which results in more copies of the relevant alleles being projected into future generations will be selected, such that the population will eventually come to be composed of individuals, each of which attempts to behave in a fitness-maximizing manner. On the other hand, because of linkage disequilibrium, the vagaries of mutation and back mutation, and the complexities inherent in multi-locus, polygenic control (7), as well as the idiosyncratic vagaries of individual experiences, exact fitness maximization will rarely, if ever, be achieved in nature. Nonetheless, this central postulate of sociobiology provides us with a new opportunity to make predictive testable hypotheses concerning behavior (8), as well as a new way of looking at behavior in general.

This evolutionary approach asks a different kind of question from that which characterizes most of science. It is concerned with ultimate or distal causation—the adaptive significance of the behavior in question, rather than its immediate or proximal causation. For a psychological example, research on love could focus on its hormonal correlates, or on the role of previous interpersonal experiences, or physical attractiveness, or behavioral inclinations by the "significant other," and so forth. These are all immediate, or proximal, causes and, while significant, they do not exhaust all possible ways of investigating the phenomenon. An evolutionary approach to love would be concerned with its distal or ultimate causation: the factors that through our evolutionary history have conferred a reproductive advantage on genes that responded to certain personal relationships with the behavior and emotion we designate love. Indeed, both romantic love and the love of parent for child and vice versa can profitably be viewed as an evolutionary stratagem, insuring that each participant behaves toward, and is behaved toward by others, in a manner that maximizes the reproductive success of each. In this sense, proximal causes accord with ultimate ends. Neither is better as an explanation; no behavior can be considered explained unless both approaches are considered.

In fact, proximal and distal causation, although logically orthogonal, are actually complementary as well. Given the ultimate strategy of maximizing fitness, this end is achieved by responding appropriately to various situations in one's environment—it is likely that most forms of human behavior (at least, those generally considered to be normal), represent adaptive, fitness-enhancing responses to proximal events.

Of course, in considering behavioral strategies, it must be emphasized that no intentionality is necessarily implied (just as it is also not necessarily excluded).

My Random House Dictionary defines "strategy" as a "plan, method, or series of maneuvers for obtaining a specific goal or result." In an evolutionary sense, then, all living things are strategists, whether they know it or not. The specific goal or result is the maximization of their inclusive fitness—the total number of their genes projected into the future. In the performance of that strategic end, many different behavioral tactics are employed. One set of these tactics is the topic of this volume: behaviors relating to families.

Having gone this far, a further *caveat* is in order: Though animals (and incidentally plants as well) appear to behave in a manner that maximizes their fitness, this emphasis on the self-perpetuation of genes should be distinguished from crude genetic determinism, the notion that living things are simply helpless automatons, mere puppets who dance at the end of strings pulled by our imperious DNA. An evolutionary approach to behavior relies heavily on the role of genetic *influence,* as opposed to determinism (9). The nature-nurture debate is one of the oldest and least productive in the history of science, having generated considerably more radiation in the infrared than in the visible spectrum. This conflict has essentially been resolved by the recognition that neither genes nor experience, acting alone, produce any phenotype, and behavior, surely, is a phenotype no less real than structure or physiology. This "Interaction Principle" (4) has buried the hatchet between ethology and comparative psychology, with the mutual recognition that all behavior derives from the interaction of both genes and experience, instinct and learning, nature and nurture (10).

Accordingly, genes do not determine behavior, any more than experience does. An evolutionary approach to behavior, whether focusing on families or anything else, is simply an effort to understand the genetic component and how it influences responses to environmental contingencies—in other words, the strategic consequences of gene-environment interactions. Although intrinsic and extrinsic factors are involved in all behavior, for all organisms, certain behaviors clearly reflect a larger contribution from one or the other interactant. Similarly, certain animal species are likely to rely more heavily on either genes or experience as the source of information to guide behavior. In this regard, the strategy of *Homo sapiens* clearly has been to rely differentially on experience, producing a behavioral program that is probably more flexible than that of any other species. But it is not infinitely flexible—from African pastorialist to New Guinea highlander to Park Avenue analyst, there is a consistency to being "human"—this is the very stuff of our lives.

Evolution by natural selection is the one construct that underlies and unites all the life sciences, and quite possibly the social sciences as well. However, it is subtle and easily misunderstood. Perhaps never have so many people said so much about something they understood so poorly. For example, a recent exchange in the *American Journal of Psychiatry* concluded that "the evolutionary value of neuroticism lay originally in promoting more rapid elimination of poorly adapted individuals" (11, 12). It may well be that an evolutionary, sociobiologic approach will shed new light on neuroses and psychoses, as I have discussed in another context (5). For our purposes, however, the point is that, given our current understanding of evolutionary biology, there is simply no way that a trait can have evolved whose purpose is the elimination of individuals bearing that trait. Errors of this sort abound in enthusiastic but uninformed efforts to apply evolution to human behavior, including those of biologists as eminent as Konrad Lorenz (13) and psychiatrists such as John Bowlby (14, 15).

The consistent error in such treatments comes from failure to appreciate the level at which selection operates (16). Natural selection modifies gene frequencies, causing a displacement from Hardy-Weinberg equilibrium, via the differential reproduction of individuals, and hence, their genes. The sifting and winnowing of natural selection is not a mechanism whose purpose is to eliminate the unfit and thus make the species better; it is the consequence of individuals and their genes competing, whether directly or indirectly, with other individuals and their genes. It is true that recent computer simulations have shown that group selection is a mathematical possibility (17, 18, 19), but the necessary conditions seem so restrictive as to make such a process very unlikely in nature (20, 21). Most important, when and if group selection is shown to occur, it too will operate strictly by differential reproduction of alternative traits. Tennyson notwithstanding, natural selection is not a fount for human ethical or moral systems; it is a mechanistic process that proceeds with no foresight and no grand design for betterment. Evolution can be legitimately invoked as an explanation for behavior only when that explanation shows how genes influencing the behavior in question can spread at the expense of alternative genes, influencing alternative behaviors. We shall now explore infrahuman families with this evolutionary perspective.

Mate Attraction and Mate Choice

Among the various strategic decisions to be made by a would-be reproducing individual, one of the first is "With whom should I mate?" Issues of mate attraction and mate choice necessarily precede many others associated with family structure and function, and have profound consequences for the fitness of the individuals concerned. Both males and females are selected to exercise discretion in this choice, since matings with individuals of the same sex or a different species are unlikely to contribute to evolutionary success. Hence, selection should operate strongly on the tactics of mate selection, with genes that influence their carriers to make good decisions being ultimately more successful than alternatives that inclined toward choice of poorer mates.

However, issues of mate selection are not symmetrically distributed between males and females, largely because of the biologic asymmetries that characterize the two sexes. Thus, the biologic definition of "male" is that sex which produces a larger number of relatively small gametes—sperm—whereas females are defined as that sex which produces a small number of relatively large gametes—eggs. Much of the behavioral asymmetry of males and females derives from this basic, underlying distinction. Biologist George C. Williams (20) has pointed out that, in general, males are the aggressive, sexual advertisers, whereas females are the careful comparison shoppers. This is true for virtually every animal species—females tend to be relatively coy, discriminating and drab, both physically and behaviorally, whereas males tend to be larger, flashier, more brightly colored and inclined toward eye-, ear-, and nose-catching displays, both aggressive and sexual.

The biology of male-female differences necessitates that the consequences of a bad reproductive decision lie more heavily on females than on males. For example, imagine the evolutionary fate of two alternative alleles, one influencing its body to be relatively undiscriminating in choice of a sexual partner, while the other influences it toward insisting on the best possible mate. When housed in a male body, the less discriminating allele would not be at a substantial disadvantage compared with the more discriminating one. In fact, it may well prosper, since the generally low level of male parental involvement does not obligate a dallying male to compromise his reproductive future because of one, or even several, reproductive indiscretions. By contrast, females make eggs, and women get pregnant; they must literally bear the consequences of their reproductive decisions. As a result, alleles which generated a nondiscriminating sexual career when housed in a female body would be strongly selected against, relative to the same strategy in males. There is no "scarlet letter" in evolution, but among most animals, as among most people, a double standard applies, with females being more severely punished for infidelity and also less likely to practice it. (Incidentally, in this and all other applications of evolutionary biology to behavior, an important distinction must be made: Natural selection may be especially valuable in helping us understand *why* behavior patterns occur. However, this does not in any way legitimize such behavior. As David Hume pointed out, *is* does not in any way imply *ought.*)

A valuable conceptualization of this difference is suggested in the notion of "parental investment" (22), defined as "any investment by the parent in offspring that increases the offspring's chances of survival, and hence, reproductive success, at the cost of the parent's ability to invest in subsequent offspring." By definition, because of their large investment in eggs vis-à-vis the males' small investment in sperm, females of most species provide a larger initial parental investment than do males. Among birds, for example, females may produce a clutch of eggs comprising 30 percent of the female's body weight, whereas among mammals, the relatively small initial female investment necessitates the much larger investment of placenta, intrauterine nourishment and, following birth, lactation. By contrast to this large obligatory female investment, the obligatory male investment in most species is very small—a few drops of sperm and the time necessary to deliver them to the appropriate place.

In such circumstances, the sex investing more becomes a limiting resource for the sex investing less. Females, with their large initial parental investment, quickly find their reproductive potential used up with the production of a relatively small number of offspring, while by contrast, the production of a comparable number of offspring by a male does not cause a comparable decrease in his reproductive potential. To use the human case, a woman simply cannot produce more offspring than one per nine months—in reality, much less than that—whereas a man can theoretically sire an almost unlimited number of offspring during the same time period. The result of this near-universal disparity is a near-universal disparity in reproductive strategies: Males, as the sex investing less, are selected to compete among themselves for access to females, the sex investing more.

As a result, if a territory is defended, it is nearly always the males who do so; if aggression commonly occurs, it is nearly always the males who do it, generally to intimidate other males and/or to attract the females, depending on the species. Parental investment theory therefore suggests that polygyny—one male mated to several females—is the preferred strategy of males, whereas monogamy is typically preferred by females. (Incidentally, William James is reported to have come to a similar conclusion, although with the aid of opium, rather than evolutionary biology, when he proclaimed "higamous, hogamous, woman monogamous; hogamous, higamous, man is polygamous.") This prediction has been supported for numerous species (23, 24, 25, 26), and is almost certainly the primitive human condition as well (27). Since on the average equal numbers of males and females are produced in most species (see Fisher (28), for explanation), any tendency for polygyny necessarily means that the variance in male reproductive success will exceed that for females, even though males and females, taken together, are exactly equal. Since some males will be highly successful, whereas others are evolutionary failures (29, 30, 31), we can expect additional pressures for male-female competition not normally found among females.

Although parental investment does not explain all male-female differences in mate attraction and selection, it does account for a great deal of the variance found among infrahuman families. What is more impressive, it even accounts for the exceptions as well. Thus, those few animal species characterized by large, aggressive, showy, and sexually forward females tend to be those such as the jacana, tinamou, and seahorses, in which male parental investment is very large, and the comparable female investment quite small. As predicted, in such cases, females—the sex investing less—are selected to compete for access to the males—the sex investing more.

Among many species, the intense level of male-male competition has resulted in highly aggressive males who dominate females, almost incidental to their dominance of each other. In the extreme cases, as among members of the seal and elk family, females have relatively little role in selecting a mate; they simply become part of the harem of a victorious male. Of course, even in these cases, such acquiescence is adaptive for the female, since by passively accepting the sexual advances of victorious males, females are likely to bear children who will themselves be successful.

However, since females are generally a sought-after resource, they often have sufficient leverage to drive a hard evolutionary bargain —that is, they can insist on mating only with males that maximize their (that is the females') fitness, withholding matings from males that will benefit them less. To some extent, therefore, we can expect that *hypergamy* ("marrying up") would be especially a female strategy—this seems generally to be the case for most species, including humans. (Indeed, this pattern is so common cross-culturally that anthropologists reserve the term hypergamy for marrying up by a woman.)

For convenience, we can divide female choice of a mating partner into several categories, depending on the type of trait being evaluated, and bearing in mind that these categories are not necessarily mutually exclusive.

Good Genes

The haploid gametes of each individual must be combined with the haploid gametes of another, to produce offspring. Hence an evolutionary advantage will accrue to every individual that hitches his or her genes to other genes that are maximally likely to be of high fitness. Furthermore, for reasons we have already discussed, this decision is likely to be especially crucial for females. There are many ways that females evaluate the genetic quality of prospective mates: Insofar as courtship is an important component of reproductive success, then males who are successful courters are likely to be chosen as maters as well, since the male offspring of such females are likely to court similarly and therefore be successful themselves, ultimately bringing enhanced fitness to the discriminating female through the number of grandchildren she produces. Among lek species such as sage grouse, for example, females preferentially mate with a small number of grotesquely-displaying males that occupy the central, preferred positions in the lek arena (29).

Similarly, by simply choosing older dominant males, females of many species assure themselves of good genes from their partner—the genetic quality of a prospective mate is to some extent guaranteed by the fact that individuals with that genotype have demonstrated both longevity and success in male-male competition. In addition, females occasionally incite actual competition among males, presumably so as to mate with the best of those available. Among elephant seals, for example, females scream loudly when mounted; this activates the dominance hierarchy among nearby males, after which the females mate with the most dominant (32).

Finally, appropriate genetic characteristics of a potential mate also appear to include the probability of producing excessively inbred offspring, a situation which would reduce the fitness of both parents involved. Among animals, disadvantageous homozygosity is generally prevented either by dispersal, which normally occurs just prior to attaining sexual maturity, or by a behavioral inhibition such that among litter-mates, for example, play patterns established during infancy interfere with the possible establishment of sexual patterns among adults (33). Of course, both dispersal and negative sexual imprinting of this sort would serve as *proximal* mechanisms which subserve the ultimate goal of maximizing fitness, in this case by minimizing inbreeding, with its depression of fitness.

Good Behavior

Among species lacking parental care, or those in which the female cares alone, females are predictably more concerned with the genetic quality of a prospective mate than with his behavioral inclinations and abilities. However, among monogamous species in which both male and female make a substantial contribution toward care of the offspring, we would expect members of either sex to evaluate a prospective partner in terms of the likelihood that he or she will *behave* adequately after the mating. From the perspective of natural selection, genes which made a reproductive commitment to a mate whose behavior did not contribute to their own success would eventually be replaced by others that were more choosy.

Certainly, among species in which both male and female must help care for the offspring, female fitness would not be advanced by mating with a "love 'em and leave 'em" type of male, no matter how much the male might benefit. Not surprisingly, therefore, courtship in such species typically involves prolonged pre-copulatory betrothals, during which time the inclinations of each partner are revealed, along with any additional reproductive commitments.

Even if there is no eternal triangle, would-be mates often have more to learn about each other. For example, I recently watched the courtship antics of a pair of sparrow hawks: For about 30 minutes they soared and pirouetted through the air in remarkable synchrony. Alternately, one would drop a small mouse and the other would dive and catch it in mid-air, only to drop it again, after which the first would catch it and then drop it for the other, and so on. For predatory birds in particular, the behavioral characteristics of a potential mate are crucial in determining its suitability; both male and female must be capable of hunting successfully if any offspring are to be fledged, and therefore it is especially fitting that their courtship involves demanding aerial acrobatics. I never observed a sparrow hawk drop the mouse during courtship, but if this happened, I would not have been at all surprised to see the other fly away in disdain!

Among certain fishes, notably the Pomacentrids or damselfishes, females typically deposit their eggs within the territory of a male, who then has sole responsibility for caring for the developing fry during the next week, after which they take up a free-living existence in the oceanic plankton. Males defend territories on the floor of the coral reef, and females travel in schools above these territories. When a school of females hovers above a male's territory, he typically begins courtship activities, after which a gravid female may or may not detach herself from the school and spawn with the male, then leaving him to care alone for the just-fertilized eggs. For the female damselfish, choice of the right male is crucial to her fitness, her evolutionary success; she will produce only one clutch of eggs per season—to what type of male should she entrust her precious store of eggs?

I recently completed a field study, investigating this question for the endemic Hawaiian damselfish, *Dascyllus albisella* (8). I found that the primary parental behavior of males involved defending the developing eggs against predators. Tropical reefs teem with fishes, many of them eager predators on damselfish eggs. In fact, when the defending male was experimentally removed, his eggs were invariably consumed within one minute! Accordingly, males devote nearly all their parental attention to driving off would-be predators, and therefore I predicted that female damselfishes would be especially attuned to a male's defensive prowess when choosing a mate. (In gene language, genes that predisposed their bodies to mate with strongly-defending males would leave more successful copies of themselves in succeeding generations than would alternative genes that were less discriminating of male behavior.) This prediction was realized; females spawned significantly more with highly defending males than with others that were more lethargic. Furthermore, males behaved more aggressively toward other, egg-predator species when female damselfishes were nearby than when they did not have such an audience.

Finally, we can expect mates and potential mates to make use of a variety of behaviors to minimize the likelihood of their being cuckolded, since there is no evolutionary pay-off in rearing someone else's offspring. I have observed that male mountain bluebirds respond aggressively to indications of adultery by their mates, but that they restrict this behavior to times when their mates' behavior may have compromised their own genetic parenthood (33a). Similarly, I have found that male mallard ducks respond in predictable and adaptive ways to rape of their mates (34), a not-uncommon event among mallards; also, male ring doves have been found to reject females who show by their behavior that they have been courted—and presumably, inseminated—by another male (35).

Good Resources

Good genes and good behavior are clearly important considerations for many species, but in other cases, the most crucial contribution that one mate can provide for the other is access to resources that contribute significantly to reproductive success. Owing largely to the asymmetry in male-female initial parental investment, described earlier, males—since they compete with each other—are likely to be more aggressive and to defend reproductively relevant resources which they acquire in competition with other males. Females thus may be thought of as bartering their cherished resource—their eggs—for the resources controlled by the male.

Accordingly, many species demonstrate "resource-based mating systems" (36), especially those inhabiting environments that are sufficiently heterogeneous to provide what may be called "polygyny potential"—that is, in proportion as reproductively relevant resources are clumped, the variance in male reproductive success is likely to be great and skewed toward the relatively small number of males that competed successfully for the resources in question and that are able to provide them in exchange for reproductive access to females. For example, Himalayan honey-guides are small brilliantly-colored birds that preferentially eat beeswax. Males compete for territories containing beehives, and in a recent study, all observed copulations were performed by the very few males who defended beehives (37). In such a system, of course, females gain doubly, receiving not only a share of the valued resource, but also getting to pair their genes with males who have already proven the likely quality of their genes.

Gordon Orians and his associates at the University of Washington have pioneered analyses of mating strategies emphasizing female choice as a determining factor. In particular, consider the case of the red-winged blackbird. Males defend individual territories in the spring, prior to the arrival of females. Females then settle on one territory or another. In doing so, they arrange themselves such that a small number of males may have three or four females nesting within their territory, while other males may go unmated altogether. Given that, by mating with an already-mated male, a female foregoes the paternal assistance that could be available to her if she chose a previously unmated male, what explains the female's preference for polygyny? Apparently, red-winged blackbird habitat is quite heterogeneous, such that certain "wealthy" males are proprietors of exceptionally good real estate—either substantial food reserves or nesting places safe from predators. As a result, females elect to mate with already-mated males when the extra fitness advantage provided by the resources within their territories exceeds the fitness cost of foregoing parental assistance (24).

In some cases, the providing of resources is even more direct, and constitutes a major part of courtship itself, most notable in the form of courtship feeding. Ethologists have long recognized that among many species, females especially are likely to mimic infant behavior, actually food-begging, in response to which behavior males feed them (38). Such behavior may actually contribute directly to the females' nutritional status, while also evaluating the capabilities of the male. Among certain insects, courtship feeding by the male has even been extended to cannibalism of him by the female. Randy Thornhill (39) has demonstrated that, in such cases, the protein contribution provided by the male contributes significantly to female nutrition, thereby selecting for female insistence on this final, lethal investment by males in their own evolutionary success.

As with other evolutionary analyses of human behavior, the sociobiology of mate attraction and selection in *Homo sapiens* is strongly suggestive, although as yet unproven. It seems reasonable that the basic significance of sexually-appealing human physical traits lies in a high probability of fitness return to individuals mating with those possessing such traits. For example, regularity of features, and other general standards of physical appearance may owe their attractiveness to the adaptive value of such individuals as potential mates. Although standards of sexual attractiveness have varied historically, there appears to be a biological wisdom underlying such apparent vagaries: The Earth Mother Goddess of ancient times obviously was somewhat immune to periods of resource scarcity, either because of the fat reserves she already possessed and/or because of her demonstrated competence in accruing such resources—probably no small consideration for prehistoric *Homo sapiens*. More recently, it is probably no coincidence that the vogue for slim, narrow-hipped women has developed only after obstetrics has permitted such individuals to be reproductively competent. A prehistoric Twiggy was probably unlikely to bear many successful children.

Resource-based mating systems are well-established among human beings, and if one looks cross-culturally, they are certainly the rule rather than the exception. Furthermore, a man's number of wives correlates nearly everywhere with access to resources. With increasing age comes increasing wealth, and more wives. Similarly, the lack of resources, especially among males, generally correlates with a lack of reproductive opportunities, and much human courtship, worldwide, consists of males' showing off their suitability as mates, whether via physical prowess such as dancing, athletics, bringing back trophies, warfare, or access to resources as in bride-wealth, or social prestige as through singing, story-telling or social leadership. Furthermore, males almost universally have a harder time growing up than do females, consistent with their being the more competitive sex, with a higher expected variance in reproductive success. Not surprisingly, young men the world around typically must endure stressful (possibly lethal) rites of passage; in most human societies, girls become women simply by growing up, whereas men are forced to prove themselves as "success objects," a prerequisite to famliy and social initiation, and an endeavor that is unlikely to terminate before senility.

An incest taboo, in one form or another, universally proscribes mating between siblings, father and daughter, and mother and son. Indeed, anthropologists have suggested that the incest taboo is the distinguishing characteristic of humanity (40). Anthropologists have consistently downplayed the biological relevance of incest prohibition, preferring instead to interpret the phenomenon in terms of the facilitation of social ties and networks, avoidance of intrafamilial competition, or psychoanalytic constructs. However, the biological disadvantages of inbreeding are real (41). Furthermore, recent studies by Israeli sociologist Joseph Shepher (42) have revealed a powerful and apparently unintentional persistence of negative sexual imprinting in Israeli kibbutzim. Thus, Shepher found that of more than 2,000 *kibbutz* marriages, not one occurred between adults who were raised together from infancy as pseudo-siblings in the communal nurseries known as "children's houses." Such avoidance was also directly contrary to social pressures which actually encouraged intra-kibbutz pairings. This finding admits of more than one interpretation, of course, but it does appear that whereas childhood familiarity does not necessarily breed contempt, it certainly does not breed.

Negative sexual imprinting is further suggested by an anthropologic study of "Shim-pua" marriage in traditional Chinese society (43). In this little-known and rarely-practiced custom, infant girls were adopted into the homes of future husbands, who were generally very young boys at the time. Of 17 such attempted marriages studied in a Taiwanese village, the young couples refused to consummate all but two, and in these cases, the girl had entered the family shortly before puberty, rather than during infancy or early childhood.

The Ecology and Evolution of Social Systems

Mating is one thing; living together is another. A second strategic question, then, after "with whom to mate?" is "with whom to live?" or more generally, "in what social system to live?"

Monogamy is a rarity among animals. It is found most often among the passerine birds, whose alricial young and very high metabolic rates often necessitate food-gathering efforts by two committed adults. Among mammals, monogamy is very rare, best developed in the gibbons, a rather unusual group of New World monkeys—the marmosets, beaver, and certain foxes (44). By far the most common pattern is polygyny or promiscuity (that is, the absence of post-copulatory male-female social bonds). The rarity of monogamy among mammals appears to result largely from lactation and the male's inability to nourish his offspring. As a consequence, males often contribute more to their fitness by interacting with other adults, seeking to garner social status and reproductively relevant resources.

There is substantial evidence that monogamy among human beings has been greatly fostered by Judeo-Christian doctrine and modern industrial technology—*Homo sapiens* is a quite typical mammal in terms of its reproductive biology, and like most mammals, shows definite signs of polygyny. Thus, prior to Western imperialism, over 75 percent of human societies were polygynous in the sense that multiple wives for men was the preferred state (27), although in practice this was achieved by only a small number of exceptionally successful men. The majority appear to have been monogamous—but by necessity rather than choice—with another minority polyandrous, generally at the bottom of the socioeconomic level.

Human beings show a moderate degree of sexual dimorphism, with males larger—as expected in a mildly polygynous species. Furthermore, we show pronounced *sexual bimaturism* (45, 46), with females becoming sexually mature significantly before males. This also is the general pattern in all polygynous species (30, 47), since the relatively fierce male-male competition gives a selective advantage to males, delaying their entrance into the competitive arena until they have attained sufficient size, strength and experience to have a reasonable expectancy of success. By contrast, despite the physiological strain of pregnancy and childbirth, the near absence of female-female competition in polgynous species selects universally for earlier reproductive competence among females.

It seems likely that in humans, as among most mammals, the biologically-based and enduring social bond is between mother and offspring, rather than between man and woman. This, of course, also fits with a conception of *Homo sapiens* as primitively polygynous. The mother-with-offspring unit serves as the basic building block of human family systems, as with all other mammals; these blocks may be organized in different ways, but are never abolished.

The significance of the mother-offspring unit is emphasized in an evolutionary approach to families, since in terms of natural selection, parental solicitude toward offspring occurs because offspring share one-half the genes of each parent, and unlike the male, females are guaranteed that 50 percent relatedness. Accordingly, it is of no small theoretical interest that the mother-offspring unit remains virtually unchanged through all mammals and through all human societies as well. However, there are also certain predictable regularities governing the involvement of males, additional females, siblings, and so on. Not surprisingly, these regularities also involve genetic patterns in which individuals engage in social systems that permit them to maximize the number of copies of their genes projected into the future, either by insuring their ability to benefit copies of their genes within the bodies of others, or by providing their own genes with opportunities to be invested in by others.

This discussion now requires the notion of *inclusive fitness* or *kin selection, one of the central concepts* of sociobiology. Consider one of the enduring puzzles of evolutionary biology: the phenomenon of sterile worker castes, or eusociality. Among bees, wasps and ants, colonies consist of many individuals, the vast majority of which are sterile, laboring—altruistically, it seems—for the reproductive success of the queen, instead of themselves. Such behavior is paradoxical in the extreme, since any mutant allele that induced a nonreproductive organism to be a parent rather than a helper for another should experience an enormous fitness and spread rapidly through the population.

The paradox seems to have been largely resolved by the brilliant insight of British population geneticist W. D. Hamilton (1), who recognized essentially that parental behavior is but a special case of the more general phenomenon: concern for others in proportion as they share genes with the individual in question. In particular, insect eusociality has evolved independently on 12 different occasions. Of these, 11 occurred among the Hymenoptera, an insect order that is characterized by a peculiar genetic system, haplo-diploidy, such that the females (both queens and workers) are diploid, being produced in the usual sexual manner from fertilized eggs, whereas the males are haploid, being produced parthenogenetically from unfertilized eggs. A few moments with paper and pencil should convince anyone that with such a system, individual female workers share three-quarters of their genome with their sisters—whom they help rear—as opposed to a potential one-half shared with their own offspring, if they were to attempt to reproduce. As a consequence, workers do more to project copies of their genes into future generations by staying home and helping to rear siblings than they would if they were to set out to rear a family of their own.

Accordingly, genotypic selfishness is simply masquerading as phenotypic altruism, and the apparent paradox is resolved by the recognition that genes may, so to speak, be acting for their own benefit even when they appear to benefit another individual. In the most general sense, Hamilton's point is that apparent altruism will occur when the benefit derived by the recipient of the altruistic act, multiplied by the genetic coefficient of relationship between altruist and beneficiary, exceeds the cost incurred by the altruist. In this system, benefits and costs are measured in units of fitness, and the coefficient of relationship is simply the proportion of genes shared by two individuals by virtue of their common descent: one-half for parents and offspring, and full sibs; one-quarter for grandparents and grandchildren and for half sibs; one-eighth for cousins, and so on.

It seems increasingly apparent that these insights, originally derived from observations on the family structure of Hymenopterous insects, have profound significance for the social behavior and family organizations of a wide variety of living things, including the vertebrates (48, 49). Alarm-calling in vertebrates provides a particularly instructive example: Among many species, individuals that perceive a predator give alarm-calls which alert others, thereby reducing the likelihood of their being taken by the predator. However, such behavior is likely to *decrease* the personal survival of the alarm-calling individual. The question then is: How can selection favor the persistence of an allele or set of alleles that induces its carriers to behave in a way that reduces the fitness of those alleles? The answer is that, in theory, such alleles can actually experience a higher "inclusive fitness" than alternative alleles that influence their carriers to keep quiet selfishly, provided that the alarmist alerts a sufficient number of relatives, who, in turn, have a sufficient probability of carrying the alleles in question. "Inclusive fitness," then, is the sum of genetic fitness derived via the reproductive success of offspring, as well as the ultimate success of all other relatives, with the importance of each relative devalued in turn as he or she is more distantly related—that is, as the prospective altruist and its beneficiary share fewer genes.

In the comparatively simple case of alarm-calling, numerous recent studies have demonstrated convincingly that it is closely correlated with the number of living, nearby relatives (50, 51). A recent study of social behavior in free-living Japanese monkeys has also shown rather precise correlations between genetic relatedness and the frequency of affiliative behavior, with inverse correlations between relatedness and the frequency and severity of aggressive behavior (52). Indeed, the demonstration that social behavior closely tracks genetic relatedness is one of the major recent trends in animal behavior research.

Family structure in a small, grouse-like bird, the Tasmanian native hen, frequently consists of trios made up of two males and one female. This pattern is very unusual for vertebrates, since participating males seem to be acquiescing to a degree of fitness less than that which would be available to them in a monogamous or polygynous situation, where they would be guaranteed a degree of reproductive success without having to share this with another male. Significantly, however, polyandrous matings among these birds typically involve two males who are themselves full siblings, so that each partner is guaranteed being either a father (if he successfully inseminates the hen) or, in the worst case, an uncle (if his brother does so). Combined with the slightly higher reproductive success of trios over duos, the maximization of ***inclusive fitness*** seems to explain this otherwise puzzling family system (53). A similar pattern obtains for the North American turkeys, in which male-male duos, composed of brothers, compete with other such duos for access to females. Within the victorious duo, then, the subordinate male defers to his brother, who achieves all the matings (54). Once again, the benefit derived by the subordinate male is revealed when we consider that he gains, via his inclusive fitness, when his brother is reproductively successful.

The evolutionary process whereby individuals maximize their inclusive fitness through the reproductive success of relatives in addition to their own offspring has been termed ***kin selection*** (55), and there seems every reason to think it is a major force in the evolution of much animal sociality, human as well as infrahuman. Thus, anthropologists have recognized for some time that the one universal underlying all human social systems is kinship. Although different cultures tend to define kinship relationships in somewhat different ways, the fact remains that a solid core of biology underlies the pan-human perception of the family. And even today, among Westernized industrial societies, appeals to social solidarity and altruism under the guise of kinship terminology have profound emotional appeal: Witness the common and generalized usage of brother, sister, the family of man, father figures, and mother figures. Furthermore, nepotism is another human universal: We all tend to favor relatives, our family members with whom we share our genes. Now we have a better understanding why.

Not surprisingly, polyandry is extremely rare among human societies. Also not surprisingly, however, when it appears it is quite likely to be found as fraternal polyandry, in which brothers share the same wife (56)—shades of the Tasmanian hen, or the turkey. Similarly, the preferred form of polygyny is often sororal polygyny, in which a man marries each of several sisters: In such a system, co-wives are less likely to compete among themselves for benefits of their own offspring (a common difficulty in human polygyny), since the other offspring in such a family are also the nieces or nephews of each co-wife.

In addition, cross-cultural sampling of human societies reveals a frequent pattern which appears to contradict the expectations of inclusive fitness theory, but which, on closer examination, provides further support instead. I refer to matriliny, or the "mother's brother" phenomenon. In approximately 30 percent of human societies, primary responsibility for a child rests with its mother's brother—its maternal uncle—rather than with the mother's husband and presumed genetic father. This situation seems to contradict biology in that uncles, who share only one-quarter of their genes, are expected to invest in a woman's children, as opposed to their fathers, who share one-half their genes. Two facts emerge here of particular interest to the evolutionary biologist. Firstly, matrilineal societies are notoriously unstable, much of the instability deriving from avuncular refusal to meet their socially defined responsibilities combined with their own efforts to funnel resources toward their own children instead (56). Secondly, societies in which the "mother's brother" system works relatively smoothly tend to be those in which male confidence of paternity is inordinately low (57), and by consequence, a maternal uncle is, in fact, more likely to share genes with his sister's child (since he is guaranteed genetic relatedness through their common mother) than is the purported father (since socially defined marriage does not assure genetic paternity for the husband). For example, a classic case of a matrilineal society was found in the

Trobriand Islands, among whom the anthropologist Malinowski reported that no connection was recognized between sexual intercourse and human reproduction. Thus, husbands typically returned from several years at sea to find that their wives had borne them one or several new children, which they "cheerfully accepted" as further proof that intercourse had nothing to do with bearing children! Not surprisingly, in the Trobriands, the mother's brother was more concerned with her offspring than was her husband.

Having briefly considered such strategic decisions as "With whom to mate?" and "With whom to live?" I would now like to focus more directly on the reproductive aspects of infrahuman and human families, in particular the strategic questions "What type of children to produce, how many, and how much parenting should they receive?"

Strategies of Offspring Production

The pioneer mathematician and evolutionary geneticist Sir Ronald Fisher (28) demonstrated that selection should, on the average, favor the production of equal numbers of male and female offspring. This result obtains mathematically for any sexually reproducing species in which the average reproductive success of males and females is equal, regardless of differences in the variances. However, among polygynous species with a high variance in male reproductive success, it can be shown that individuals will be favored if they produce males when they are in especially good physical condition and/or socially dominant, and females when in relatively poor physical condition and/or socially subordinate (58). This follows from the fact that healthy, dominant individuals (especially females) are likely to produce offspring who become healthy and dominant, whereas the offspring of less favored adults are likely to be less successful themselves. Accordingly, individuals at the top are most fit if they invest in males—who are likely to succeed in competition with other males and therefore enjoy great fitness. Individuals at the bottom are most fit if they invest preferentially in females—who, because of the low variance in female reproductive success among polygynous species, are likely to experience approximately the same fitness regardless of whether they are the offspring of high- or low-ranking parents. In short, the production of males is a risky strategy, likely to pay off especially when parents have an increased likelihood of producing offspring who are particularly successful, whereas the production of females is a more conservative strategy, especially appropriate to individuals whose likelihood of producing competitively successful offspring is low.

In general, this prediction has been verified for a wide range of animal species (58; see also 59). For human beings, it provides a new perspective on the higher mortality of male versus female fetuses—stressful intrauterine conditions may select for an adaptive jettisoning of male fetuses over female. Recent efforts by anthropologist Mildred Dickeman (60) have revealed a cross-cultural human pattern of infanticide, exactly as predicted by this sociobiologic theory. In highly stratified societies for which such data are available, such as medieval Europe and pre-colonial India and China, infanticide of female infants was selectively practiced by upper-class families, often on an enormous scale. This enabled such families to invest preferentially in males, who were likely to mature into successful polygamists, with very high reproductive success. The other side of the prediction, preferential male infanticide among lower-class families, has proved harder to evaluate, although the meager data are suggestive.

In addition to the (perhaps rather surprising) question of whether to produce males or females, evolutionary and ecologic theory also sheds light on the issue of how many children to produce and how much to invest in each. The basic prediction is that individuals should be selected to produce the number of offspring that maximizes the total lifetime reproductive success of each parent. Under the reasonable assumption that individuals are limited in the amount of resources—chiefly time and energy—that they can invest in offspring, it then seems reasonable that various combinations of offspring number versus investment in each offspring should obtain for different organisms, depending on the biological characteristics and ecological niche of each.

In short, parents can produce a large number of offspring—but if they do, they generally must be content with small size and little parental care for each. Alternatively, they can produce a small number of offspring—this seemingly less fit reproductive strategy proving advantageous if, by investing more heavily in each, the total reproductive success of the parents is thereby increased. Ecologists refer to the former strategy—quantity—as "r-selection," with r being the Malthusian parameter of geometric population increase. By contrast, the latter strategy—quality—is known as "K-selection," after the symbol for environmental carrying capacity (61). This notation was adopted because r-selection regimes appear to maximize the crude reproductive rate of individuals, whereas K-selection regimes appear when populations are near the carrying capacity, and added investment, in the form of greater offspring size, enhanced parental care, and so on, are necessary in order for offspring (and hence parental) fitness to be maximized.

Thus, mice are K-selected relative to codfish, who may shed a million gametes at a single spawning. Needless to say, these gametes are each small and do not receive a great deal of personalized parental attention. On the other hand, mice are r-selected relative to human beings, who produce most commonly only one offspring at a time, and who invest very heavily in them, often producing in a lifetime fewer offspring than a mouse generates in a single breeding season. On the other hand, both mice and *Homo sapiens* are about equally fit, insofar as populations are more or less at equilibrium and parents in each case are simply replacing themselves. Thus, the differences between r- and K-selection typically involve a higher mortality among r-selected offspring.

In general, K-selection occurs when the parents have relatively large body size, with low mortality, inhabiting environments in which competitive pressures are high and in which social organization tends to be relatively complex. Human beings, then, are among the most K-selected of animals, producing a small number of utterly dependent offspring, each of which typically receives a great deal of parental care, including nourishment, defense, and teaching, extending at least until adolescence and often beyond that time as well. Interestingly, with the advent of Western industrialization, there seems to be an enhancement of K-selection in human beings, as family size tends to drop in proportion as per capita income rises. This so-called "demographic transition," well-known to demographers, sociologists, and anthropologists, may well reflect an increasingly competitive environment in which offspring must receive increased parental resources—such as money for education—if they are to be biologically successful.

In most of these strategic parenting decisions, we tend to expect that both parents and offspring will agree as to the best possible course of action. That is, that which maximizes the inclusive fitness of the offspring should also maximize that of the parents, and therefore, little or no conflict between parents and offspring is predicted. Indeed, the technical literature of both developmental psychology and child psychiatry repeatedly emphasizes the "symbiotic" relationship between mother and child, paralleling the heart-warming notions of mother love that pervade most televised documentaries of animal behavior.

It may therefore be quite surprising that evolutionary biology does not predict that the course of parent-offspring relations should always be smooth. In fact, the basic genetics of sexually-reproducing diploid organisms suggests some precise areas of expected cross-generational conflict (see 62). This conflict derives basically from the simple fact that mother and offspring are not genetically identical; mother and offspring share only one-half their genes, and this asymmetry can be seen to generate asymmetry in preferred behavior, since that which maximizes the fitness of one does not necessarily maximize the fitness of the other. In fact, the interests of parent and child can be seen to conflict in several respects.

Imagine a female mammal that has a single offspring. When it is young, the offspring benefits from any maternal investment it receives; furthermore, the mother benefits her fitness by giving it. Accordingly, conflict is not expected. However, as the offspring develops, the time will come when the mother's fitness will be increased by her reproducing again and investing in a new offspring. At this time, the mother can be expected to value the two offspring about equally, since she is equally related to each—sharing 50 percent of her genes in each case. The offspring in question, however, can be expected to disagree. It shares 50 percent of its genes with its mother; hence, it can be expected to be only 50 percent as concerned with her fitness as she is. Viewing this another way, the original offspring is 100 percent related to itself, whereas it would be only 50 percent related to a second offspring, if its mother were to reproduce again. (Of course, this applies only to full siblings, the joint offspring of the same parents. If a different adult male sires the subsequent offspring, then the coefficient of relationship between them drops to only 25 percent.)

As a result, one can expect that, whereas the mother will be selected to cease investing in a given offspring whenever the benefits she derives from doing so exceed the costs incurred by ceasing to invest in the current offspring, the offspring itself should be selected to resist this withdrawal of maternal attention until the benefits derived by the mother exceed *twice* the costs. Again, this is because mother and offspring are related only by a factor of one-half, as a result of which offspring are selected to devalue maternal costs by one-half, and vice versa for the mothers. In summary, then, mothers and offspring are expected to agree on continuing investment in the offspring, so long as the cost-to-benefit ratio (for the mother) of continuing such investment is less than one. This cost-to-benefit ratio can be expected to increase during development, such that once it is greater than one but less than two, the mother is selected to resist such termination. Once the cost-to-benefit ratio exceeds two, then mother and offspring are expected to agree once more, with their interests this time converging on termination of investment.

This predicted conflict may well coincide with weaning conflict in most mammals, including human beings, and in the latter case it may also coincide with conflict over toilet training as well. By offspring age of two or three years, mothers are biologically prepared to commence reproducing once more, and at this time they may well be expected to push their offspring into less dependent behavior patterns, which, in turn, the offspring can be expected to resist.

The parent-offspring conflict model presented above concerns conflict over the time of termination of parental investment. A similar treatment applies to the amount invested at any one time—a nursing bout, for example. Thus, parents can be expected to behave toward their offspring in a manner that maximizes the difference between benefits and costs. The offspring, however, can be expected to seek a different optimum level of investment, endeavoring to maximize the difference between parental benefit and *one-half* the cost, since offspring should devalue parental cost by one-half, because they share only one-half their genes.

As sociobiologist Robert Trivers has pointed out, since offspring cannot physically fling their mothers to the ground and nurse at will, they can be expected to have evolved psychological techniques to aid their side of the conflict. Since parents should be strongly selected to respond to genuine offspring need, offspring should be selected to exaggerate that need whenever possible. Parents, in turn, should then be selected for the ability to distinguish false from genuine need. In addition, since parents presumably have some teaching that is of value to impart to their offspring, offspring should be selected to receive teaching from parents. Parents, in turn, should be selected to exaggerate their didactic roles and to take advantage of any offspring capacity for being manipulated. In this cross-generational conflict, increased experience should increasingly favor the parent. Furthermore, the phenomenon of regression could have its roots in parent-offspring strategies, since parents should be especially responsive to infantile, as opposed to juvenile, needs, insofar as the former are more likely to correspond to shared parent-offspring strategies for fitness maximization, while the latter are more characteristic of conflict.

Even after parents have provided an offspring with a sibling, one would not expect parent-offspring conflict to cease entirely. Thus, parents should be selected to encourage altruism from one offspring to another any time the beneficiary profits more than the altruist loses. As a result, since the parent is equally related to each offspring, the net fitness benefit to the parent is positive. Once again, however, the offspring can be expected to disagree. Since each offspring is entirely related to itself but only one-half related to its sibling, it can be expected to behave altruistically to a sibling only when the benefit derived by the act exceeds *twice* the cost incurred by the altruist. Once more, then, parent-offspring conflict is predicted over sibling-sibling interactions, with parents seeking to induce their offspring to be more altruistic, play more nicely with, or share more with his or her siblings than is in the biologic interest of the offspring itself. In other words, evolutionary biology provides a new and, I think, a rather powerful interpretation of sibling rivalry as well as of the generation gap.

Parent-offspring conflict should also be apparent over the behavioral inclinations of offspring toward other individuals with whom the parents and the offspring are differentially related. For example, offspring share a coefficient of relationship of one-eighth with their first cousins, whereas their parents, by contrast, share one-quarter of their genes with these same individuals, their nieces or nephews. As a result, we can expect parents to seek to induce their offspring to behave more altruistically toward cousins than the offspring themselves would be inclined. There are, in fact, a host of predictions of this sort that cry out for empirical testing, both among infrahuman and human families. For example, cousin-cousin altruism is expected to decline following death or departure of parents. Sibling rivalry is expected to be higher among half-siblings than among full siblings. Older parents can be expected to experience less parent-offspring conflict than younger parents, since the older a parent, the less its future reproductive potential and, therefore, the less should it hold back current parental investment in the expectation of future reproduction gain.

The parent-offspring conflict model presented here is clearly greatly at variance with the traditional view of socialization, according to which the infant is gradually but smoothly "encultured" into adult society, albeit with occasional disagreements, but generally with parents and offspring moving ultimately toward the same end. An evolutionary view, by contrast, emphasizes that families are composed of individualists, each of whom is selected to maximize his or her fitness and not that of anyone else. This is but scratching the surface of a brand-new and potentially stimulating area for research, as well as practice. Appeal to enlightened self-interest might just do wonders in rearing cooperative children.

Who Cares for the Offspring

A final strategic, familial decision is simply "Who cares for the offspring?" As stated earlier, among birds both parents usually care for the offspring, apparently because the large metabolic needs of growing nestlings necessitates such biparental efforts. Significantly, uniparental families among birds are found most commonly among precocial species such as pheasant, grouse, and the flightless or ratite birds, in which the young are able to forage for themselves immediately after hatching. In such cases, the caring parent is usually, but not always, the female. Among fishes, curiously enough, the situation is often reversed: Uniparental care, when it occurs, is often the responsibility of the male—the reasons for this are unclear, but they seem to be intimately tied up with territorial maintenance and the simple fact that with external fertilization, the female gets to deposit her eggs before the male covers them with sperm, thereby giving her the opportunity to desert him, and not vice versa (63).

Among mammals, parental care is overwhelmingly the responsibility of the mother. Indeed, for the great majority of mammal species, the only enduring social bond is between mother and her offspring, with male-female associations generally limited to copulation itself and a brief period of consortship, with paternal care in mammals almost unheard of. There are undoubtedly several factors responsible for this, among which the most cogent seem to be confidence of genetic relatedness and potential contribution to offspring success. Among all species practicing internal fertilization, females enjoy an enormous advantage over males: They can be entirely confident of their genetic relatedness to their infants, whereas males simply cannot. As a result, alleles that coded for paternal solicitude would generally experience a lower fitness than alternative alleles that influenced their carriers to maximize their fitness in other ways (largely by interacting with other adults and potential competitors and/or predators from other species), while leaving the child care to the adult females. This tendency is further enhanced by the anatomy and physiology of mammalian reproduction, such that all mothers —and only mothers—lactate. Accordingly, females are uniquely equipped to nourish their young, while males not only cannot, but they actually may compete with mother and young for needed resources.

Of course, these two considerations are not independent. In fact, it is entirely likely that the fact of guaranteed maternal relatedness to offspring has itself been largely responsible for the fact of maternal lactation. If one were to inquire why males do not lactate, the answer might well be that, given the significantly lower level of confidence of relatedness, alleles that necessitated such a substantial investment in offspring would be at a substantial disadvantage if cuckoldry were sufficiently frequent.

Among hoary marmots (western mountain-dwelling relatives of the eastern woodchuck), males virtually ignore their offspring in large social colonies consisting of several adult males and females. They occupy themselves with defending their females against invading males, while also soliciting copulations with neighboring females, generally being repulsed by their proprietor male. By contrast, at isolated family units, adult male marmots are the very model of doting paternal solicitude (64). Thus, when males can enhance their fitness by interacting with other adults, they tend to do so; when the avenue is closed, they may then explore the next-best route—interacting with offspring, wherein they appear to provide some extra survivorship through enhanced watchfulness for predators. Significantly, devoted paternal behavior among primates is limited to the marmosets, gibbons and siamangs, species whose extreme monogamy virtually guarantees each male's genetic relatedness to his offspring. Nonetheless, facultative male parenting is still the rule (as opposed to obligatory parenting by females). For example, among Indonesian orangutans, males are involved in the family unit on the island of Sumatra, where they help to defend the female and young against predators and inter-specific competitors, whereas on Borneo, where these dangers are absent, orangutan fathers show virtually no paternal behavior, concentrating instead on the defense of territories against other males (65).

Finally, given the large initial female investment of pregnancy, as well as lactation, it is no surprise that female mammals are invariably the more nurturant sex—the cost to a female of loss of her offspring, regardless of its developmental stage, is invariably greater than the cost to a male, in that significantly more maternal than paternal resources would have to be expended to replace lost offspring with others. Consequently, since the stakes are higher for females, it is not surprising that their nurturance is greater.

Given the profound evolutionary cost of rearing unrelated offspring, we can expect that parent-like behavior should be limited to the biological parents. In general, this is true. Aside from humans, some interesting exceptions are found in the so-called "helpers at the nest" phenomenon, occurrences that once more confirm rather than refute the value of an evolutionary approach to family structure. Among certain bird species in particular, yearlings (especially yearling males) frequently assist adults in rearing additional offspring rather than attempting to reproduce on their own. This situation is somewhat similar to the eusocial insects, described earlier, and as in that case, the explanation is entirely consistent with a sociobiological perspective. Thus, helpers at the nest have almost invariably been shown to be offspring of the previous year. These juveniles are therefore helping their parents rear additional siblings for themselves. Accordingly, their apparent phenotypic altruism is actually genotypic selfishness, since they profit via their inclusive fitness—that is, through kin selection (e.g., 66, 67). It is interesting, however, that selfish considerations are relevant here as well, since female helpers are rarely found, and females—even juvenile females—are generally able to reproduce, whereas the competitive pressures faced by juvenile males render them more fit biding their time and rearing relatives rather than entering the competitive fray with older, more experienced adults.

An evolutionary perspective suggests not only that parenting behaviors should be predisposed by genetic relatedness to the infants in question but also, conversely, that such behavior should be denied in the absence of genetic relatedness. A study of mountain bluebird confirmed this expectation (68). When 20 male bluebirds were removed from their females, 17 were replaced by new males who consorted with the females but had not sired the nestlings, which had already hatched. Not one of these "stepfathers" fed the young or gave alarm calls when the experimenter approached the nest. Male mountain bluebirds invariably do this when they are presiding over their own, intact families.

Recent studies have revealed further that within infrahuman families, not only is parental solicitude unlikely in the absence of shared genes, but further, infanticide by males is a remarkably frequent phenomenon. The langur monkeys of India and Ceylon are a particularly good example (69). Among these slender, semi-arboreal primates, a typical reproductive group consists of one breeding male, several females and their juveniles and infants. Since the sex ratio is approximately equal—as it is in nearly all mammals—this type of family system results in a large population of bachelor males. These unmated males form all-male social groups, which periodically attempt to oust the dominant male and take over his females. Once successful, the dominant male among the newcomers quickly evicts his former colleagues and assumes control of the troops. Significantly, the usurper male almost invariably then embarks on a program of infanticide, methodically killing all nursing young. Since he did not father these infants, such behavior has no evolutionary cost to the usurper male, while it also provides the immediate benefit that females, bereaved of their infants, commence cycling once again, mate with the usurper male and thereby provide him with an evolutionary return for his behavior. This pattern of infanticide following male take-overs has also been described for colobus monkeys (70), lions (71), ground squirrels (72), and howler monkeys (Crockett, personal communication), and indeed, it has been turning up recently just about wherever it has been looked for.

A human parallel, less extreme although nonetheless unpleasant, also seems likely. Thus fairy tales from Cinderella to Snow White have invariably portrayed the stepparent as less than committed to a child's welfare, and a recent review of data compiled at the Center for Child Abuse in Denver has revealed that children residing in a home with one or more stepparents are significantly more at risk for abuse and/or neglect than are children living with both biological parents (73). In a society with an increasing divorce rate and in which double careers necessitate an increasing frequency of parenting by non-biological parents, these data and their biologic interpretation are likely to be resisted. Certainly, alternative interpretations are also available, but an open-minded appraisal of the situation among infrahuman families suggests that an evolutionary viewpoint on human behavior should not be overlooked.

Finally, stepparents in this context should be distinguished from adoptive parents, since the latter have made active efforts to achieve their parental status, whereas the former more frequently find themselves associated with offspring only incidentally, often as a result of their association with the biological parent. However, adoption per se, so prevalent among *Homo sapiens,* also appears to contradict evolutionary prediction. In this regard, several points are worth emphasizing. First, in nearly all cases, adoption is a second-best strategy: Given the opportunity, nearly all human beings, like other animals, would prefer to make their own children. Second, during the portion of our evolutionary past that doubtless shaped most of our biologically-mediated inclinations, we lived in small hunter-gatherer groups, within which genetic relatedness was certainly quite high. As a result, adoption of orphaned children probably enhanced the inclusive fitness of the adopters either directly, through kin selection, or indirectly, through reciprocity (74), from other relatives of the adoptees. Lastly, it is interesting to note that among animals, the ability of parents to recognize their offspring varies directly with the likelihood of an unrelated individual being substituted for their own offspring: Herd-dwelling ungulates such as wildebeest, and ground-nesting bulls, for example, reject strange young, whereas cliff-dwelling gulls and den-dwelling mammals such as rats do not. In the latter cases, adults are unlikely to encounter young other than their own, and hence, they lack the appropriate identification and rejection mechanisms. It seems apparent that human beings are similarly non-equipped: It is only in modern, over-crowded maternity wards that infants and mothers can be separated, and indeed, the fact that such accidental switches occasionally occur is testimony to our lack of innate ability to recognize our young. Among primitive hunter-gatherers, a mother ran no risk of misidentifying her baby; hence, we have an "open program" when it comes to accepting infants. This lack of innate discrimination permits us to be successful adopters today, especially when our own biological inclinations are somehow thwarted, either because of disability or an overriding ecological superego.

In summary, I believe that the use of evolutionary principles has substantial promise for adding to our knowledge of human behavior. Like the physical sciences, evolutionary biology is well-grounded in both data and testable theory. For good reasons, the behavioral sciences have long felt somewhat inferior to the physical sciences—suffering what one might call "physics envy." In this respect, evolutionary biology might help provide some welcome therapy.

REFERENCES

1. Hamilton, W. D.: The genetical theory of social behavior: I. and II. *Journal of Theoretical Biology*, 7:1-52, 1964.
2. Dawkins, R.: *The Selfish Gene*. London: Oxford University Press, 1976.
3. Wilson, E. O.: *Sociobiology: The New Synthesis*. Cambridge: Harvard University Press, 1975.
4. Barash, D. P.: *Sociobiology and Behavior*. New York: Elsevier, 1977.
5. Barash, D. P.: *The Whisperings Within: Explorations of Human Sociobiology*. New York: Harper & Row, 1979.
6. Barash, D. P. and Lipton, J. E.: Sociobiology. In: A. M. Freedman, H. I. Kaplan, and B. J. Sadock (Eds.), *Comprehensive Textbook of Psychiatry*, 3rd Ed. Baltimore: Williams & Wilkins, in press.
7. Karlin, S.: General two-locus selection models: Some objectives, results and interpretations. *Theoretical Population Biology*, 7: 364-398, 1975.
8. Barash, D. P.: Predictive sociobiology: Mate selection in Hawaiian damselfishes and parental defense in white-crowned sparrows. In: G. Barlow and J. Silverberg (Eds.), *Sociobiology: Beyond Nature/Nurture?* Washington, D.C.: A.A.A.S., 1979.
9. Dobzhansky, T.: The myths of genetic predestination and of tabula rasa. *Perspectives in Biology and Medicine*, 19:156-170, 1976.
10. Hinde, R. A.: *Animal Behavior*. New York: McGraw-Hill, 1970.
11. Galanter, M. Dr. Galanter replies. *American Journal of Psychiatry*, 135:1430, 1978.
12. Sloman, L. Maladaptation in prehistory. *American Journal of Psychiatry*, 135:1429-1430, 1978.
13. Lorenz, K. *Evolution and Modification of Behavior*. Chicago: University of Chicago Press, 1965.
14. Bowlby, J.: *Attachment*. New York: Basic Books, 1969.
15. Bowlby, J.: *Separation*. New York: Basic Books, 1973.
16. Alexander, R. D.: The search for a general theory of behavior. *Behav. Sci.*, 20:77-100, 1975.
17. Wilson, D. S.: A theory of group selection proceedings. *Proceedings of the National Academy of Sciences*, 72:143-146, 1975.
18. Wilson, D. S.: Structured demes and the evolution of group-advantageous traits. *The American Naturalist*, 111:157-185, 1977.

19. BELL, G.: Group selection in structured populations. *The American Naturalist,* 112:389-399, 1978.
20. WILLIAMS, G. C.: *Adaptation and Natural Selection.* Princeton: Princeton University Press, 1966.
21. WILLIAMS, G. C.: *Group Selection.* Chicago: Aldine-Atherton, 1971.
22. TRIVERS, R. L.: Parental investment and sexual selection. In: B. Campbell (Ed.), *Sexual Selection and the Descent of Man.* Chicago: Aldine, 1972.
23. EISENBERG, J. F.: The social organization of mammals. *Handbuch der Zoologie,* 10:1-92, 1966.
24. ORIANS, G. H. and HORN, H.: Overlap in foods and foraging among four species of blackbirds in the potholes of Central Washington. *Ecology,* 50:930-938, 1969.
25. DOWNHOWER, J. and ARMITAGE, K.: The yellow-bellied marmot and the evolution of polygamy. *The American Naturalist,* 105: 355-370, 1971.
26. CAREY, M. and NOLAN, V.: Polygyny in indigo buntings: A hypothesis tested. *Sci.,* 190:1296-1297, 1976.
27. VAN DEN BERGHE, P. L.: *Man in Society.* New York: Elsevier, 1975.
28. FISHER, R. A. *The Genetical Theory of Natural Selection.* New York: Dover, 1928.
29. WILEY, R. H.: Territoriality and non-random mating in sage grouse. *Animal Behavior Monographs,* 6:85-169, 1973.
30. LEBOEUF, B. J.: Male-male competition and reproductive success in elephent seals. *American Zoologist,* 14:163-176, 1974.
31. HAUSFATER, G.: Dominance and reproduction in baboons (*Papio cynocephalus*) *Contrib. to Primatology,* 7:1-150, 1975.
32. COX, C. R. and LEBOEUF, B. J.: Female incitation of male competition: A mechanism in sexual selection. *The American Naturalist,* 111:317-335, 1977.
33. HILL, J. L.: *Peromyscus*: Effect of early pairing on reproduction. *Sci.,* 186:1042-1044, 1974.
33a. BARASH, D. P.: The male response to apparent female adultery in the mountain bluebird, *Sialia currocoides*: An evolutionary interpretation. *The American Naturalist,* 110:109711101, 1976.
34. BARASH, D. P.: Sociobiology of rape in mallards (*Anas platyrhynchos*): Responses of the mated male. *Sci.,* 197:788-789, 1977.
35. ERICKSON, C. J. and ZENONE, P. G.: Courtship differences in male ring doves: Avoidance of cuckoldry? *Sci.,* 192:1353-1354, 1976.
36. EMLEN, S. T. and ORING, L. W.: Ecology, sexual selection and the evolution of mating systems. *Sci.,* 197:215-223, 1977.
37. CRONIN, E. W. and SHERMAN, P. W.: A resource-based mating system: The orange-rumped honeyguide. *The Living Bird,* 15: 5-32, 1977 .
88. EIBL-EIBESFELDT, I.: *Ethology: And Biology of Behavior.* New York: Holt, Rinehart & Winston, 1975.

39. THORNHILL, R.: Sexual selection and parental investment in insect. *The American Naturalist,* 110:153-163, 1976.
40. LEVI-STRAUSS, C.: *The Elementary Structures of Kinship.* Boston: Beacon Press, 1969.
41. CAVALLI-SFORZA, L. L. and BODMER, W. F.: *The Genetics of Human Populations.* San Francisco: W. H. Freeman, 1971.
42. SHEPHER, J.: Mate selection among second-generation Kibbutz adolescents and adults: Incest avoidance and vegative imprinting. *Archives of Sexual Behavior,* 1:293-307, 1971.
43. WOLF, A.: Childhood association, sexual attraction, and the incest taboo: A Chinese case. *American Anthropologist,* 68:883-898, 1966.
44. KLEIMAN, D.: Monogamy in mammals. *The Quarterly Review of Biology,* 52:39-69, 1977.
45. WILEY, R. H.: Evolution of social organization and life history patterns among grouse: *Tetraonidae. Quarterly Review of Biology,* 49:201-227, 1974.
46. RALLS, K.: Sexual dimorphism in mammals: Avian models and unanswered questions. *The American Naturalist,* 111:917-938, 1977.
47. SELANDER, R. K.: On mating systems and sexual selection. *The American Naturalist,* 99:129-141, 1965.
48. WEST EBERHARD, M. J.: The evolution of social behavior by kin selection. *Quarterly Review of Biology,* 50:1-33, 1975.
49. HAMILTON, W. D.: Innate social aptitudes of man: An approach from evolutionary genetics. In: R. Fox (Ed.), *Biosocial Anthropology.* New York: Wiley, 1975.
50. SHERMAN, P. W.: Nepotism and the evolution of alarm calls. *Sci.,* 197:1246-1253, 1977.
51. DUNFORD, C.: Kin selection for ground squirrel alarm calls. *The American Naturalist,* 111:782-785, 1977.
52. KURLAND, J. A.: Kin selection in the Japanese monkey. *Contributions to Primatology,* 12:1-145, 1977.
53. MAYNARD SMITH, J. and RIDPATH, M. G.: Wife sharing in the Tosmanian native hen, *Tribonyx mortierii*: A case of kin selection? *The American Naturalist,* 106:447-452, 1972.
54. WATTS, C. R. and STOKES, A. W.: The social order of turkeys. *Scientific American,* 224:112-118, 1971.
55. MAYNARD SMITH, J.: Group selection and kin selection. *Nature,* 201:1145-1147, 1964.
56. VAN DEN BERGHE, P. L. and BARASH, D. P.: Inclusive fitness theory and human family structure. *American Anthropologist,* 79:809-823, 1977.
57. KURLAND, J.: Primate matrilines and the avunculate. In: I. DeVore (Ed.), *Sociobiology and Human Social Behavior.* New York: Academic Press, in press.
58. TRIVERS, R. L. and WILLARD, D. E.: Natural selection of parental ability to vary the sex ratio of offspring. *Sci.,* 179:90-92, 1973.

59. MYERS, J. H.: Sex ratio adjustment under food stress: Maximization of quality of numbers of offspring? *The American Naturalist,* 112:381-388, 1978.
60. DICKEMAN, M.: Female infanticide and the reproductive strategies of stratified human societies: A preliminary model. In: N. Chagnon and W. Irons (Eds.), *Sociobiology and Human Social Organization.* No. Scituate, Mass.: Duxbury Press, 1979.
61. PIANKA, E. R.: On r- and K-selection. *The American Naturalist,* 104:292-297, 1970.
62. TRIVERS, R. L.: Parent-offspring conflict. *American Zoologist,* 14: 249-264, 1974.
63. DAWKINS, R. and CARLISLE, R. T.: Parental investment, mate desertion and a fallacy. *Nature,* 262:131-132, 1976.
64. BARASH, D.: Ecology of paternal behavior in the hoary marmot: An evolutionary interpretation. *Journal of Mammalogy,* 56:612-615, 1976.
65. MACKINNON, J.: The behavior and ecology of wild orangutans (*Pongo pygmaeus*). *Animal Behavior,* 22:3-74, 1974.
66. BROWN, J. L.: Alternate routes to sociality in jays—with a theory for the evolution of altruism and communal breeding. *American Zoologist,* 14:63-80, 1974.
67. WOLFENDEN, G. E.: Florida scrub jay helpers at the nest. *Auk.,* 92:1-15, 1975.
68. POWER, H. W.: Mountain bluebirds: Experimental evidence against altruism. *Science,* 189:142-143, 1975.
69. HRDY, S. BLAFFER: *The Langurs of Abu.* Cambridge: Harvard University Press, 1977.
70. STRUHSAKER, T. T.: Infanticide and social organization in the redtail monkey in the Kibale Forest, Uganda. *Zeitschrift fur Tierpsychologie,* 45:75-84, 1977.
71. SCHALLER, G. B.: *The Serengetti Lion.* Chicago: University of Chicago Press, 1972.
72. STEINER, A. L.: Mortality resulting from intraspecific fighting in some ground squirrel populations. *Journal of Mammalogy,* 53: 601-603, 1972.
73. DALY, M. and WILSON, M.: Child abuse and neglect in sociobiologic perspective. In: R. Alexander and D. Tinkle (Eds.), *Natural Selection and Social Behavior.* Ann Arbor: University of Michigan Press, in press.
74. TRIVERS, R. L.: The evolution of reciprocal altruism. *Quarterly Review of Biology,* 46:35-57, 1971.

Part III

8

Family Therapy

Donald A. Bloch, M.D.

Several important changes in psychiatric theory and practice preceded the development of the family approach to psychiatric matters. In the decade following World War II, roughly from 1945-1955, a number of innovative themes were gathering force in American psychiatry. While the psychoanalytic movement consolidated its position, new approaches became theoretically influential. There developed, for example, new definitions of the proper locus of pyschiatric concern as being the interpersonal field (K. Lewin, H. S. Sullivan),* as well as psychiatric interest in sociocultural factors (Horney, Thompson, Redlich), linguistics (Sapir), sociology and small group psychology (Parsons, Bales), communication theory (Reusch, Bateson), and general systems theory (Grinker, Sr., Spiegel, Von Bertalanffy). Somewhat later, microkinesthesiologists (Birdwhistell, Scheflen) undertook an exploration of the previously unnoticed areas of non-verbal communication.

On the clinical side, there was growing attention in that decade to the effects on the patient of the social milieu, as in the studies

This article is based in part on an earlier work co-authored with Kitty Laperriere, Ph.D.

* References are not intended to be complete, since extensive bibliographies exist in all these areas.

relating hospital environments, individual psychological performance, and treatment outcome (Stanton, Schwartz, Caudill). Conceptions of the therapeutic community as a treatment modality were also having profound influence on developing concepts of psychotherapy (Jones). Group therapy flourished, as did psychodrama. Of particular importance were fine-grained studies of the psychotherapy of schizophrenia (Sullivan and Fromm-Reichmann), which revealed a carefully articulated relationship between the bizarre, apparently incomprehensible symptomatology of the schizophrenic and events taking place in the ongoing interpersonal field.

Common to this welter of activity was a consideration of the psychiatric patient and his treatment in terms of the social systems of which he was a part. In a sense, the process of abstracting the patient and his symptomatology from the background of interpersonal and social context—which had characterized the psychiatric and psychological advances of the previous hundred years—began to be reversed. Treatment came more and more to be conceptualized in terms of its relationship to the overt, current experiences of the patient. An interactive rather than in-dwelling model of mental illness was increasingly advocated, and an interactive model of psychotherapy came to dominate the thinking and practice of a number of clinicians and theoreticians. A principal feature of this change was the emphasis on the systems qualities of the phenomena being considered and of their conceptualization in communications terms.

An interest in the family system as it related to psychiatric disorder inevitably evolved out of these trends. Clinically, there was a burgeoning effort to conceptualize psychiatric disorder in family terms and to bring family methods of treatment to bear on issues previously viewed primarily as expressions of intrapsychic processes.

The Diverse Roots of Family Therapy Techniques

Child analysis was technically and conceptually invaluable; indeed, Freud's celebrated "Little Hans" case was the first case of both child analysis and family therapy, since the boy was treated through the agency of his father. As a single instance of the contribution of child analysis, we may note the relation of play therapy to family therapy. The earlier use of dolls and art materials to represent primary objects in play therapy with children led to a format in family therapy where primary objects, i.e., mother, father, siblings, are used to represent themselves.

Group therapy in its diverse modes has made, and continues to make, technical contributions to family therapy. More recently, concepts and methods of group therapy have been extended into the development of therapeutic formats in which couples (Framo) and families (Laqueur) are seen in groups. *Gestalt, transactional* and *encounter* styles or orientations have been picked up for use in the techniques of family therapy (Napier). *Games theory* and *communicational analysis* also have provided technical inputs, with some of their research procedures becoming a part of the therapeutic armamentarium, for example, the Ravich interpersonal game test (RIG/T).

In the same way that primary objects in family therapy replace the dolls and toys of play therapy, so the actors of *psychodrama,* when it is used with families, are partly or wholly replaced by the original figures in the plot of the family story. (In some cases a mix of family and nonfamily members is recruited to act out significant events in the family life.) Specific techniques of psychodrama have also been adapted for use in family psychotherapy: Role playing, simulations, and "doubling" are among those which may be mentioned.

The field has had a steady orientation towards *direct* observation of the phenomena under consideration, as opposed to dealing with *reports* about the phenomena (and directly observing only the reporter). Thus it has developed a teaching technology largely built around live supervision utilizing the one-way mirror or in-the-room consultation. The clinical home visit has been developed as a diagnostic and treatment tool. In the same vein, there is growing interest in the use of devices that can provide the family with additional vantage points for viewing their own behavior and patterns of interaction and the opportunity to study these in sequence and in detail. Modern television equipment is particularly useful in this regard, and innovative hardware and software are flowering in this area.

Some Characteristics of Family Therapy

Any attempt to distinguish family therapy as a technique must begin with a word of caution. While perhaps no more variegated than other psychotherapies, this field is certainly no less so. Thus, one generalizes at one's peril. No single set of rubrics quite captures the cool intellectuality of the theories and practice of Murray Bowen or the dramatic élan of Virginia Satir; one cannot really do justice to these highly individual styles or those of other leaders in the field in a brief description. Yet the characterization we attempt below is largely correct. An attempt at generalization is made possible by the realization that *what unites family therapists is the intention to change the family system.*

To characterize specific family therapy techniques is, then, in large degree, to make distinctions of emphasis rather than of sharply defined differences. As noted earlier, the essence of family therapy as a technique is that it deals directly with a natural system, some substantial part of the family of the index patient (at least, where one has been defined). A series of technical and stylistic consequences flows from this: Thus, family therapy is an action therapy; a do, show, and tell technique; a therapy of primary objects and first order symbols in which people are used to symbolize themselves; a therapy of confrontation; a therapy oriented towards direct exploration of systems feedback loops; a therapy oriented towards exchange of alternate vantage points; a therapy of actual exploration and trial of alternate modes of adaptive interaction. It is a modeling technique in which the therapist's use of self offers interpersonal modes for the family to copy. Very often, it is an affective, liberating technique. The family therapist may be actively involved in systems maintenance operations, such as nurturance, power balancing, and role and boundary definition.

The therapist is available as a whole person, actively using his or her own affective responses and, in a deliberate way, the full range of personal response patterns as measures and indicators of the nature of the events taking place.

> In the course of a family interview a male therapist began to become aware of his own growing anger at the father of the

> family, who seemed to be using deft, humorous, self-deprecating remarks to reduce awareness of painful feelings and particularly to avoid noticing pleas by other family members for support and contact. The therapist in an irritated tone said that he did not like being "fobbed off" by the father. There followed an intense moment of silent eye-to-eye contact, after which the father said, "I don't want to fight with you." More silence followed, and the father added, "Either we would destroy each other, or I would have to back down, and I prefer to back down." The therapist then became aware that his own anger was replaced with a profound sense of sadness; tears welled in his eyes and he said to the father, "Would this be the only possible solution?" As the two men continued looking at each other, not a sound was to be heard in the room. After a moment the therapist became fully aware of the emotion that had been moving him and so said to the man, "I know what it feels like to be an isolated father." As he said this, tears began to stream down the father's face. Throughout the interchange, the family watched in silence.

This example illustrates a number of aspects of family therapy technique. The scene described was played out in the presence of the other family members: the index patient, an adult daughter, her older brother and the mother of the family. It was confrontational of the father's defensive distancing; the confrontation was by direct action rather than by interpretation. An interpretation of the father's isolation and, by implication, of the family's *complicity* in it was made by breaching it, rather than by referring to it. By allowing his own anger and sadness to be clearly visible and by using them as guides to the meaning of the events, the therapist demonstrated an alternative mode for the father and the family.

From this point of view the therapist is a person able to provide inputs that are vivid, flexible, and unexploitive. A family session is a safer place to do this than is the one-to-one dyadic interview. By its public nature it provides opportunity for experimentation with human interaction that might not be possible elsewhere.

Issues of the therapist's personal involvement (or lack of it) permeate all psychotherapies. In family therapy they are somewhat more out in the open because the anonymity of the therapist is less taken for granted. In many other therapies personal interaction takes place against the old ideal of non-involvement; in family therapy, non-involvement is not recommended. While transference expectations still exist, the format reduces the intense, quasimagical quality of dependent, erotic, and hostile fantasies for all family members. Jokes about sexual contact between therapist and patient which are ubiquitous regarding psychoanalytic therapy, for example, are practically unknown regarding family therapy.

Like all psychotherapies, family psychotherapy clearly sets limits as to the nature of the real, i.e., action, involvement of the therapist with the patient family. He will make a clinical home visit, but will not move in, be sexually appreciative, but not have a sexual relationship, angry, but yet protective and facilitating. The symbolic nature of the psychotherapeutic encounter and the proscenium arch of therapy exists here as it does for all other psychotherapies, at least as far as the therapist is concerned. He is moved by the drama, but it is not his life.

Family therapy is explicitly concerned with the role of power in the therapeutic work. Power does not develop only transferentially, but by interference with the system's options. The family therapist, aware of the highly stable nature of bio-psycho-social systems, is trying to grasp power. To this end, family therapy uses paradox, quirkiness, inconsistency, and reversals, as deliberate systems disequilibrators. The promotion of disequilibration, the anti-homeostatic theme in family therapy technique, is a profound and important one. Many of the innovators in the field (Haley, Whitaker, Bowen) have been extraordinarily imaginative and inventive in developing such an armamentarium.

As noted earlier, in family therapy the therapist actually demonstrates alternate moves in his behavior toward family members: being kind to a frantically manipulative mother; unafraid of a tyrannical father; supportive of a pregnant 15-year-old as she advises her parents about sex and love. Paradoxical and political elements as well as modeling techniques may be seen in all these instances.

In this context, issues relating to qualities of the therapist as a person are prominent. It is important to note that the personal limitations of the therapist are often useful adjuncts to the therapeutic work; the inability of a therapist to deal with something is frequently as important as his ability to cope with it. He may be revealed as baffled or guarded, as responsive to the same pressures of social role, male or female power concerns, nurturant needs and wishes as other members of the family. He can be induced by the family into response patterns that mimic and, in fact, reveal the very difficulties the family itself is experiencing.

This overt indication of countertransference is different from what one sees in individual psychotherapy.* In addition, co-therapy teams may be used to display to the family an interaction that reflects splits, competitiveness, communication difficulties, role confusions, and so on. The subtle, textural elucidation of these interactional issues is extremely difficult in a dyad when one person, the pyschotherapist, must be the screen on which these complexities are projected. Richness and complexity are added when family members can use each other directly as well as the therapist(s) for these purposes.

By its very nature family therapy is likely to be a proselytizing therapy. The orientation towards the family involved in this choice of format bespeaks a value and belief system which generally holds that a famliy or family-like system is, in fact, needed for the maintenance of mental health, that a human being functioning in isolation is underfunctioning or malfunctioning. In attempting to do justice to the basically social nature of human beings, to the fact that human life thrives only in intimacy, in taking into account the sociocultural system in which we all live, the assumption is that the family, despite its many drawbacks, and uncertainties, is the most reliable and responsive system for maintaining the interpersonal connectedness of people.

Indications and Contraindications

Indications for family therapy may be categorized under two headings—those situations in which it is mandatory and those in which it is the most desirable approach. (I shall assume that family therapy means some kind of prolonged and regular contact with the family beyond an initial diagnostic-therapeutic assessment interview.)

---

* Although, of course, countertransference, if recognized, can often be useful in individual therapy as well (*Eds.*).

Family therapy is clearly the only suitable treatment in situations where the presenting problem appears in systems terms. It may involve conflict at one level of the system, for example, severe marital conflict or severe sibling rivalry, or intergenerational conflict and disturbance. All these are increasingly prevalent as presenting psychiatric complaints; they are essentially problems at the family systems level.

Symptomatic outbreaks associated with developmental transitions in the family are comparatively easy to conceptualize and demonstrate in family system terms and often provide the tyro family therapist with good treatment cases. As the family moves through time, there are nodal developmental points in the flow of events, such as entrance of a child into puberty or of a grandparent into senescence. They are well-known, usually associated with a change in status for one or more family members, almost always accompanied by a reshuffling of functions and of power relationships, and therefore almost always accompanied by stress.

A full recounting of these periods of transformation is inappropriate here, nor is it possible simply to relate symptomatic pictures to the stress source. Families are uniquely able to provide pooled information that will elucidate these issues, however; and there is no substitute for the conjoint family interview as a diagnostic tool in this regard. A general principle is that the degree to which these periods will be stressful is closely related to the reactivation of similar unresolved issues in the parental life.

Early childhood is critically important in that the infant's requirements for nurturance, dependent support, and protection are likely to intensify competition for such supplies when they are scarce in a family. This is, of course, particularly true when there are two infantile, immature, and undernurtured parents. Marital conflict will frequently erupt in such families, usually around some symbolic representation of nurturance, such as money. At times desperate efforts to solve the parenting needs of the young couple will lead to a rapid production of additional children, particularly in families from cultures which accord position and status to women and men with large numbers of children.

The young mother of an Italian, Catholic family came from stock close to its peasant origins in Calabria. Her first marriage was dissolved because of the infertility of her husband. She married a devout, modern Italian-American Catholic businessman, whose first wife had died shortly after the birth of their only child. The issue of child production and care was basic to the marriage; the husband was chosen for his demonstrated fertility, the wife because of her interest and apparent emotional investment in this purpose. The signal event in the courtship, from the husband's point of view, was the young woman's extravagant concern when she accidentally burned his child with a cigarette, although this event might also have forewarned him as to the ambivalence of her motives.

With the birth of two children of her own, the mother became increasingly neglectful of the child of her husband's former marriage. The child eventually died of a condition ambiguously related to this neglect, whereupon the family began to experience the most severe stress, all of this leading in turn to separations alternating with three more pregnancies. At the time of referral, there were five children in the family under the age of seven and two walled-off, isolated parents, living in separate worlds of home and business, with further catastrophic breakdown threatening.

The least adaptive solutions to human stress situations are, of course, those which, in an effort to relieve the stress, in fact add to it. In systems terms, one would speak of this as error-amplifying or positive feedback. The undernurtured, poorly integrated parents in the above example consistently make the wrong moves in an effort to solve the parenting problem by producing more children. The referral for treatment was based on the issue of marital incompatibility. The strategy of family treatment was to identify and reverse the pattern described above by initially providing large amounts of nurturant support for the parents.

Vulnerability to stress in the family often is accentuated by the arrival of children in similar sex and sibling positions in relation to the new family as the parents were in relation to their families of origin. When this occurrence is coupled with a reactivation of relationship issues, a still more potent disequilibrator is brought into being.

> A family organized itself around issues of control and dominance. The mother defined herself as a "battler" in relationship to her cruel, dominating, tyrannical father. Her husband was chosen for his apparent docility. The mother was a first-born daughter. At the point at which her oldest daughter became increasingly autonomous around the age of two, severe stress began to appear in the marital relationship, along with phobic symptoms in the wife.

The foregoing examples were given to illustrate the possibilities of systems interpretations related to the experience of stress associated with developmental change. One further example, coming from the other end of life's continuum, may also be useful.

> An oncologist, the identified patient, experienced attacks of acute, disabling anxiety at work. Two family systems appeared to be involved in this phenomenon. This man, in his early forties, was required in his work often to attend cancer patients with hopeless outcomes; his own father was severely senile and worsening at the time. During the same period, there had been a reduction in the usually close support given him by his wife, because she had reached the end of her child-bearing years and was reorienting herself to a status less tied to her home. The physician-husband's dependent push towards her was asynchronous with her moves toward autonomy, and she had been somewhat resentful of his increasing demands upon her.

In this last example, two developmental shifts act to disequilibrate a previously stable system. The move of the husband's father into severe senescence was associated with the wife's leaving the child-bearing role and moving into a more separate and autonomous pattern of relatedness to the family. The husband's work as a cancer specialist, with the exposure to the stresses associated with a continuous series of dying and mutilated patients, set the stage for his symptomatic breakdown. (An associated factor is the lack of an adequate social support system for those in stressful occupations. The unspoken assumption is that the family will fill this gap.) These stresses, however, had been reasonably well tolerated over the years, until the developmental shifts had taken place in both the family of origin and family of procreation.

The ideological and epistemological stance of the mental health clinician determines the format and scope of the inquiry and the nature of the concepts developed regarding the therapeutic approach indicated. All of the examples presented could have been treated with other modalities. (For example, the physician last described had been previously placed on large doses of chemotherapeutic agents which, understandably, had failed to stabilize the situation.)

Thus, the entire progression of life's stages is somewhat disequilibrating in the sense described above: the birth of successive children, particularly those in important sibling positions; the separation and departure of children for school; the achievement of sexual roles, identities, and work statuses; mid-life and the developmental stages of later life. In this sense, of course, they are much like other intercurrent events—illness or death, financial reversal or good fortune—all can operate in this way to require adaptation on the part of the family system, or to activate latent conflictual areas.

Since the relationship of the symptom or subjective disturbance to the systems property of the family is not always obvious, many observers may hold that there is little warrant for family study and therapy. Thus, early on it becomes an act of faith for the neophyte family therapist to ask the entire family to be part of the therapeutic work. This is most true where the presenting problem seems to be the property of one indiviual—a symptom in the classic sense. Where the problematic behavior is at the family system level—marital discord, for example—it is easier to invite the entire family to come to the consultation, although, unfortunately, children are often left out of such meetings as if, somehow, they did not know there was trouble between the parents—or were not part of the family.

The Phenomena of Family Therapy

Family therapy, for any therapist, consists of his engagement, with or without a co-therapist, with a social unit called the family in a therapeutic venture. He may have observed simulated interviews, seen videotapes, watched motion pictures, read articles and books, listened to lectures. He may be a solo practitioner, distant from large teaching centers, or a mental health trainee at an institute or in a university department. He may be at one or another developmental stage in regard to his family of origin and in regard to his family of procreation. Whatever the nature of these prior events and circumstances may be, there is a final engagement with the family in the therapeutic venture, and the systems properties and informational properties of this engagement generate the phenomena of family therapy.

Since the family system has the longest tenure for individuals and is operative both at the earliest ages and during the years of highest learning rates, the mutual integration of such patterns takes place most effectively among family members. One important feature of the phenomenology of family therapy concerns the large quantities of data and the multiple channels of data transmission which must be attended to. Initially, the experience of shifting from a dyadic form of therapy to an interview session involving a family group is overwhelming. The data are more numerous by far, and the interaction rate is high; of particular importance is the fact that a natural social group having lifetime tenure together is producing the information, very often idiosyncratically, coded with considerable condensation, and with high specificity of messages.

Thus, the sense of bewilderment and of transformation overload that characterizes the therapist in a family treatment situation is understandable. Theory building and the development of a set of basic treatment maneuvers and regularities help the therapist to stay afloat in a sea of data. Most important is an altered relationship with his/her own inner experience. This might be generally described as a shift from slower, controlled, cognitive examination of data towards more rapid affective processing. Minimal bodily and affective clues within the therapist become highly significant aspects of the therapeutic process.

Because of the special information-processing characteristics and the theory building requirements that are forced upon him by his engagement with the material under these circumstances, the family therapist is less able (should he wish to do so) to isolate and exclude the experience by excessive professionalism or intellectuality.

The family therapist becomes increasingly aware of the effect on the nature of the encounter of the social circumstances of his or her own personal and professional life. These affect the nature of the possible contractual relationships that can be established. With the family itself defined as the patient, the therapist's philosophy of health and illness is tested, and alternative models of illness must be considered, leading frequently to conflicts with the other social fields in which he operates. The terms "reality" and "pathology" may come to have lessened applicability as useful concepts to those involved in this kind of engagement. Associated with this phenomenon is an altered distinction as to the nature of the barrier between work and personal life. The impact on the life of the therapist and his or her own family, as these are forced into an altered state of relationship with the events of new professional experiences, must be considered.

Faced with this experience, the family therapist first of all has to revise some of his concepts of psychopathology. He is led into issues of family dynamics, into concepts related to systems; he begins to think in terms of family functions, family tasks, family developmental issues, family interfaces with other systems, rather than thinking primarily in terms of success or failure of the coping mechanisms of an individual. He thinks in terms of the historical, multigenerational family; he thinks in terms of maintenance and restoration of function rather than in terms of cure. Theory building becomes increasingly important. At this point, there are several theoretical emphases available, none of which is comprehensive and rigorous, or sufficiently defined as to be predictive in a statistically reliable way. However, the theories are sufficiently formulated to inform the clinician how he is to proceed further and to make him look at the families he works with in a particular way. Most useful are those approaches conceptualized in general systems terms, an approach which has come increasingly to dominate family therapy theorizing.

The interested reader may consult Grinker, Gray and Duhl, and Von Bertalanffy, among others. Certain orienting points, however, are of value in conceptualizing the relationships of the family systems approach to other modes of intervention.

Political Issues

If one speaks of politics as those behaviors concerned with the acquisition and maintenance of power or which bear on shifts in power balance, it is well to know that political consequences flow from the assumption of a family therapy stance.

The recognition of the power orientation of supposedly nonpolitical social units, such as the mental health apparatus or the family, is often experienced as distressing and cynical, yet the failure of such recognition is seriously handicapping. With respect to the family, such perceptions must move in three directions: (a) to an understanding of the internal politics of the family; (b) to an awareness of the political nature of the therapeutic encounter with the family (the therapist's interest in acquiring power); and, (c) to knowledge of the political effects in the mental health institutional world of a shift from a basically individual orientation toward the family orientation.

The process of identifying a psychiatric matter in family terms is, among other things, a political act. It shifts the power relations within the family, for example, by improving the status of the identified patient or by redirecting control operations away from a scapegoated person. In addition, as we have noted, the family therapist is concerned with the acquisition of power in the family and uses many techniques explicitly for this purpose. He interferes directly in the family political system, making covert operations explicit and, on occasion, shifting weight in the direction of redistribution of power.

The politics of family therapy, as of other mental health postures, extends into other arenas. The institutions involved to the greatest extent are those directly concerned with the provision of mental health services: clinics, child care agencies, residential treatment facilities, hospitals, and the private practice apparatus. Briefly, family therapy blends into work modes and technologies habitually associated with lower-status elements of the mental health professions. Psychologists, social workers, nurses, paraprofessionals, guidance personnel—all participate in such work to the degree that there are no clearly defined, exclusive tools or techniques. The guarding of guild-like vocational interests is far more difficult under such circumstances.

To the extent that the medical model of a "diseased person" is deliberately eschewed, it is more difficult for the physician to claim the authority of special expertness. The spread of family therapy is facilitated by other pressures in the modern world, principally society's need for less costly, more widely available health services. This leads to the inclusion of nontraditional disciplines as part of the health care delivery team. The net effect of this spread is to produce a *lateralization* of power and to reduce the influence of the traditionally organized vertical hierarchies of psychiatry, psychology and nursing. Established institutions deal with these political issues in a variety of ways; the manner in which they have been handled has in turn impinged on the acceptance of family therapy. Thus, the choice of this approach for any practitioner becomes, in part, a political as well as a clinical act.

Finally, too, one may speak of the position of family therapy with respect to moral values. For a variety of reasons the family is no longer easily recognizable as an institution organized around task functions or structures. More and more we expect to find our innermost needs for recognition, expression, validation, and intimacy satisfied with some family-like structure, or perhaps—as adults—chiefly within the marriage relationship. Communication, openness, connectedness, and genuineness become more highly prized under these circumstances than insight, personal growth, self-actualization, autonomy, and independence. In this sense family therapy may be a statement for authenticity, for confrontation, for affective expression, and for open conflict rather than for an unchanging maintenance of a structure, a clearly defined fulfillment of a task, a clearly expected social function. The interface between family and society is more permeable and less clearly defined, the expectations and inputs are many, and consequently a family represents a meeting place of many cultural subsystems negotiated via their individual representatives. No family therapist would claim that his work aim is to save families; he would maintain that he treats people in the context of a family. Nevertheless, there is an underlying bias in favor of some such ongoing interrelatedness as that in families, with consequent effect on the therapeutic choices to be made.

9

Indications and Contraindications for Family and Marital Therapy: An Illustrative Case

Marshall D. Schechter, M.D.
and
Harold I. Lief, M.D.

Introduction

Harold I. Lief, M.D.

Marital therapy and family therapy have had different origins, and until recent years have served different sorts of patients. Marriage counseling began in 1932 in Great Britain and the United States and was organized professionally in the United States in 1940. Family therapy began in the period between 1950 and 1955. Marital therapists treated minimally disturbed couples, whereas family therapists treated severely disturbed families. Marital therapy arose out of the demands of couples for help with troubled marriages, whereas family therapy had to be initiated by therapists, who attempted to persuade families that treating the family as a unit was preferable to treating the family member who was the indicated patient. Until recently, marital and family therapies were not received warmly by psychiatrists, who placed greater emphasis on intrapsychic processes and who tended to look down on the nonmedical therapists engaged in marital and family therapy.

Today, marital therapy and family therapy are going through a process of convergence. Increasingly, marital therapists see other family members, and family therapists spend more of their professional time dealing with the marital relationship. The American Association of Marriage and Family Therapists now has HEW provisional sanction to speak for the entire field of marital and family therapy. Whatever the merits of the opposition to this by certain family therapists, conceptually the merger of the two fields has great merit.

The conceptualization of marital and family therapy depends on a systems approach, which incorporates psychodynamics, communications, and behavioral concepts. The unification of these approaches is based on the belief that relationships are at least as important in human behavior and in therapy as are intrapsychic events. The nature of requests for help underscores this position. Forty-two percent of the people coming for help define their mental and emotional problems as marital; 17 percent emphasize other disturbed family relationships. Other surveys show that 75 percent of the clients are concerned primarily with family problems.

Results of Treatment

An excellent review of results of marital and family therapy has been written by Gurman and Kniskern (1). Their review of many studies has been condensed and simplified for this paper. Table 1

TABLE 1

Results of Nonbehavioral Marital Therapy*

Type of Therapy	No. of Studies	No. of Patients	% Improved	% No Change	% Worsened
Conjoint Therapy	9	296	70	29	1
Individual Therapy	7	406	48	45	7
Conjoint Group Therapy	15	397	66	30	4
Concurrent and Collaborative Therapy	5	429	62	36	2

* After Gurman & Kniskern (1).

shows the results of nonbehavioral marital therapy and indicates that the best results for patients with marital problems are by conjoint therapy. Not far behind is conjoint group therapy, in which couples are treated in groups. All forms of marital therapy seem to be superior to individual therapy.

Similar results are demonstrated with nonbehavioral family therapy (Table 2), although these studies did not compare family therapy

TABLE 2

Results of Nonbehavioral Family Therapy

Focus	No. of Studies	No. of Patients	% Improved	% No Change	% Worsened
Child as the Identified Patient	12	370	68	32	0
Adolescent as the Identified Patient	8	187	77	23	0
Adult as the Identified Patient	11	390	71	27	2
Mixed	8	467	81	17	2

with either marital therapy or individual therapy. The range of improvement was from 68 percent to 81 percent, which certainly compares favorably with other forms of treatment.

Direct comparison of nonbehavioral treatments for marital problems demonstrates that conjoint marital and conjoint group therapies are superior to individual and other forms of treatment in 70 percent of studies reviewed, whereas individual psychotherapy was superior in only 15 percent of studies (Table 3).

When marital-family therapies with nonbehavioral methods were compared with individual therapy in 29 studies, marital-family therapy turned out to be better in 21 of those studies (Table 4). These studies were not controlled. When controlled studies are examined, one finds that the treatment groups had better results than did the control groups in 10 out of 15 studies (Table 5). Similarly, in 11 other studies of family therapy, treatment was better than control in 7 (Table 6).

One must be mindful that these studies vary in quality. Some of

TABLE 3

Direct Comparison of Nonbehavioral Treatments for Marital Problems (26 Studies) (Conjoint, Individual, and "Others"*)

Conjoint Marital and Conjoint Group**		Individual Psychotherapy	
Two compared ———no difference			
Superior to Individual and Other Treatments	70%	Superior to "Others"	10%
Inferior to Individual and Other Treatments	5%	Superior to Conjoint	5%

* Other forms of treatment included concurrent, collaborative marital therapy; community care; drug therapy; communication training; encounter groups.
** Concurrent and collaborative methods less effective than conjoint.

TABLE 4

Comparison of Nonbehavioral Marital-Family Therapy with Individual Therapy

No. of Studies	Marital-Family Therapy Better	No Difference	M-F Therapy Worse
29	21	7	1

TABLE 5

Controlled Studies of Nonbehavioral Marital Therapy (15 Studies)

Treatment better than Control	10
No difference	4
Control better than Treatment	1

them were very good, using therapists with similar training and with matched patients. Others had many deficiencies in that they often

Table 6

Controlled Studies of Family Therapy
(11 Studies)

Treatment better than Control	7
No difference	4

would compare therapists with different levels of training and experience and use treatment populations that differed considerably. Yet, the overall impression one gets from surveying 156 studies is that these forms of treatment for marital and family problems are far superior to individual psychotherapy. The studies also demonstrate that when both partners are involved in therapy, especially when they are seen conjointly, maximum benefit occurs.

Part I

Marshall D. Schechter, M.D.

A number of functions of family life are essential to the understanding of circumstances that may go awry in either the total family or its individual members. It is necessary to consider two functioning axes of family life: (a) the generation separation with the division of parents, who nurture and teach and are sexually active with each other, from the younger members; (b) the division between the two different sexes for the development of gender identity. In the normal family it is necessary for the parents to have a coalition about the beliefs that determine family values; it is necessary that the parents are willing to undertake the tasks of nurturing; it is necessary that the family teach the functions of the culture to the younger generation; it is necessary for the family to emancipate its offspring when they get into the middle and later adolescent phase; and lastly, it is necessary for the family to exemplify and teach coping with crises. Generally speaking, the father's role in our current society still determines the family's social position, whereas the mother's role is often more responsible for the affective and emotional climate within the family. These nurturant roles of the mother must have the support of the father; if effective, this arrangement establishes basic trust in each of the children within the family. Therefore, it is clear that the parental roles ought to be sufficiently complementary, permitting the parents to share the tangibles and intangibles necessary to maintain the functions of the family. Because of the long developmental period of the human infant, separations begin with weaning, continue for some years, and then, under favorable conditions, conclude at the end of the adolescent period with complete separation and individuation. The following case history helps identify some of these issues and highlights some of the indications and contraindications for marital and family therapy.

Case History

Barbara was just 14 years of age at the time of the referral. For the previous six months she had frequently talked about death, but it was difficult for the parents to tell if she was obsessed with the philosophical meaning of death, fearful of her own death or of someone else's dying, or expressing thoughts having suicidal implications. It was only when Barbara began to speak of methods whereby she might kill herself that her parents consulted a psychiatrist, who made the referral to the writer.

This delay should not be considered a lack of interest or concern of the parents about Barbara. Their attitude and confusion were a reflection of the way Barbara acted and characteristically responded. The initial phone call was from Mr. Rosen (fictitious name), Barbara's father, who indicated that he was uncertain as to whether there was a definite problem or whether this was merely a particular phase of adolescent development through which Barbara was passing. There was considerable difficulty setting up an appropriate consultation time since Mrs. Rosen worked as a high school physics teacher but, more particularly, because the father, a university physics teacher, had innumerable departmental and university committee meetings. He attempted to bargain about time to meet at his convenience (as later he attempted to bargain over the fee).

When the three—Barbara, Father, and Mother—did come for their first appointment, I decided to see all of them together—to get a sense of how they related to each other and how they tended to confront each other regarding Barbara's symptom. Mrs. Rosen walked in first, followed by Barbara, and then Mr. Rosen. Mrs. Rosen, 40 years of age, had white hair but a youthful face and figure. She was dressed in a wool suit, stylish blouse, and boots, carrying a briefcase filled with papers and books. She spoke softly during the visit, looking pensive and, at times, guilty as she questioned her parenting. Barbara wore overalls, a t-shirt, a down vest, and shoes whose soles were about to fall off. Mr. Rosen was about six feet tall, with tousled hair, sport shirt, jeans, tennis shoes, and parka. He looked younger than his chronological age of 41. Barbara and Mrs. Rosen sat on opposite ends of the couch, while the father sat on an easy chair closer to Barbara, only a short arm's-length away.

Barbara, clearly the center of attention, looked very comfortable. She argued and quipped with her parents. She moved easily in her seat, sometimes addressing me or criticizing her parents for their lack of appreciation, understanding, or memory of her life's experiences. Her vocabulary and sentence structure were very advanced. Barbara had long, light-brown hair, which she flounced imperiously; she was small-boned and had few of the curves which her mother evidenced. There seemed to be a closeness between Barbara and Mrs. Rosen.

During the first 15 minutes, all three agreed that Barbara had only one close friend—a next-door neighbor two years her senior—and that for years she had seemed to antagonize her peers. Academically she had always done well but, it was emphasized by all three, not as well as her brother, four years her senior, who was a freshman at Yale. During these first few minutes it was evident that Barbara's attachment to her father had a seductive aspect in the way she coyly looked at him, touched him with her hand on his arm, or played "footsie" with him. Barbara emphasized that she had been preoccupied with suicidal thoughts for at least two years, but as she spoke there was no evidence of sadness or depression, nor was there any increase or decrease in bodily activity or rate of verbal production. She stated that for some time she had wanted to see a psychiatrist, and the only way she felt she would get her parents' attention was to talk about taking pills to end her life. I decided to ask the parents to leave so that I could talk to Barbara alone.

Barbara continued her easy conversation, looking at times like a 14-year-old girl going on 24; at other times like a 14-year-old feeling, thinking, and acting like a three-year-old. Specifically, when she spoke of boys, with whom she had had no actual romantic contact, she acted like she was sex-starved and had had considerable post-adolescent experience. When she spoke of her peer group, however, and how they didn't understand her, she acted like a youngster wanting to take her jacks and ball home with her as she left the group. Her attitude was that of arrogantly assuming everyone else was wrong and she was right, this rightness confirmed, she felt, by her parents' agreement with her. Barbara talked of how her brother, Robert, had plagued her in her growing up, but also mentioned with considerable pride that he was one of the youngest students from their local high school to get an early-decision major university acceptance.

As I asked about the neighborhood in which the Rosens lived, she indicated that their family was the poorest but the best educated. She told me that the other families exhibited their wealth, but the Rosens all enjoyed the simple things of life together. These included playing musical instruments, discussing all of their problems and experiences, democratically deciding how to spend their money and how to deal with family problems by defusing their anger. There was a moment of minor annoyance as Barbara described her father's way of ending an argument, particularly with her, by holding his fingers in the peace symbol. She found this irritating, often wishing to continue the argument while he decided to end it at his discretion and, from her standpoint, prematurely. She said she liked the peace symbol, but when she wasn't finished arguing she felt like holding the middle finger up to her father's face, signifying she was only half finished arguing.

I discussed with Barbara the need for an evaluative process in which I would see her a number of times and might decide to include psychological testing. I also told her that I would see her parents at the end of the evaluation, telling them only those matters on which Barbara and I agreed ahead of time, and keeping confidential all of the other thoughts and experiences that we discussed. She agreed to this and also to my seeing them with her at this time to discuss the conduct of the evaluation. Before calling in her parents, I requested of Barbara that, if her parents agreed to the evaluation, she would note significant life events, dreams, daydreams, and periods of sadness, anger, and anxiety.

When her parents returned, they both looked very concerned and asked if I thought Barbara was actively suicidal and needed intensive psychotherapy. I suggested an evaluation and indicated the potential costs of psychological testing and the individual sessions with me. The father asked whether he might get a reduction in view of his not only being a fellow academic, but also having the enormous tuition costs for his son at Yale. When I indicated that the fees for my services and the psychological testing already took into account his circumstances, he acquiesced without further question. The family left after this two-and-one-half hour session with Mrs. Rosen leading the way and Barbara following with her father's arm around her shoulder.

On subsequent visits I was impressed with the disparity between the depressive content of dreams and life events and the relative absence of any similar affect in Barbara's speech and expression. In fact, while reporting serious problems with her peers, she demonstrated delight and pleasure at her clearly maladaptive fashion of coping with them. For example, she spoke of her concern over her lack of friendships, and yet she described how she was the only one in the class who told the teacher that another student had left class early. She also spoke of telling the vice principal, when he became aware of the distinctive odor, which students were smoking pot. Barbara could not imagine why the other students labeled her "narc," saying that she, Barbara, couldn't abide smoking marijuana herself and knew that it was illegal. She indicated parental support for both of these positions and could not understand why, even if one did not agree with the peer group, it wasn't acceptable to oppose them openly by joining forces with the establishment.

Barbara also described how she discussed these and other items with her father before her mother came home. Since he was a senior member of his department and its vice-chairman, he was able to arrange his classes and time schedules fairly much as desired. Without too much effort, Barbara, upon demand, could get her father to leave whatever activity which he was engaged in to sit with her in her room or on the living room couch to discuss the problems of the day. It was a rare occasion when, despite some disagreements, the father was not able to get Barbara to laugh and feel better when she came to him troubled. By the time Mrs. Rosen returned from her work, she was greeted with a report of an activity and the conclusions reached by Barbara and the father, having little or no opportunity to voice her opinion if it in any way differed from theirs. On a number of occasions during this evaluation, I commented that it appeared that peer friendships seemed unneeded and unwanted in view of the close ties Barbara maintained with her parents—particularly with her father.

The diagnostic process spread over a few months because of a number of meetings and out-of-town lectures with which I was involved. Barbara seemed genuinely pleased about the visits, and yet I could see no awareness by her of her role in the difficulties with peers. It became obvious that Barbara's superiority and even arrogance were shared and supported by her parents and her brother. They saw themselves as very special people, to be considered correct even if the mores of the surrounding social group considered their actions incorrect. When Barbara reported that she turned in a classmate who had cut his car in front of the school bus, she smiled, expecting me to compliment her as her parents did. When asked why they agreed with Barbara's action despite their awareness of her rejection by her classmates, both parents indicated that they were always insistent on their children's telling the truth. They could not appreciate the weight of the group mores against tattling, nor that Barbara had the option of not speaking and allowing some other member of her class to reveal the offender.

There were a number of occasions when Barbara came home from school to discuss with her father the disappointments of the day. Mr. Rosen comforted her by cuddling and agreeing with her understanding and handling of her peer relationships for "fear of further diminishing her self-esteem." By the time Mrs. Rosen came home, Barbara and her father had taken the edge off the situation, signifying the coalition between Barbara and her father, with his assuming a greater nurturing and modeling role for Barbara. With the firm, superior position of her brother and her father, Barbara presented a picture of an individual whose gender identity was ambivalent and whose feelings as a female were those of a disparaged and degraded individual. These feelings were enhanced by Mrs. Rosen's feelings that she herself was powerless and her conflict over assuming an authoritarian, critical position, as had her own mother.

Family therapy was considered because of the dynamics involved. It appeared to me that Barbara was still trapped within an unresolved oedipal situation supported by the complementary seductiveness of her father and the passivity of her mother. It appeared to me also that two axes of family life were deficient. Specifically, generational bonding was insufficient to permit adequate separation between the parents and Barbara, and the parents' confusion over their own gender identities and gender-role behavior prevented adequate development of secure gender identity in Barbara. Besides these factors, an inadequate parental coalition with respect to their roles and tasks interfered with the nurturant role and functions generally assumed by a mother. Since the father's nurturance was heavily spiced with seduction, Barbara's development of basic trust was damaged.

Before presenting these thoughts to Barbara and her parents, I decided to have Barbara psychologically tested to help to clarify the possibility of an incipient psychosis. Also, because Barbara's object ties were so fragile, I decided that she might benefit from a period of individual therapy before instituting a family approach. The salient data derived from this testing are the following: On cognitive functioning, Verbal IQ was 127; Performance IQ 141; Full-Scale IQ 139. There was no evidence of intrusion in the cognitive realm of the adverse effects of any emotional disturbance. Because the details are germane to this case, I quote the entire section on personality functioning.*

> Despite Barbara's dislike and hatred for the unstructured tasks, the material she presented to the projectives was marked by considerable elaboration of detail and clear presentation of conflicted dynamics. The most striking feature of her functioning is the presence of many polarities in her functioning. On one hand, there is a push for a hypermature, sexualized, hysterical façade, appropriate for an older woman, balanced by the giving of childlike regressive responses on the Rorschach. By the same token, the expression of very strong aggressive drives cannot be allowed to consciousness, yet one sees people around her constantly threatened with harm and her felt need to be supportive of them. Along the same lines, she views herself as "prim and proper," superior to others, yet underneath one sees a profound sense of vulnerability, helplessness, and need for closeness. This controlled young lady constantly fears and anticipates a breakdown in control of instinctual life as she moves into adolescence. In general, Barbara has a rather pessimistic view of life, feels she can never get support from men and, in that respect, she sees herself as very much like her mother. She sees herself as weak but with a façade of strength and a strong sense of righteousness. As much as she maintains this façade, she hopes that it can be penetrated by others and the distance between them thereby reduced (at the very moment she tries so hard to maintain her distance). She is a perfectionist, yet feels she had not been provided the adequate tools by her parents to obtain her level of perfectionism. She rages at them (not openly) for leaving her so ill-prepared. Despite her perfectionistic attitudes she feels there is no sense to attempt to meet parental standards which she sees as not being for accomplishment as much as for maintaining behaviors consistent with adulthood. In essence, she feels her childhood has never been accepted and to be childlike is threatening and "bad." Her sense of superiority allows her to differentiate partially both from her parents and from her peers, but there is a deep desire for closeness. Her fear of vulnerability especially related to stimulation of dependent needs prevents her allowing such closeness to take place.

---

* Alvin Gerstein, Ph.D., Irving Schwartz Institute, Philadelphia, Pennsylvania.

Although she appears to be sexually mature, oedipal issues, per se, are not basic to her problem areas. Rather, one sees a felt need for nurturant satisfaction and a generalized insufficiency in what was obtained from either parent, each of whom presents a very different, but clear, view of male and female roles. The mother is seen as an individual who pushes control and superego development. In essence, "be good," meet your obligations. Barbara is quite protective of her and does not openly show any disagreement with her on such issues, complying in a passive-aggressive way. Yet mother (and women) tends to regress badly when her desperate search for love is unsatisfied. There is a depressive, almost tragic, chord to her view of women (consequently, Barbara feels that she cannot let herself fully identify with her mother and run the risk of such periodic breakdowns in controls).

The fact that women are unfulfilled relates to the fact that men are seen as capable of giving little. Barbara seems too closely related to her father and has not been able to shunt her sexual interests to males of her own age. There is an indication that one time she felt much closer to him and that something has happened so that the relationship no longer provides this. Men in general are seen as providing little in the way of nurturance or protection and are basically geared to devoting themselves to the development of their intellectual interests. They denigrate females and are suspicious of their intentions. Still, relatively speaking, they offer the hope of being a source of warmth. Yet they rarely provide what they seem to promise.

Barbara seems very comfortable in a fantasied world which allows aberrant thought processes ready expression without any great anxiety on her part. There is a tendency to be overly ideational and preoccupied with the fantasy of being a "grand dame" and a seductive woman. There is a stubborn insistence upon seeing the world in an unbending fashion. Hypercriticalness is pronounced in her view of all interpersonal relationships, especially those where feelings may be readily stimulated. If she were a 20-year-old rather than an adolescent, the picture presented would be consistent with a person with marked paranoid ideation with underlying thought disorder if she had to function in a give-and-take fashion without clear guidelines or social amenities and appearance to fall back upon. Her judgment regarding people may frequently be quite inadequate and she has a poor assessment of social reality. Object relations seem

> to be not well established and more dependent on an entrenched view of people and not current experiences. Sublimation appears to be poor, and childhood conflicts not well resolved.
>
> The picture as presented would indicate a rather difficult treatment situation, although obviously Barbara is very much in need of help. To reiterate: She is extremely vulnerable, yet insists upon maintaining a façade, yet at the next moment wishes it were broken; she is seductive and appears to look like she wants closeness and the next moment denigrates others and is anti-instinctual; she is quite comfortable with bizarre fantasy and shows no anxiety about idiosyncratic autistic preoccupation. It is apparent that a developmental delay has been quite profound. She has considerable conflict about acceptance of her own adolescent and childhood needs and is torn, but not readily open toward a helping hand at this time. I would anticipate without treatment we could eventually expect considerable psychopathology, great difficulty maintaining even the most meager relationships, but with the capacity to maintain herself in a formal academic learning environment. Any therapy that would be undertaken would be of a protracted nature.

My findings and those of the psychologist were presented first to Barbara to see if there was anything in my presentation and recommendation she wished me to modify in my discussion with her and her parents. (In neither presentation did I include the question of possible psychotic elements nor the feeling of women being unfulfilled or of men denigrating women.) I emphasized the split in her character structure and how, in many ways, the family seemed to support her defenses. Even during this presentation, the sympathetic looks among all of them, the amount of physical touching, and their sitting in similar formation as they did on the initial visit, as well as the tears that both parents shed, made me suggest again that with friends like her parents I could imagine it might be difficult for Barbara to find others as close within her own peer group. I suggested that the three of them might want a week or so to think about my recommendation for family therapy on a weekly basis (with the option of my seeing Barbara individually as needed). Both Mr. and Mrs. Rosen immediately turned to Barbara and, simultaneously, said they wanted to proceed with treatment if it were all right with her. She agreed, as she had when we discussed it prior to meeting with her parents, and we made an appointment for the following week.

On subsequent visits I pointed out the repartee and humorous digs which went on between all of them, particularly Barbara and Mr. Rosen. I inquired if this were typical of the interactions within the family. Mrs. Rosen said it was not only typical, but, at times, she felt very frustrated because of the length of time this kind of bickering took place, not only with Barbara but with their son, Robert, during his junior and senior high school period. Mrs. Rosen also brought out that Robert was an isolate to a great degree like Barbara, but he was able to spend time in one of the school's laboratories where he was doing independent research. The other positive aspects of Robert's interpersonal relationships related to a general appeal he had for older people, enhanced by the fact that Robert was at least a year-and-a-half younger than most of the students in his class. Mr. Rosen said he enjoyed these exchanges because he felt it strengthened both children's argumentative skills, which they would need when they got to college, especially if either one were to go into law.

Barbara brought up a number of times how her verbal skills were her only weapon against Robert. He frequently attacked her physically, while she fought with cutting remarks. When Barbara mentioned this, her parents recalled that they first consulted a psychiatrist when Robert was five years old because of the violence of his rivalrous feelings toward Barbara. It appeared that Mrs. Rosen had exhausted all of her resources and energies in attempting, without much success, to control Robert. Mr. Rosen was a student completing his doctoral thesis at a major university when Robert was five, and Mrs. Rosen felt that he shouldn't be, or couldn't be, bothered with disciplinary matters.

By the time Barbara was five, the family had moved twice across the country and had been to Europe twice. During each of these moves Barbara became more clinging. By the time they moved to the Philadelphia area, she was unable to leave her mother's side without considerable anxiety. Mrs. Rosen, nevertheless, started to work, placing Barbara in the public school kindergarten, an arrangement which seemed to go fairly well both behaviorally and academically. From that point on in her life, her best friend was her next-door neighbor, a girl two years her senior.

Mr. Rosen rose rapidly in the university ranks because of his original research, his personality, and his excellence as a teacher. Since his university valued publications in major journals, he devoted considerable time to writing, a circumstance which kept him at home much of the time Barbara was not in school. Barbara and he played many physical games together which included his being in charge of Barbara's pre-bedtime activities. He would carry her, sometimes piggyback and sometimes in his arms, to bed, where tickling games would ensue prior to hugs and kisses before turning off the light. These activities continued through the time of our family sessions, and both Barbara and Mr. Rosen spoke of their pleasure in them. When I raised questions as to the appropriateness of continuing these games at this age, Mr. Rosen indicated that on my advice he would discontinue them, but he felt it was so much fun for them both he couldn't imagine any harm occurring.

It became evident in the sessions that father was the head of the house in the sense that he got what he wanted. There were frequent allusions to the episode that brought Mr. and Mrs. Rosen to see the referring psychiatrist. The social position of the family clearly revolved around Mr. Rosen's academic acquaintances and schedules. His pleasures and involvements became the family's. Ski trips were planned for Robert and Barbara, with Mrs. Rosen going along and patiently waiting until the three came off the slopes. When Robert went off to college, the father arranged two trips with Barbara alone. Both the parents and Barbara felt this was an excellent arrangement, but reconsidered when I raised the question about whether the parents ever took vacations by themselves without the children. The generational gap not only had not been considered; it had been avoided and obscured, really obliterated, by the force of Mr. Rosen's view of family life. It became evident that Mr. Rosen assumed many of the nurturant roles in the family, interfering with Barbara's normal psychosexual development. The marital boundaries were diffuse and confused. The closeness of the bond with her father tended to engulf Barbara, handicapping her from interacting with the peer group and also preventing her from the adolescent drive to separate. She was confronted with a double-bind situation of being rewarded at times for remaining a young child, and at times for being a mature woman. Parental ambivalence and role diffusion became evident during the session in which Barbara talked about her boredom at home, her annoyance with her peer group, and her desire to visit her brother. Barbara said that the previous evening, while her parents were out, she had thought about running away without leaving a note. Her father looking momentarily shocked, and then calmly began to express understanding of her feelings and to say that he had felt the same when he was growing up. I asked him to go back and examine his feelings when Barbara talked of running away. He first looked puzzled, and then spoke of his anger with her for even considering such a move. He went on to describe how, early in his life, he learned to smile when hurt, like a boxer, to throw off his opponent whom he then could subdue with his logic. With this, Mrs. Rosen responded with her feeling that Mr. Rosen was always in the power position and cared little for others' feelings. She admitted, as did Barbara, that Mr. Rosen was better during the few months since our sessions began.

During subsequent interviews, we focused on Barbara's ineptness in handling a boyfriend with whom she had fantasied an intimate relationship. This was a young man, a year her senior, who was a counselor-in-training at the camp she attended the previous summer. The camp had a Christmas get-together during which the young man ignored her. When he called her in the spring, she greeted him on the phone by saying, "Boy, you sure acted like an ass last Christmas." Barbara insisted that he acted like an ass, but finally, with pressure from her parents, she did admit that perhaps she had spoken without sufficient thought, discouraging rather than encouraging closeness. The same coalition and consolidation of parental opinion helped Barbara to see that her response to being pinched by one of the girls in the school chorus was inappropriate. As the annoyance continued, Barbara shouted, "Look, girl, if you have to touch, pick on some female who will appreciate it."

With her parents remaining out of the sympathetic and buddy roles, it was interesting to note how rapidly Barbara found the means to attract friends rather than to repulse them. Although Mr. Rosen continued some of his behavior with his students and colleagues, both parents were very pleased with Barbara's growing involvement with her peers, her developing interests of her own (rather than following competitively her brother's interests), and her increasing involvement with extracurricular activities. When Barbara found that she was not able to maintain her thoughts and feelings to herself during our family sessions, she found it necessary to announce that she wouldn't be attending the sessions anymore. She said that the therapy had been helpful and that there might be some time in the future when she would return. She said that it would be all right if her parents wanted to continue, and that if her brother ever wanted to come, this, too, would be all right with her.

The parents agreed to come themselves to review what Barbara was doing and their responses to her life events. They reported that in all her relationships she was doing well. A brief argument occurred when Barbara answered the phone and refused to tell her mother to whom she was speaking. Mrs. Rosen insisted, and when Barbara continued to refuse, threatened her with grounding for a day. Barbara took the punishment because she felt her mother had no right to infringe on her privacy.

Barbara knew of her parents' visits with me and said to tell me how much she appreciated the help and how much she received from our sessions together. Her brother, Robert, came in for the holidays and also reported a significant change in Barbara. To him she seemed more like a teenager, was not as clinging to him or to the college friend he brought home with him, and the relationship to their parents seemed more like that which he had observed in other homes. The last point distressed him somewhat, as he still felt the unique quality of the family enmeshment. He spoke with Barbara about the reputation their father maintained on his, Robert's, campus. He suggested that she consider going into their father's and mother's field, missing completely his parents' advice to him to leave Barbara alone so as to permit her to establish her own psychological identity. He also instructed Barbara to let go sexually and "go all the way" with boys as a means of increasing her popularity. Robert emphasized to Barbara in their parents' presence that he was 14 years old when he engaged in sexual intercourse and felt that this activity was positive for his development. The parents reported this interchange and also that Barbara felt that bras were old-fashioned and that breasts were a public matter, there being no inhibition to permitting boys to fondle her breasts to some degree, even in public.

Mrs. Rosen was shocked and angered by Robert's insensitivity and by Barbara's inability to establish protective boundaries. Mr. Rosen verbally backed his wife's position, but did so with a smile. It was evident that Mr. Rosen approved of and was pleased by Robert's sexual activities, and also that he was stimulated by Barbara's views. Noticing his attitude, Mrs. Rosen paled. She said that she and Mr. Rosen were again having profound marital problems. However, they indicated that Mr. Rosen was reevaluating taking Barbara on a ski trip, and probably would go with his own brother at a time when Barbara was involved in school. Mrs. Rosen stated that Barbara herself said that she would rather go with her peer group on some of their trips. The parents set another time for getting together with me to continue to track Barbara's development.

* * * *

My criteria for undertaking family therapy can largely be illustrated by references to the Rosen family situation. Direct contact with members of the nuclear family is indicated as a potential background for any therapeutic modality. Family therapy per se is of prime consideration 1) when there are amorphous communications between family members; 2) when there is an acute family crisis; 3) when the complaints are mainly interpersonal; 4) when there are acting-out behaviors related to forces within the family; 5) when marital disturbances can be seen to influence the behaviors of the children; and 6) when there has been an unsuccessful trial of individual treatment.

The contraindications to family therapy include the following conditions: 1) when there is a stable family system despite a highly inappropriate system of roles and relationships; 2) when one of the members of the family is in a severely psychotic state, whether depressive or paranoid schizophrenic (although recognizing that much of the history of family therapy revolves around treating the families of schizophrenics); 3) when a severe sadomasochistic relationship is present between members of the family; 4) when there are certain very debilitating psychosomatic conditions (e.g., ulcerative colitis); 5) when there is a refusal of significant family members to come in to family treatment; 6) when there is the potential for violent physical attacks within the family; 7) when one of the adult members of the family is firmly and actively sociopathic; and 8) when the problem is that of an older adolescent attempting to separate psychologically.

I fully recognize, of course, that the view of other authors as to contraindications to family therapy range widely. Some authors admit no contraindications; some offer lists at variance with mine. I also acknowledge that the availability of a trained family therapist is a practical matter of great importance.

Insofar as this family is concerned, it is apparent that Barbara's presenting complaint of preoccupation with death is no longer present. She seems to have progressed actively into adolescence with a determined effort to separate and individuate fully. The father's narcissistic tendencies may still be enough in evidence to create other crises and could be the limiting factor for family progress, perhaps again directly affecting Barbara's development. In similar fashion, Mrs. Rosen's lack of assertiveness and her relinquishment of power and control to her husband may also be damaging to the development in Barbara of an adequate female identity. The hope is that with the detailing of such case histories and adequate long-term follow-up research, we can better determine the effectiveness of such treatment approaches and refine the indications and contraindications for family therapy.

Part II

Harold I. Lief, M.D.

We have chosen the Rosen family as an illustrative case history because its situation required a variety of treatment methods at different times in the course of treatment. Multiple therapy has the advantage of being flexible: The therapist uses the treatment most appropriate for patients in a particular situation at a given time.

This allows the therapist to fit the treatment to the needs of each patient, rather than offer the patient a single mode of treatment with which the therapist is familiar and comfortable. All too often this mode is unsuitable. The flexible approach carries with it the disadvantage that the therapeutic contract may be confused. At the outset, the therapist and patient may have different expectations about the goals of treatment. Moreover, treatment goals may shift without the shift becoming explicit, a circumstance which is likely to create a good deal of therapeutic confusion. A flexible approach requires that the therapist be very explicit about the expectations and directions of treatment every time a new therapeutic arrangement is negotiated. Even this is not a fail-safe method of preventing ambiguities in the treatment process.

If we return to the Rosen family, we have the opportunity to explore their situation over three years earlier than the treatment outlined by my colleague. At that time in their lives, Mr. and Mrs. Rosen came to see me at a point of crisis revolving around his infidelity and attempt to persuade his wife to accept an "open marriage."

Case History

Mrs. Rosen was depressed and distraught; she had lost 10 pounds in several weeks. Her whole life was wrapped up in her husband and in her family, and her pride was severely damaged. They had been childhood sweethearts, had "gone steady" in high school, and had married in college. (Her father had died when she was four, and her mother had never remarried.) Up until the time they had married, neither of them had had other romantic or sexual partners. This was still true of Mrs. Rosen. She could not countenance the idea of her husband's having the freedom to have other partners while being married to her, nor could she countenance separation. She was demoralized, because neither alternative was possible for her.

Mr. Rosen had had no extramarital relations until three years before during a working holiday in Europe without his wife, when he had a week-long affair with a Belgian girl. He had been intensely attracted to her and had been altogether pleased by her adulation, which had not lessened despite his impotence in repeated attempts at intercourse. For about two years before coming for help, he had had a number of sexual encounters with the wife of a colleague. The colleague knew and approved of these encounters; the couple had an open marriage and the wife had several concurrent boyfriends. Mr. Rosen had a very close relationship with this couple; indeed, he had worked on a number of projects with his colleague and had been with the two of them at a variety of professional meetings. His colleague's wife had been attentive, romantic, witty, and charming, and had bolstered Mr. Rosen's self-esteem with many flattering remarks. Despite the intense sexual arousal, he was again unable to perform sexually, usually being completely impotent, at best losing his erection on penetration.

During the initial session he made light of his sexual difficulties. For many weeks he denied that there were any signfiicant sexual problems and only some months into treatment did he recognize and acknowledge that a lot of his motivation for extramarital sex was to prove his sexual competence.

His entire life had been dominated by a need for performance, to be "number one." When he began to talk more freely of his sexual problems, it became clear that only rarely was he able to penetrate sexually and ejaculate. On most occasions he would have noncoital ejaculation without erection. When erect, he would attempt intercourse but, even if successful, only rarely would he ejaculate. In brief, he had a combination of impotence and retarded ejaculation. He developed an elaborate system of scoring his sexual performance. He would give himself points for sexual interest, erection, noncoital flaccid ejaculation, noncoital ejaculation with erection, coital erection with and without ejaculation, and finally the number of minutes taken up during intromission. It was perhaps the most elaborate method of monitoring one's own sexual performance that I have ever encountered.

Later, it became apparent that since his teens he had had the conviction that his penis was small. Moreover, an attack of mumps orchitis had left him with a shriveled testicle. Another source of embarrassment was his extreme difficulty urinating in public. In one session he disclosed that, beginning when he was seven, his father would check on him nightly to make sure that his hands were above the bed-covers. Between the ages of 13 and 17 he masturbated without ejaculating, and at 17 ejaculated for the first time during heavy petting with his future wife. His masturbatory fantasies involved being tied to a bed by a dominating and controlling woman, having sex with a huge, heavy woman who pressed him to the bed, being a woman himself during sex with his wife, being a sandwich with his wife on top and a man beneath, with the man's penis in his anus. The bondage fantasies had several times been acted out in reality, aided by marijuana, by inhaling chloroform, and on at least one occasion, by inhaling carbon tetrachloride. As one might imagine, this extreme passivity was defended against in many situations by an aggressive, dominating posture and even outright physical violence within the family. At work he was friendly, agreeable, anxious to be regarded as a good fellow. In therapy, his usual mode was to be very friendly, agreeable, and compliant, carefully concealing, usually from himself as well, any aggressive impulses.

Mrs. Rosen, deprived of a father at a very early age, projected on to her husband the image of an idealized father and protector, despite his being only a year older than she. Her self-esteem, which had been lowered by a demanding and critical mother who had taken over the family business, was maintained by basking in the reflected glory of her husband-to-be. He had been a child prodigy in science, music, and tennis, the recipient of scholarships, and had graduated first in his class from a major university. The wife's worth and security were totally dependent on the relationship with her husband. Desertion by him would repeat the early loss of her idealized father at age four. She had even undertaken graduate studies in the same field as her husband, despite the less-than-adequate support and encouragement for women in physics.

The husband's pride was fed fairly well by his wife's love, support, and admiration for about 13 years of marriage. About the same time that he encountered a serious blow to his self-esteem at work, his sexual problems at home increased in severity. (Fortunately for their relationship, his wife had had no difficulty in rapidly responding to noncoital clitoral stimulation, and was almost invariably orgastic, although rarely during coitus.) Mr. Rosen's tenuous masculine pride was suffering increasing blows at the time he had his first extramarital relationship. This encounter was a mixed blessing, for although it was clear that the young woman was very interested in him, he had failed in sexual performance, and performance was everything. A skilled tennis player as a youth, for example, with the possibility of playing competitive tournament tennis, he had given it up almost entirely when he recognized that he could not be the very best in the field.

It appeared that we were dealing with a couple who had never experienced and worked through a genuine separation from their families in late adolescence. It was a pseudo-separation and maturation. This was more obvious in the wife, with her glorification of her husband; yet it was equally true, although more complex and insidious, in the husband. He had never worked through the oedipal conflict with his father, was fearful of retaliation, and warded off castration anxiety in sexual experiences by an identification with women and the fantasy of absorbing the penis from behind so that he could put it out in front. These defenses were only partially successful, and the passivity and dependency had to be guarded against or his vulnerability would be exposed (hence, his denial of sexual problems for some months). In addition to the extramarital sex, his techniques of reassurance included adventurous pursuits, such as skiing on the highest and most dangerous slopes and white-water canoeing in the Rockies (the same type of defenses commonly seen in transvestites). He partially understood his wife's anxiety and consequent refusal to join him in these dangerous pursuits, but did a poor job of hiding his contempt. This, in turn, led to a degree of isolation in their recreational activities, which increased her feeling of desertion.

His defenses provided some positive elements as well. His great need for new experiences and for new sensations included enormous pleasure in meeting new people and making friends, although only a very few remained close. His intense curiosity about people and new experiences, however, was all related to their impact on him, rather than to enlarging his concept of others. Yet the split between his masculine and feminine selves was bridged in all but the explicit sexual side of his life by a creativity in science and a love of music. He was a capable pianist who spent may hours a week practicing.

Many of the marital problems were clear from the outset—not only his extramarital adventuring and a wish for an open marriage and its significance to his wife, but his boredom with her clinging possessiveness and her unwillingness to join him in his adventures. Despite their mutual interdependence, there was a good deal of unpleasant competitiveness between them, so that even a ping-pong game became difficult. Some of the playful quality Mr. Rosen could have with other women was lost because of this competitiveness.

Above all, Mr. Rosen regarded the family as special and unique. There was a sense of superiority which he imparted, especially to his children. It was this uniqueness which made him eschew the marital norms, codes of dress, and concern for the attitudes of others. At the same time, he could exhibit a good deal of superficial tenderness toward his wife, although on a larger scene he was being cruel. Although he wanted to be loved by everyone, he managed to create a good deal of hostility around hin not only from his wife but from his son and daughter.

There was a sufficient revelation of each one's personality difficulties to suggest the need for individual psychotherapy for both. It was felt that individual therapy could be the major focus, with occasional conjoint sessions with the two therapists providing some refocusing on their marital interactions as therapy progressed. My immediate goals in treatment were to get Mr. Rosen to make a decisions about whether he wanted to commit himself to the marriage within the constraints that his wife found necessary to impose, or to leave and be free to experience the sexual and romantic adventures which he yearned for so intensely. In short, I was trying to see whether the reality principle could partially replace the pleasure principle which seemed to be guiding his life. While a full-scale psychoanalysis was out of the question for financial and time considerations, intensive psychotherapy might give him enough understanding to change his priorities. While this was going on, the goal of his wife's treatment was to increase her self-reliance and self-esteem, to give her more of a sense of worth as a separate person and not merely as the reflected image of her highly successful husband.

A marital evaluation was chosen at first because the couple presented themselves as a couple in a crisis which they were unable to resolve. The onset of depression in the wife was directly related to the marital conflict. The couple seemed to be generally committed to the marriage, although there was some doubt at first about the husband's commitment to the permanency of the relationship.

One problem with marital therapy was that the partners each had different goals and expectations, the husband believing that the therapist might be able to convince his wife to go along with an open marriage, while the wife expected that the therapist would convince her husband that this was an unrealistic expectation. When the personality disorder of the husband became more and more apparent, the therapist had the option of trying to confront him with his narcissism and sadism in conjoint sessions. This course would have been destructive to his self-esteem, the fragility of which was protected by a veneer of superiority and grandiosity and, perhaps at the same time, would prematurely threaten the wife's still-present need to see her husband in an idealized light. While marital therapy might have worked, it would have been a very difficult assignment and risky at best. The therapist thought it would be more reasonable to try individual concurrent therapy, with the idea of having the couple come back for conjoint sessions from time to time, especially when individual therapy was close to completion.

Mrs. Rosen was seen weekly for a year by a social worker-marital therapist. Gradually her feelings of self-worth and self-confidence increased. She changed her teaching job to a better one, in which she derived more of a sense of appreciation from the students and faculty. She no longer was as dependent on her husband, and began to be able to enjoy periods of separation from him.

To be sure our goals were consistent, about six months after the beginning of treatment I asked Mr. Rosen to list his goals in treatment. He wrote, in part: "My wife's hope is that in understanding and coming to peace with my views of my own sexuality, I will also see that I have involved S. (the other woman) in my life principally as a means of working out my troubled views. If these can be worked out instead in therapy, the main need for S. will disappear, and I will be able to part with her for the sake of our marriage. My reaction to this is skeptical, but if I became convinced of its truth, I'm willing to face it."

Six months into treatment he still was not willing to accept the idea that his concern about his sexual ability was a principal factor in seeking extramarital sex. Despite this limitation, he went on to describe his problems in these words: "Sexual performance depends heavily on how well I think I've been performing lately in making love with F. (his wife). Performing, in my mind, seems to be equated with screwing well rather than with overall erotic pleasure and making love. Sometimes F. and I are aware that we are screwing just to earn me a brownie-point. Sometimes it works; sometimes it doesn't. I seem to hold as the ideal performance standard the ability to screw at the slightest impulse. I would like to see myself as the kind of person who could take a plane, pick up the stewardess, go to bed with her that night, make beautiful love, and continue on my way."

He recognized that in making love he was "screwing perhaps half the time," and he went on to say that, "I thought that the rest of the world might be more oriented toward screwing, and began both to judge my performance by such standards and to alter it towards more screwing." In the statement of his problem, he also mentioned that it was painful for him to look at himself in the mirror, see the wrinkles around his eyes, and be aware that he was getting older. There was a curious note which might be a reflection of his total behavior. He said, "Sometimes I let my eyes go hazy when doing this (looking into the mirror), with the result that I see myself out of focus and looking somewhat better." A clear statement about denial and self-deception.

A good part of the work in ensuing months was devoted to his sexual problems and their implications for his extramarital sexual activities. There was gradual improvement, especially following some behavioral exercises, until more frequent coital ejaculation began to occur.

Not much material was brought in about the children, except for passing references as to how bright, clever, and talented they were, until about a year after treatment began. At this time, he brought in a group of dreams in which his son was killed, and he associated to the dream content that this would be the price for abandoning his marriage and maintaining his extramarital liaison. At another level, there was enormous rivalry with his son. Although he was proud of him, he was also afraid that his son would be more talented and more productive than he. Gradually he began to bring in material about his being abandoned and alone. This became accentuated in the same week that his extramarital affair was terminated. Although his mistress actually terminated the relationship, he had provoked this reaction by acting in an indifferent and rejecting fashion. This was followed by dreams and associations dealing with his fear of being supplanted in his wife's affections by a stronger and more potent man. In his fantasies and dream life he was testing out the consequences of having an open marriage. Over the next few months, the marital relationship became closer as he began to abandon some of his James Bond type fantasies.

The first indication of how serious the rift was between himself and his son came about two years after the start of treatment. Mr. Rosen had gone to South America for three weeks and had written several letters to his son. The letters remained unopened, and on the envelope of one letter his son had scrawled in large hand, "OUT." On Mr. Rosen's return, there followed a period of some weeks in which the son acted as if his father did not exist, as if he were not actually present. He would not look at him or talk to him or respond to direct invitations to communicate. Because my contract was for individual therapy which, by this time, was psychoanalytic in nature, I felt that a family therapy consultation with another therapist was in order. The family therapist did not suggest family therapy, but made suggestions as to how the father should interact with his son, in essence trying to overcome the communication barrier between them. This was only partially successful.

Treatment continued for another year in which individual gains were increased and maintained, and several conjoint sessions were rewarding. Therapy was subsequently terminated, with the clear understanding that if difficulties arouse, the Rosens would consult me again. About six months later, I was consulted because of the daughter's despondency, depression, difficulty with her peers, and suicidal thoughts. It was then that I made the referral to my colleague.

In response to a routine, follow-up questionnaire, Mrs. Rosen wrote: "Working with you and then with Mrs. G.S. (her individual therapist), I learned to like myself (most of the time) and to recognize, accept, and, if necessary, to fight for my needs and desires. J. (Mr. Rosen) and I have enjoyed two comfortable years in our relationship; simple lack of anxiety and pulling has been sufficient for me (and I believe for him, too). However, I'm beginning to feel now 'what else?' We are very different people. I have come to recognize and accept that, and have stopped trying to attach his values to my existence. Perhaps I am still looking for too much from our relationship. I still feel that although our love for each other is deep, I am constantly working and fighting for him to see my real values. For me that exists beyond the loving wife and mother."

I wonder whether this couple is now finally ready for real marital therapy. If so, it has been a long, circuitous route. It was four-and-a half years ago that they originally came to see me for a marital consultation.

* * * *

This case illustrates some of the complexities in deciding on the appropriate treatment at a given point, not only in an individual's life but in the context of the marriage and the family in which the individual exists and transacts. Leaving out consideration of group therapy, we have selected a case that illustrates the possibilities of using individual therapy, concurrent marital therapy intermixed with conjoint sessions, and family therapy. This case also illustrates some of the problems dealing with the two functioning axes of family life, namely the generation-separation and the division between the two sexes. Both of these issues are controversial, and one might better talk of an optimum separation of the generations. Too great a separation may interfere with appropriate communication, understanding, and nurturance. Too small a gap may produce confusion about how to deal effectively with authority, and may easily interfere with appropriate moral development, as well as difficulty in separation. The current attack on gender-stereotyping may lead one to assume that any gender differentiation between the parents is harmful. It is our view that some separation of expressive and instrumental roles and functions on the part of the parents is necessary, although it hardly seems necessary that these follow the social stereotypes in every instance. If the family decided to be quite different from the surrounding community (social class, ethnic group, etc.), it would have to be able to cope with sometimes serious problems of socialization during childhood and adolescence. At any rate, in our case illustration the confused gender identity in the daughter arose not from a deliberate parental reversal of gender stereotyping, but from the confused gender identities of the parents themselves.

The difficulties in establishing hard-and-fast guidelines about indications and contraindications for family therapy are also illustrated in this case. Despite my colleague's list of contraindications, one finds that in the Rosen family 1) there was a highly inappropriate system of roles and relationships; 2) there was at least a moderate amount of sadomasochism in the marital relationship; 3) there had been a degree of physical violence in the family; 4) there was an element of sociopathy in the father; and 5) there was an older adolescent attempting to separate psychologically. Yet the family did respond to family therapy—although, to be effective, family therapy could not be the entire approach. The clinician will find many marginal cases: Routine guidelines must give way to clinical judgment. But then, flexible interpretation of guidelines is what makes clinical judgment as much art as science.

REFERENCE

1. GURMAN, A. S. and KNISKERN, D. P.: Research in marital and family therapy: Progress, perspective, and prospect. In: S. L. Garfield and A. E. Bergin (Eds.), *Handbook of Psychotherapy and Behavior Change: Empirical Analysis* (revised edition). New York: Wiley, 1978.

BIBLIOGRAPHY

1. ACKERMAN, N., PAPP, P., and PROSKY, P.: Childhood disorders and interlocking pathology in family relationships. In: E. J. Anthony and C. Koupernick (Eds.), *The Child in His Family: Children at Psychiatric Risk.* New York: Wiley-Interscience, 1970, pp. 241-266.
2. ANTHONY, E. J.: Children at risk from a divorce: A review. In: E. J. Anthony and C. Koupernick (Eds.), *The Child in His Family: Children at Psychiatric Risk.* New York: Wiley-Interscience, 1970, pp. 461-479.
3. BERMAN, E. M. and LIEF, H. I.: Marital therapy from a psychiatric perspective: An overview. *Am. J. Psychiat.,* 132(6):583-592, June, 1975.
4. FRAMO, J. L.: Rationale and techniques of intensive family therapy. In: I. Boszormenyi-Nagy and J. Framo (Eds.), *Intensive Family Therapy.* New York: Harper & Row, 1965, pp. 143-213.
5. GURMAN, A. S.: Dimensions of marital therapy: A comparative analysis. *J. of Marital and Family Therapy,* 5(1):3-16, 1979.
6. HALEY, J.: *Problem Solving Therapy.* San Francisco: Jossey-Bass, 1976.
7. HOLLENDER, M. H.: Selection of therapy for marital problems. In: J. H. Masserman (Ed.), *Current Psychiatric Therapies,* Vol. 2. New York: Grune & Stratton, pp. 119-128.
8. KAPLAN, H. S.: *The New Sex Therapy.* New York: Brunner/Mazel, 1974.
9. LOPICCOLO, J. and LOPICCOLO, L. (Eds.): *Handbook of Sex Therapy.* New York: Plenum, 1978.
10. LYNN, D.: *The Father: His Role in Child Development.* Belmont, CA: Brooks/Cole, 1974.
11. OFFER, D. and VANDERSTOEP, E.: Indications and contraindications for family therapy. In: M. Sugar (Ed.), *The Adolescent in Group and Family Therapy.* New York: Brunner/Mazel, 1975, pp. 145-160.
12. PEARSON, G.: *Handbook of Child Psychoanalysis.* New York: Basic Books, 1968, pp. 120, 194-195.
13. STEINHAUER, P. and RAE-GRANT, Q.: *Psychological Problems of the Child and His Family.* Toronto: Macmillan of Canada, 1977, pp. 53-55.
14. THOMAS, A. and CHESS, S.: *Temperament and Development.* New York: Brunner/Mazel, 1977, p. 80.
15. WYNNE, L. C.: Some indications and contraindications for exploratory family therapy. In: I. Boszormenyi-Nagy and J. Framo (Eds.), *Intensive Family Therapy.* New York: Harper & Row, 1965, pp. 289-322.

10

Panel Discussion: Controversial Issues in Family Therapy

Donald A. Bloch, M.D., Saul L. Brown, M.D.
Harold I. Lief, M.D. and
Jerry M. Lewis, M.D.

JOHN C. NEMIAH, M.D., *presiding*

DR. NEMIAH: We shall start the discussion from the floor rather than from within the panel to achieve maximum group involvement. May we have comments, questions, and discussion directed to the panel members?

IRVING PHILLIPS, M.D.: Would the panel members talk about the prerequisites for training in family therapy? Is training in individual therapy a necessary prerequisite? What is the relationship to psychoanalytic training?

DR. BLOCH: One way of going about it might be simply to say what we do at the Ackerman Institute. We train mental health professionals who have already had their basic training in their own disciplines. We have tended to look on family therapy as a postgraduate form of training. On the average, our trainees work with us during a period of two years on a half-time basis. Of that time, they spend about half in direct treatment of families in our clinic and half in some kind of training situation. It is a highly experiential form of training. We get trainees into direct contact with families immediately and work hard on this issue of the nature of their own personal involvement, but stop short of therapy of the trainees. We like people to have individual therapy, whether it is formal psychoanalysis or intensive psychotherapy. It does seem important for them to have spent some time looking inward. At the same time, we want to enlarge the bent to an understanding of themselves in an interpersonal context and to working with families from that point of view. We have used this training model now for almost 15 years. It keeps changing, of course, as the field keeps growing. We keep adding didactic material, but it is the basic format that we use, and it seems to work well for us.

DR. BROWN: I think Don Bloch's situation at the Ackerman Institute is a relatively ideal one. There is no absolute ideal. It is very difficult—sometimes the effort is dismaying—to weave family therapy training into a general psychiatric residency, doing it on the run or in rotation. Family therapy requires total immersion for at least some considerable period to get the full feel of it, and residents or other trainees don't get it if it is only a small part of their assignment. I would not want to complicate the discussion with the issue of analytic training, which I think is a whole other area, but it is certainly doubtful that one can manage well the enormously complex series of internal feelings that a family interviewer and therapist must experience unless he or she has had a lot of individual treatment.

* * * *

NORMAN BRILL, M.D.: I would like to address this chiefly to Harold Lief, primarily because the results of family therapy described in the tables presented in his paper are so outstanding that I would like a little clarification. Are the results described here long-term or short-term results? What is implied by improvement? For example, in an instance in which there was special marital difficulty and where the marriage dissolves but both spouses feel happy about it, is this regarded as improvement or not? I also wonder about the competence and qualifications of the persons who are doing the individual therapy, since in many studies in the literature, one finds beginning residents, medical students, or relatively untrained persons doing individual therapy.

DR. LIEF: The length of time of therapy varied, of course. These were often relatively short-term therapies rather than psychoanalytic or psychoanalytically-oriented. Most of the studies were based on relatively short-term therapies of both kinds, although, as I remember them, the individual treatment tended to be somewhat longer than the marital or family therapy. Since criteria for improvement tended to vary from one study to another, when you lump together studies like this, you are using quite varied standards for improvement. With regard to an existing marriage, improvement varies depending upon how it is defined. Most marital therapists do not consider keeping the marriage together as a *sine qua non* of improvement. Value orientations come in, of course, but most therapists will take individual self-realization as an indication of improvement, so keeping a marriage together cannot be generally taken as the index.

The question you raised about the experience of therapists is a vital one. I think this is a weakness of these studies. They often compared individual therapy carried out by inexperienced therapists with marital and family therapy carried out by experienced therapists. You are quite right; these are some of the problems we have with this sort of research.

* * * *

GENE USDIN, M.D.: Many therapists are doing individual therapy without ever having been in therapy themselves. One would certainly question trying to do psychoanalysis without having been analyzed. It has been said that the best way to learn to do group therapy is to be in group therapy oneself, and I think that has, in fact, been the experience of most group therapists.

I see another problem. Because of my own background, I am struck by the wide range of ages with which we see skilled family therapists dealing. I think one needs to empathize sometimes with a

45-year-old father who is being manipulated by his 13-year-old child in a family therapy session in the protective environment of the therapist's office. I understand that the experienced family therapists may not see this as a problem; yet coming from where I do, I find it a problem. Would the panel comment on this issue?

DR. BROWN: In a sense, I have agreed with everything that you have said. Entering into a system as a therapist, whether it be simply a marital couple or a larger family group, if the therapist is still relatively immature in life's experiences, makes for a pretty difficult problem. The quickness of empathy with parental dilemmas and parental discomforts, for example, is greater if one has been a parent than if this is not the case, and still greater if one has been a parent of an adolescent. Similarly, the ability to recognize very quickly the enormous pressure on, let us say, a couple with children under the age of seven, becomes far more substantial if the therapist has been a parent of such children than if not. And so on. All of this enters in, creating occasional doubts in me as to what the optimal age is for someone to be trained to do family or marital therapy.

Certain measures can be taken. Although the technique was not described today, I think many of the people here are familiar with a procedure in Minuchin's clinic. The supervisor sits in an observation room, observing and calling in on the telephone when he sees the therapist missing the boat. The therapist answers the telephone, says something, and hangs up. The family doesn't necessarily know that the telephone call was about them. They may think the therapist was just getting an emergency call. I gather that, remarkably enough, many families don't even discern that the therapist then rather suddenly starts doing something different from what he was doing a minute before. This shows that patients can accommodate to a quite wide range of error on the part of the therapist—but we know that that is also true in psychoanalysis and other psychotherapies.

DR. LEWIS: I should like to add that the dilemma of when you begin training in family therapy is a little different for me. On the other side of the issue is the difficulty that if you do not introduce residents to at least some kind of experience with multiple modalities, some kind of pluralistic base, many of them are going to close their conceptual stance, and so shall continue to do what many psychiatrists have always done—that is, treat every clinical situation with the one modality they know.

* * * *

KIM WEISS, M.D.: We know that, in general although not invariably, we do better in individual therapy with patients who are from the upper socioeconomic classes, who are articulate, educated, intelligent, with some capacity for self-scrutiny. Does this also apply to marital and family therapy? Is it the same, or is there something different in this respect about working with the unitary group that makes it more widely available?

DR. BLOCH: I'll try to answer, especially with regard to marital therapy. I think some of the same qualities apply here as well. One of the difficulties we have is in terms of people who happen to come from different backgrounds from our own. We have had the experience of training indigenous black workers to work in a community mental health center and found that when they called themselves "marital therapists" or especially "sex therapists," nobody came. All they had to do was to change their title to "family therapists," and people were knocking at their door. They could then enter the delivery system and focus wherever indicated. There is a great deal of stigma in certain social groups with respect to having any difficulty in marriage, especially if it is a sexual problem. That's one thing I can report on. Insofar as the ease of introspection goes, this is somewhat less of a problem when you are dealing with interpersonal phenomena than when you are dealing with intrapsychic material.

DR. BROWN: One or two remarks. I recently heard Gerald Zuk, the editor of the *International Journal of Family Therapy*, say that, based on his experience in Philadelphia, he views the openness to family therapy of persons from working-class backgrounds as relatively limited. He has found it unusual to work with such families for more than just a few sessions, maybe three or four, and he contrasted this with an upper-middle-class group. Drawing on my knowledge of some of what goes on at the Los Angeles County General Hospital, a working-class center, I should like to add that in that population group treatment modalities veer in the direction of reinforcement and behavioral modification techniques and direct educational kinds of interventions.

* * * *

EMANUEL STRAKER, M.D.: In his presentation Dr. Lief mentioned that family therapy was probably not suitable for severe psychoses or severe psychosomatic conditions. Some of the questions already addressed to the panel suggest an interest in finding some kind of agreement as to the suitability of families and therapists for family therapy. Is there, in fact, much agreement among those doing family therapy as to when you get into the system to do family therapy, when you stay out, and when, having gotten in, you get out? To Dr. Brown I'd like to address a second question: What is the difference between family interviewing and family therapy? When does the interviewing become therapy?

DR. LIEF: I agree that Dr. Schecter does feel as stated. It is an area of controversy. Family therapy grew up and developed in the treatment of severely disturbed patients, and many people doing family therapy don't see a need to draw a line in terms of individual psychopathology. But I'm interested to hear what the family therapist on the panel has to say about this.

DR. BROWN: I should like to reemphasize a guiding notion, which I did allude to this morning, but perhaps without sufficient elaboration. This notion is the one of resistance to change in a system and of differentiating this from the classical resistance of the psychoanalytic framework. For me, at least, the continuing process is to attempt to discern the locus of resistance to change. Resistance to change in a family system may take a dynamic form; that is, resistance to change may appear in the marital relationship. I'm talking about developmental change and therapeutic change: I assume that every family is in constant process of developmental change. Everybody in this room knows this, but I suspect that a lot of you don't pay attention to it when you work with an individual patient. The family as a system is proceeding through developmental change. In the very first area, as was pointed out in some of the other talks, for example, nurturance is a major issue when babies are first being born, but it isn't just nurturance of the baby. The babies are nurturing the parents. All you have to do is look at the smiles on the faces of the parents to know the baby is also nurturing them. That's a developmental process.

Now, when does this developmental process meet resistance, and, if it does, what is the origin of that resistance? Is the development failing because of a lack of knowledge, because of a marital conflict, because of dynamic factors, because of the mother's depression, because of the baby's congenital defects—what is resisting that progressive change of this family? I take the same notion and overlay it, when I work with a family in therapy. What is resisting the progress of therapy in this given situation, say, the emancipation of an adolescent from the family? If I keep that as my guideline, if I keep looking through that particular lens, then I have something to guide me when doing just a family interview or two or when engaging in something more elaborate called family therapy. It guides me with questions such as: How do we switch foci back and forth? When does it seem as though resistance to change in a family system has so organized itself that individual therapy is indicated, or that marital therapy is now indicated? When should we pull the whole crowd back in, if we can get them, including the grandparents, because Grandpa over there who controls the money through a trust fund is now making it hard for therapy to continue? Is this back-and-forth process the therapy of the whole family? Is it therapy of the individual? Is it just a couple of interviews here and there to find out where things are? I use the notion of resistance to change in a systems sense to guide me.

* * * *

PAUL FINK, M.D.: The indications and contraindications for family therapy may deserve further discussion. Dr. Lewis pointed out that we generally do the treatment that we know how to do. This is, of course, true, not only of individual therapists but of family therapists. I am curious about Dr. Brown's last statement. What I thought I heard was that one finds out whether people need, or can use, family therapy after they're in it. Could we have further discussion on this question?

DR. BLOCH: I think it is very important to stress an orientation that is essentially an epistemological one towards human events, an orientation that would consider them as natural systems or general living systems. If you think of family therapy in such a conceptual framework, I believe you're always required to do some kind of systems therapy. The choice, then, becomes which format you can use to give you the best scope in the sense of identifying the nature of the problem: the resistance (in Saul's terms), and then the level and mode of intervention that are likeliest to produce change. This is a way of thinking about the problem that really takes into account all the levels in the hierarchy of systems—including, let's say, the molecular, psychological, personal, familial, and cultural—as possible levels of intervention. To answer the question properly, it has to be asked in the terms I've just used, not in terms of indications or contraindications. The family therapist would say that your best initial approximation consists of an entry into this hierarchy at the family systems level. That gives you the best initial chance. It's like getting a picture of the area within which you're ultimately going to make your major intervention.

Let me illustrate with a clinical problem. You might talk about depression in a female patient, and you might think about it as related to the menstrual cycle, that is, as somewhat hormonal, biochemical. You might talk about it in psychological terms as the particular expression of the management of hostility. You might talk about it in interpersonal terms as being the function of a move that is designed to structure the interpersonal field. You might talk about it as a family role position that's been defined, and you certainly can talk about it in largely sociocultural terms, in terms of women's position and the changing position and self-image that women have in this society. Then your choice of treatment would rest on the basis of an assessment that would flow from that kind of a hierarchical organization way of looking at it.

DR. LIEF: To be practical, I think the practicing clinician has to deal with the point of view of the patient who comes to him. In other words, if a patient, even though with a serious marital or family problem, comes for individual therapy and expects it, that has to be dealt with first: To move immediately into a family appraisal would cause difficulties. It might be ideal, but I try to be pragmatic about it. This issue provides many difficulties for most practicing psychiatrists. I believe one of the basic questions is: How does the patient see his problem? What does he or she expect out of treatment? If one has to modify those expectations in a given way, there are various therapeutic techniques that may have to be used. . . . Whatever guidelines we have—and they're difficult to arrive at—should be used flexibly.

* * * *

ALEX ————, M.D.: I'd like to address the question of whether there is, or is not, a good case for family therapy when there is a psychotic member in the family. A couple of years ago, we had a Stanley R. Dean lecture delivered by John K. Wing, who spoke quite extensively about how and when the family can be used as an important instrument in the treatment of psychotic patients. He reported on the research of Brown and Leff, who were able to make some predictions about which families are ecologically favorable for the return of a pyschotic person and which families are so destructive to a particular patient that a return should not be planned. Here was a clear example of contraindication for family therapy with a very disturbed member. The issue is quite important, because currently a major focus of psychiatric interest is on the proper treatment of the psychotic. As hospitals are increasingly being closed, there are fewer and fewer places where we can treat our patients. Often those families which can accept psychotic members have to be supported in doing so, in order to make up for the loss of treatment facilities. I should like to warn against the quick acceptance of rigidly exclusive statements on this subject.

* * * *

JEANNE SPURLOCK, M.D.: I have a question which is class-color related. I understand that in some areas in the country the third-party payers are raising more and more questions about payments and fees, and I would like someone to give me reassurance that there is going to be money available for adequate family therapy. How should one charge? How should one get reimbursed?

DR. LIEF: I should prefer to answer primarily for marital therapy. At the present time, this matter of payment is a really difficult proposition. There is an effort on the part of the American Association of Marriage and Family Therapists, who have a lobbyist in Washington, to insure that such therapies are included in any national health insurance and to deal with third-party carriers. I have been a consultant to an insurance firm and have been trying to get its medical director to change the attitudes of third-party carriers regarding marital and family therapy. What often happens, however, is that marital therapists—and, I think family therapists as well—have to use one person as the designated patient and put down a diagnosis for that person. All of the third-party carriers know that this is not strictly accurate, but they seem not to object if it goes through the computer.

DR. LEWIS: I agree. I am not aware of very much trouble if there is an obvious patient in the family, an individually diagnosed patient for whom treatment is covered. The problem is that one fairly often sees families before there has been any clear-cut agreement as to an identified patient. From a therapeutic viewpoint, this is a very favorable kind of position to be in. However, that's where the trouble lies at this time in terms of coverage: Third-party payers often will not cover such a situation.

DR. BLOCH: I fully agree with what Harold and Jerry have said. We have no problem where we have a clearly designated patient. In other cases it's a very ambiguous situation. I hope that DSM III will clarify the issue, but it will not be easy to do. Possibly the situation may become even more difficult.

DR. LIEF: DSM III will not help, because in it a marital problem is not a designated mental disorder. . . . This may be a losing battle, but there is one pertinent point to keep in mind. If there is a management information system in the clinical environment where one is working, one should be sure to have, within its setup, an item that therapists check off, even though there has to be an index patient. At least have an item that can be called "collateral visit" or "collateral members of the family," that goes into the management information data bank whenever appropriate. In this way, there will be a growing amount of evidence as to how frequently family groups need to be—and are—seen.

Part IV

THE STANLEY R. DEAN AWARD LECTURE

11

In Search of the Interactional Origin of Schizophrenia

Yrjo O. Alanen, M.D.

Most professionals who have experience in the psychotherapy of schizophrenic persons and their families soon become convinced of the great significance of intrafamilial pyschic processes and interactions for both the genesis and treatment of this disorder. That the atmosphere in these families is almost invariably pathological has been shown by numerous family studies. In view of this, one wonders at the fact that many psychiatrists and researchers still feel that the bearing of the family environment on the etiology of this disorder is scientifically disputable.

This is the case for several reasons. One of them is linked to the nature of our research culture, based, as it is, on the methodologies of empirical natural science. It has difficulty in accepting observations, which, though also based on experience, rest on a case-specific approach involving empathy and understanding, and which have proved difficult to confirm by the techniques of natural science. It is easily forgotten that the bulk of knowledge useful for a thorough comprehension of the nature of psychic disorders and for the alleviation of the suffering caused by them has arisen from the insights made possible by the introspective and disciplined search of Sigmund Freud, continued in the specific field of schizophrenia by the more interrelational approach of Harry Stack Sullivan, Frieda Fromm-Reichmann and Theodore Lidz.

Another reason is the intensification of the biological study of schizophrenia connected with the development of neuroleptic drugs and the demonstration of their effects on psychotic symptoms. This has also led to new etiological theories which have attracted considerable attention. However, not much has thus far been detected in this field that helps to clarify the causes of schizophrenia, and the limitations of the psychopharmacological treatment as a means of improving prognostic results seem to have become obvious to us (cf., e.g., 1, 2). I doubt that further discoveries in this direction will render useless our achievements in the field of psychological knowledge; in fact, I believe that the most promising line for us to follow is still to deepen and broaden our empathic understanding of schizophrenia and to promote the application of this knowledge to everyday practice along a wider front than hitherto. In contrast to some rather formally planned studies carried out elsewhere (3, 4), the preliminary follow-up information of our own treatment study under way in Turku, Finland, seems to indicate that psychotherapeutic treatment plans, laid out individually for each patient and considering the nature of both of his disturbance and his life situation and family environment, can add appreciably to our hopes of a favorable outcome.

I have given my lecture the title "In Search of the Interactional Origin of Schizophrenia." Even though my approach to schizophrenia had its origin in two studies based on large samples of families, it has from the beginning included an endeavor to understand what is happening in the minds of the patients and what is involved in the interactions going on in their families. My therapeutic experience—both of individual and family psychotherapy—has further strengthened this line of interest. I will not deal extensively here with the interaction which is involved in the complementarity of genes and environment, a topic which has been much in the foreground of recent American research in schizophrenia and the discussions stimulated by it. I strongly support the view that genetic factors—irrespective of whether one is concerned with schizophrenia or with a more speculative "schizophrenia spectrum" as suggested by Kety, Rosenthal and Wender and their Danish co-workers (5, 6)—should not be studied separately. Attention should be given to the interaction between them and the psychological factors of the family environment. On the basis of our own family studies (7), I advocate the view that a mother (or father) craving for a symbiotic relationship with a child may select for this purpose the child who is constitutionally the most passive and, thus, the likeliest to respond compliantly to such a request, while the other children may be more defiant and develop more autonomous patterns of interpersonal relationships. (The family dynamic roles and the interactional factors in such situations are, of course, more complicated than this simplified formulation seems to suggest.)

I expect that some of the studies now under way may elucidate this point more than my own. I am especially referring to the prospective studies going on in Rochester and UCLA (8, 9), as well as to an extensive adoptive child study initiated by Pekka Tienari in Finland. (For the planning and some preliminary results of this study, see Tienari et al. (10).

In what follows I shall first give an account of some findings of two comparatively extensive family dynamic studies and then draw inferences from these and other family studies of schizophrenia, trying to elucidate the basic pathogenic interactional forces at work in these families. I shall also make use of recent psychoanalytic studies of severely disturbed personalities, particularly those by Heinz Kohut and Otto Kernberg, because I consider them to be helpful in understanding the parents of schizophrenics and their interaction with their children. Finally, I shall consider briefly the significance of a family-centered treatment of schizophrenic patients.

Two Studies of the Families of Schizophrenic Patients

The first of my studies was concerned with the mothers and the mother-child relationship in schizophrenia. The gathering of the material for the study began in December 1952, at the Psychiatric Clinic of the University of Helsinki, at a time when the investigation of the families of schizophrenics consisted essentially of the early work of Ruth and Theodore Lidz (11) and three or four other American studies of a preliminary kind (12-15). A considerably greater number of studies had seen daylight when my results were published in 1958 as a supplement monograph to *Acta psychiatrica et neurologica Scandinavica* (16).

Employing a semi-structured interview, I investigated an unselected series of mothers of 100 schizophrenic patients under 30 years of age, and the mothers of 20 neurotic patients, and those of 20 normal controls. The distribution of this sample as to socioeconomic status was rather wide. The Rorschach test, scored and analyzed by an experienced clinical psychologist, was administered to 92 of the mothers of schizophrenics and to all mothers in the comparative series.

The distribution of these mothers by clinical category is illustrated in Table 1. I classified them on a one-dimensional scale that I devised to represent the degree of personality disturbance as estimated on the basis of both interview findings and the Rorschach.

I found that 12 of the 100 mothers of schizophrenic patients had received hospital treatment for psychotic disorders (Category A in Table 1), and that in another 11 cases the mother had psychotic features or potentials in her personality (Category B). The most surprising finding (and the most confusing to the still inexperienced investigator) was the large number of mothers whose personalities,

TABLE 1

Distribution of Mothers of Schizophrenics, Neurotics and Normal Persons by Clinical Category

Series	Clinical Category of Mothers					
	A	B	C	D	A+B+C+D	E
Typical schizophrenics	7	5	27	9	48	6
Schizophreniform psychotics	5	4	12	12	33	8
Schizophrenia plus organic brain disorder	—	2	1	—	3	2
Total schizophrenics	12	11	40	21	84	16
Neurotics	—	1	1	7	9	11
Normals	—	—	1	5	6	14

For definition of clinical categories A-E see text.
From Alanen (16).

though they could not be assigned to the group of borderline conditions approximating to the psychotic, were nevertheless severely disturbed. This group (Category C) included some clearly schizoid or paranoid personalities, as well as others characterized by schizoid features and serious emotional disorders often marked by a poorly controlled aggressiveness and a conspicious lack of empathic ability, associated with a dominating way of relating to the child. I considered it amply justified to distinguish these mothers from ordinary psychoneurotics, who were, as I stated, "in possession of a greater amount of the more sensitive components of affective life, of self-control and an ability to feel themselves into the inner life of other people" (16). Category C included a total of 40 mothers. It should be pointed out that many of the mothers who had previously had psychotic episodes also displayed patterns of emotional disorder similar to those found in Category C. Of the remaining 37 mothers of schizophrenics, 21 were neurotically disturbed (Category D), whereas 16 were within normal limits (Category E). As appears from Table 1, the distribution of the mothers in the comparative series was very different: There were only three who were found to suffer from disturbances graver than the neuroses.

Instead of summarizing all the psychodynamic findings of this study, I will refer to selected observations which seem of particular interest here.

In describing the quality of the disordered mother-child relationships, I emphasized especially a dominating and possessive pattern which, as I wrote, "was frequently of a clearly narcissistic brand, particularly in the sense that many of the mothers considered their children to be, as it were, their property, lacking the value and rights of an independent person" (16, p. 192). These mothers were inclined to project their own needs onto their children in an intrusive manner and retain symbiotic ties with them. Fairbairn (17), the Scotch psychoanalyst, had concluded that the typical attitude characterizing the object relationships of schizoid persons was "that towards a partial object, and not towards a person." Referring to his object relations theory, and also to some descriptions of the mothers of schizophrenics by Lewis B. Hill (18), I then introduced the term "schizoid pattern of interpersonal relationship" to describe this maternal attitude. I can add here that even in connection with my study of mothers, but particularly later, when I was investigating entire families (7), I found similar relational patterns in schizophrenic patients' fathers, whose disturbedness had also been pointed out by Lidz and his co-workers (19, 20).

The following case excerpt, reproduced from my monograph, illuminates how this kind of mother's way of relating to her child can be used for the maintenance of her own balance. The case no doubt represents an extreme of its kind, but for this reason it reveals features that in other cases may remain somewhat covered though still influential.

> In the interview she (the mother) gave the impression of being pronouncedly schizoid, was quite tense, and used unnaturally decorative language. She also stated that she had, ever since her youth, been prone to depression, manifesting itself in the form of apathy and a peculiar feeling of estrangement, "as if one were afraid of one's environment." She said that she regretted her marriage; F admittedly liked her, but she had not wanted to marry him. The marriage was, in fact, compulsory; i.e., due to her pregnancy, and P—who was the first of three children and the only son—was born five months after the wedding. M talked, in abstract terms, about the lack of love and of poverty; she alluded to her love for another man, who emigrated to America. The examiner got the impression of a schizoid love from a distance—nothing had ever happened between M and this man. F had been industrious and taken good care of his family, but M did not like him. She found him "uneducated and rude." M stated that she felt depressed during pregnancy. She said, however, that she had desired to have a child "of fine character," who would be the opposite of his father—and, she continued, the child, in fact, "developed into such a person." She greatly praised P's kindness and obedience, which was the result of his upbringing and the condition for M's tenderness, and his "deep mindedness." Of the children, P had been closest to M, whose attitude toward him had been strongly possessive from the very outset. She stated that P's sisters were jealous of him and, for instance, said that M would go crazy if she were to lose him. She guarded P carefully from bad-mannered playmates and had an intensely forbidding attitude toward his sexuality, stating with pleasure that P had grown up to be a "mother's boy," who had no girlfriends.

> M has been keenly interested in P's school attendance. In addition to all this, her attitude toward P contained a not very overt but all the same powerful aggressive element. Apart from the fact that it had been involved in her absolute denial of P's independence, it manifested itself in the form of constant fears and fantasies of accidents happening to him, and of bad "forebodings," which M thought had now been realized in P's becoming psychotic (16, pp. 168-9).

My conclusion was that disturbances of this kind in the mothers were not a reaction to the child's illness. Nor, I think, should they be viewed as a consequence of psychological changes in the parent resulting from the rearing of a deviant child, as has been proposed by some later critics of family studies (e.g., 21, 22)—even though what happens between the mother and a growing child naturally is an interactional process. Observations of the mothers of schizophrenics revealed that the mother's childhood had often been emotionally frustrating. I was struck by the surprisingly affect-laden words and manners with which many a mother expressed her feelings of bitterness toward her childhood environment, often especially toward her own mother, reflecting her still great—if ambivalent—dependent needs, as well as her lack of capacity for mourning. Another striking observation was the unsatisfactory state of these women's marriages, often from the very beginning and in many cases accentuated during the birth and early infancy of the child who was to become the schizophrenic patient. Still, I was more impressed by the continuity of the interpersonal disturbances than by the difficulties of the early phase. As regarded breast-feeding, feeding problems, and the child's permanent or temporary separation from its mother, the schizophrenia series did not differ from the control series.

Another extensive study was made in Helsinki during the early '60s by a team that worked under my direction (7, 23, 24). The subjects of this study were the families of orientation of 30 typical schizophrenic and 30 typical neurotic patients. Both series consisted of an unselected sample of families which included two to four children between 15 and 40 years of age. Altogether, 249 persons were interviewed individually by four psychiatrists and given an extensive psychological test battery by the same psychologist (Kalevi Takala). A detailed account of the findings of this study, sponsored by Foundations' Fund for Research in Psychiatry, was published as a monograph supplement to *Acta Psychiatrica Scandinavica* in 1966 (7).

A clinical classification similar to—though not completely identical with—the one employed in the study of mothers was applied here. The results are illustrated in Table 2. It was found that a majority of the parents of schizophrenics (not only the mothers but also the fathers), displayed severe personality disorders reflecting pathology of the ego functions, whereas milder, neurotic-level disturbances were typical of neurotic patients' parents. The dispersion of the schizophrenic patient's siblings on a psychic-disturbance continuum was notably wider than that of the patients' parents. This fact was no doubt partly, but not exclusively, related to the age of the subjects: The mean age of the schizophrenics' parents was 57.7 years, while that of their siblings was 25.5 years. I would suggest that this difference in dispersion points, on the one hand, to the fact that the

TABLE 2

Distribution of Parents and Siblings of Typical Schizophrenic and Neurotic Patients by Clinical Category

Series	Degree of Disturbance Category						
	VI	V	IV	III	II	I	?
Parents of schizophrenics	4	12	26	12	1	—	5
Fathers	1	6	14	5	—	—	4
Mothers	3	6	12	7	1	—	1
Parents of neurotics	—	1	10	25	16	2	6
Fathers	—	—	6	10	8	2	4
Mothers	—	1	4	15	8	—	2
Siblings of schizophrenics	4	6	10	11	18	—	—
Siblings of neurotics	—	—	4	17	24	4	—

Degree of disturbance categories: VI = schizophrenia; V = other functional psychoses, borderline psychotic features; IV = schizoid, paranoid and cyclic character disorder, alcoholism psychopathy, sexual perversions, very severe character neuroses; III = milder psychoneurotic symptoms or personalities; II = normal with disorder traits; I = normal without disorder traits.

From Alanen et al. (7).

production of a schizophrenic offspring is rendered more likely by the existence of two disordered parents and, on the other hand, to the influences of the differences in family dynamic sibling position revealed by our study and explicable by the interaction of genetic and environmental factors.

Considering the high frequency of severe pathology among the parents, it should be emphasized that all the index patients in our schizophrenia series were typical, that is, "process" patients. Reference can here be made to a recent report by Singer, Wynne and Toohey (25), according to which 75 percent of nonremitting ("process") patients had one or both parents who were themselves diagnosed as borderline or worse, while only 21 percent of the remitting schizophrenics had parents of such diagnoses. (One may at this point also refer to the findings of my mother study, cf. Table 1).

The classification used by us later served as the basis of the one used by Kety, Rosenthal and Wender (22, 26-28) in their adoptive material studies, with the modification, however, that the global six-category scale of pyschopathology developed by us was extended to a seven-category scale, mainly by breaking our degree of disturbance category IV into two categories, the lower of them representing moderate to marked character neurosis, the higher one representing severe character neurosis as well as moderate to marked cyclothymic characters, schizoid characters and paranoid characters.

This may be appropriate if the new line of division would differentiate better than the old one those parents who manifest significant ego pathology from those who do not—a difference, the importance of which for my thinking will shortly become apparent. However, it is very difficult for me to accept lines of division of the kind that Rosenthal (29) has quite recently applied to our material, to find numbers which would better suit his genetic theory: He places those of our parents of schizophrenics who were diagnosed as schizoid or paranoid *characters* on one side of a line of division, supposedly tracing back to a one-gene etiology, and those who had schizoid or paranoid *features* on the other side. I cannot think that our clinical findings were exact enough to justify such a play with numbers: The difference between parents involved here is certainly one in degree or quantity, not one in kind. Had another investigation been made of these parents, say, five years later, the position of some parents on the scale could well have changed.

Proceeding to the more interactional findings of our second study, I would mention that, among our families of schizophrenics, we confirmed that frequency of marital skews and schisms such as were discovered earlier by Lidz' team (30), in whose research I had had the opportunity of participating after completing my monograph on mothers. Not only separate parent-child relationships but combinations of mother-father relationships were deemed to be of importance. As to the general atmosphere in these families, we found two predominant patterns which clearly differed from those encountered in our neurotic patients' families: the chaotic and the rigid. The atmosphere in the chaotic families was incoherent and irrational, often dominated by one parent's psychotic or borderline-level thought and behavior disturbances. Typical of the rigid families was an extreme inelasticity of role constellations and an emotional impoverishment. An abundance of projective mechanisms, directed by parents onto children, was common to both. The differences among the sibling positions were considered to be of great importance in the family dynamics. Almost all of the patients' siblings whom we regarded as normal, as well as most of the neurotic siblings, came from rigid families, or from a small group remaining outside of this classification, whereas a majority of siblings who exhibited borderline psychotic features or were psychopaths were members of the chaotic families.

Judging by my later experience, both classifications, the one into schismatic and skewed families and the one into chaotic and rigid families, have important implications regarding the possibilities for and the ways of carrying out family therapy (31). The schismatic-type families seem to respond more favorably to family therapy than skewed families, although there are also differences among the families of the former type in this respect. Compared with skewed families, schismatic families offer better possibilities for the construction of intrafamilial balance. Constantly strained relations and quarreling are typical of schismatic families, but tendencies toward an increasing mutual understanding are also found in them, and these healthy elements are quite important for success in family therapy. In

the skewed families, dominated to a disproportionate extent by one parent with severe psychopathology, the situation seemed worse.

When family therapy can be started with a chaotic family, characterized by extensive disturbances of reality testing and a general incoherence, this nearly always amounts to a strongly supportive and tranquilizing intervention. Anxious or incoherent parents often have an intense need of help, and they may also seek help more readily than do parents who have settled down to follow their own paths rigidly and defensively (although these seem superficially better balanced). The experiences we have gained of the therapies of rigid families have been varied and greatly dependent on the extent to which the family has included persons possessing a motivation for therapeutic clarification.

Schizophrenia as an Interactional Process: An Introduction

During the last 10 to 11 years, while working at the Department of Psychiatry in Turku, another university center in Finland, my co-workers and I have continued both psychodynamically oriented and social-psychiatric research on schizophrenia (32-36). One of the central aims of our efforts has been the development and evaluation of broadly based psychotherapeutic care of schizophrenic patients in a community psychiatric setting (37-39). My own interest has continued to center on the families of schizophrenics and especially on the study of family therapy of young schizophrenics and their parents (31, 40, 41), as well as of marital couples in cases where one of the spouses has fallen ill with schizophrenic psychosis (42).

I will now present my current thoughts on the pathogenesis of schizophrenia conceived as an interactional process, on the basis of these and other family dynamic studies and family therapeutic experiences, as well as on inferences drawn from the psychoanalytic studies mentioned earlier.

As many of my readers would certainly remark, and as I have repeatedly said in my monographs, findings such as those presented above can in themselves be interpreted on the basis of genetic factors as well as on the basis of transactional factors. It is essential to

realize, however, that when we proceed from genetically oriented views to family psychodynamics, we simultaneously proceed to an entirely different conception of schizophrenia, or at least to a different disorder model. We no longer regard the boundaries of the disorder as coincident with those of the individual: The development of schizophrenia in a child is, according to this newer conception, connected with a disturbed state of the entire family unit. Furthermore, it also exceeds the limits of the psychology of the nuclear family, since the ultimate causes of the parents' disturbances are traceable to the disordered interaction between them and their own parents. Nor do we any longer see schizophrenia as a disorder specifically different from other psychic disorders: We view it as part of a network of disordered intrafamilial interactional processes. To be sure, it is clinically the most severely disturbed manifestation of this network; nevertheless, with respect to its genesis and often its current dynamics as well, it is intimately connected with the other parts of the network. The disturbances of various degrees in the other family members presented in our tables can also be seen as reflections of this disordered network.

Thus, this altered conception of illness means transcending the boundaries of both an individual-centered and a disorder-centered, classical medical illness model. Conceptions of this kind cannot easily be coupled with the individual-centered and often one-dimensional theories of genetic investigators.

In American research on the transactional factors bearing on the genesis of schizophrenia, the main attention in recent years has been accorded to the role of the deviant communication of the patients' parents. These play, for instance, a central part in Wynne's and Singer's recent studies (25, 43), as well as in the prospective project started by Goldstein and his co-workers (9, 44) in Los Angeles. Wynne and his co-workers note, however, that "empirically, communication lends itself to systematic research methods, including the blind comparison of different kinds of families" better than other aspects of family life, such as the family role structure, styles of relating, and family values, which also are "probably highly significant factors but more difficult than communication to study sys-

tematically and comparatively" (43, p. 421). Communication is consequently that aspect of family dynamics which can be investigated most readily by methods similar to those of natural science, and which can also best be used in the search for disturbances. Yet this is not tantamount to saying that deviant communication is the most important factor making for disturbances.

I am inclined to attach the greatest significance to even more fundamental interactional processes associated with the parent-child relationships, which can be assumed to have the greatest influence on the structural development of the child's personality. It is precisely at this point that psychoanalytic studies are likely to be of help to the family investigator, bringing in vital components associated with the psychology of needs, which, e.g., a pure systems theory approach easily tends to neglect. This is the case despite the fact that there are notable differences between an interactional approach and the psychoanalytic theory based on individual-psychological conceptions.

Such differences can be shown very clearly by considering how a matter such as the earliest developmental stage of the child is conceived. The interactional view brings the mother and her relationship with the environment into the picture in quite a different way—beginning immediately from the event of birth and even before it—than that of the individual-centered psychoanalytic approach, which sees the first object relations of the small infant originating from its second or third month of life, at the earliest, and refers to the developmental stage preceding this as that of "primary autoerotism" (e.g., 45, 46). From an interactional standpoint one gladdening exception to the general analytic view is that of the late Michael Balint (47), who described the earliest stage as one of a "harmonious interpenetrating mix-up" between mother and child, thus emphasizing the fact that the infant, "enveloped during the fetal stage by its mother in nearly the same way that we are all surrounded by the air or fish surrounded by water," is after its birth still entirely undifferentiated from her, and dependent on her, the continuity of this interpenetrating relationship still forming a vital condition for its survival in a very global sense.

Despite the fact that classical psychoanalytic investigation has strongly brought out the significance for personality development of the early interpersonal relations, limitations have been attached to it that can only be remedied through interactional views and studies. It is typical, for instance, that the mother is often conceived of in a very general and schematic way as a background for the child's development, constituting a source of stimulations, gratifications and frustrations, but as a background lacking more individual characteristics. In the description of normal development—involving, to use Hartmann's (48) very helpful term, "an average expectable environment"—this perhaps may be considered justifiable, though not sufficient. The more pathological the interactional relationships concerned, the more important it will be to investigate in detail the individual characteristics of both the mother's and the father's personality, as well as the significant transactional relationships in the family and even between the family and its environment. The mother, her behavior, emotional expressions, her way of caring for the child, and her fantasies connected with the child will only then obtain the significance belonging to them in this psychological total situation.

The early interactional relationships cannot, of course, be investigated in the ordinary clinical situation in the same way as the current transactional dynamics. Yet a better picture of them can generally be obtained through the family therapeutic approach than through the individual therapeutic approach. This is particularly so in cases where the intrapersonal psychological process of development has failed to lead to a clear-cut individuation and to maturely differentiated object relations.

I may add that the polarity formed between the impulses arising from my psychoanalytic training, on the one hand, and those from my activity as a family therapist, on the other, has created a challenge for me to strive for a synthesis which might—even if imperfect—prove useful both for the understanding of schizophrenia and for an increased mutual understanding between family therapists and psychoanalysts.

Narcissistic Object Relationships in the Families of Schizophrenic Patients

I have reviewed my findings which revealed the possessive yet unempathic quality of the parent-child relationships in the families of schizophrenics. Parents of this kind do not have a rejecting attitude toward their children. Quite the contrary, the child is often particularly close to and significant for them. However, for the child itself such parental attitudes are frustrating, because they do not include enough empathy and understanding of its own needs and strivings. Helm Stierlin (49, 50) has characterized the nature of such a relationship as the transactional mode of binding, describing how the parent thereby owns the child's inner world, as it were, at the same time that the child's sense of owning itself remains defective (51). Paradoxically, the mode of binding in its extreme form thus comes close to its opposite, the mode of expelling, in which the rejection experienced by the child is overt.*

The psychoanalytic concept of narcissistic object relationships, as developed by Kohut (53, 54), is very useful for an understanding of the binding mode of interaction. According to Kohut, narcissistic objects, or self-objects, are "objects which are either used in the service of the self and of the maintenance of its instinctual investment, or objects which are themselves experienced as parts of the self" (53). A need for this kind of object is characteristic of a child still in its early development, but it is maintained by severely disturbed adults, those with narcissistic personality disorders and with latent psychoses. As parents, they often use their children as narcissistic objects, seeking compensation for their earlier disappointments.

With the aid of this concept, it is easy to interpret many central

* It should be pointed out that there exists a group of schizophrenics whose parents' attitudes are more neglecting than binding; however, at least in our country, they form a distinct minority according to our latest findings (52). Salokangas's (38) multivariate analysis of a series of schizophrenic patients from Turku showed that overdependence in parent-child relationship was of more frequent occurrence in the group of typical schizophrenias, whereas childhood conditions characterized by lack of family cohesiveness were met oftener in the more reactive, schizophreniform psychoses.

phenomena typical of transactional relationships between severely disordered parents and their children. Some family investigators have, in fact, spoken of narcissistic relationships in describing these families; one who did so early and distinctly was Warren M. Brodey (55), who defined such a relationship as a "relationship with the projected part of one's self, mirrored in the behavior of another person." In his book *The Origin and Treatment of Schizophrenic Disorders,* Lidz (56) considers the parents' "narcissistic needs" and "a profound cognitive egocentricity" parallel to these as the most central pathogenetic factors in these families. These transactional relationships have been described empathically by Stierlin (50), who, like Kohut, stresses the fundamental normality of their origin. All relationships between parents and their children, as well as relationships of attachment in general, include binding, Stierlin says; binding becomes pathological only when it assumes forms that do not correspond to the child's age-specific developmental needs. This can also be expressed by saying that all parents experience their children not only as individuals separate from themselves but also as complements to themselves and extensions of their own lives. The narcissistic side of a parent's relationship to the child becomes pathological only if it becomes disproportionately strong, relative to the mature side appreciating the child as a separate person.

Because of the lack of empathic and accepting parental attitudes—the mirroring and idealized parental self-objects as described by Kohut (53)—the structural development of narcissistically bound children is prone to remain immature, incoherent, and fragile. With regard to schizophrenic patients, this kind of view has important therapeutic implications. Because of their hampered development these patients have an intense—if often ambivalent and easily frustrated—need for parental figures. I have termed these interactional needs for empathy and support as well as for identification, the "dependency needs of the ego" (7, 23). Following Kohut's terminology, one should rather speak of the "dependency needs of the self." These needs of our patients form one of the most important challenges to, though also one of our powerful allies in, the psychotherapy of schizophrenics, about the possibilities of which my own experience leads me to be more optimistic than Kohut seems to be.

Transactional Dynamics and the Psychoanalytic Point of View

Another significant psychoanalyst, Otto Kernberg (57, 58), has also in recent years lucidly analyzed personalities affected by disturbances more serious than the neurotic, for whose inner structure he uses the term "borderline personality organization." One who has acquainted himself with schizophrenic patients' family environments easily recognizes in Kernberg's descriptions parents of the kind he has investigated and cared for. The description that Kernberg gives of the defense mechanisms typical of his rather broad spectrum of borderline personalities is particularly helpful when one seeks to understand schizophrenic patients' parents and their family environments in general.

The defense mechanisms that are typical of the borderline personalities are splitting, primitive idealization, the early forms of projection, and especially projective identification, denial, omnipotence, and devaluation. Even though Kernberg describes these defense mechanisms from an individual-psychological (psychoanalytic) point of view, it is important to note that they very often have another side, directed at and connected with another person, this other person being used as a support to one's own balance and thus as a part of one's own system of defense mechanisms aiming at the relief of anxiety. The role of these mechanisms is also central in the psychology of many more extended interactional phenomena met in the families of schizophrenic patients, as is illustrated, for example, by the role of splitting in the psychology of double-bind (59) and pseudomutuality (60).

The unconscious defense mechanisms, which psychoanalytic research has traditionally seen as intrapsychic phenomena, may thus also occur in accentuatedly interactional forms; i.e., in forms connected with interpersonal relationships. I have proposed that these should be called "transactional defense mechanisms" (41, 52). This term has, of course, a close association with Stierlin's formulation of "transactional modes." Stierlin's conceptions, however, are based on a clearly circular model of causal relations, on a systemic or family therapeutic paradigm (61), while the concept of "transactional defense mechanisms" is meant to serve as a bridge between a psychoanalytic and a family-oriented (systems) approach.

One can, of course, argue about the concept of defense mechanism: Which psychic operations should be included in its sphere and which excluded? Stolorow and Lachmann (62) quite recently suggested that there exists a developmental line for each defensive process. According to them one should make a distinction between "prestages of defenses," reflecting an arrest in ego development and offering an indication for promotion of structuralization of ego functions, on the one hand; and, on the other, defenses—even if representing a "lower" level in their hierarchy—which are used against structural conflicts and should be approached with interpretations. Stolorow and Lachmann found this line of division meaningful with respect to its consequences in the individual treatment of patients. The family therapeutic situations illustrate this kind of distinction as well. Yet they reveal that defensive patterns can also be used transactionally to support the strength of simultaneous intrapsychic warding-off, usually by a projective identification. For example, this happens, by "locating" a "bad" or otherwise negative self-representation unconsciously experienced as dangerous to another person. In this connection, Stierlin's (50, 63) creative and useful transactional conception of delegation, as well as the family therapeutic studies of Zinner and R. Shapiro (64, 65, 66), should also be recalled.

> I treated with family therapy a young man who had fallen ill with schizoaffective psychosis while in the armed service and whose father seemed to have had, ever since his son's infancy, an image of the son as weak and delicate and needing special protection in order to get along in life. The father himself was successful but had had to fight continually against his own "weakness," which he experienced as shameful. Such a feeling had haunted him, particularly in his youth, but it still made its appearance from time to time, leading to states of melancholy, for which he used antidepressant drugs in order—as he put it—"to increase the speed of rotation." Being a highly narcissistic person in this concept's narrow meaning, he had a devaluating attitude toward the other members of his family. Still, on returning home from work, this man, considered active and even ruth-

less in his occupational life, could resort to his wife's care like a little child. He associated a sense of weakness with his image of his father, and he had always tried to avoid becoming like him. My patient was the younger of his two children and had developed somewhat more slowly than his sister. The father's attitudes toward the children were characterized by an unmistakable split: The "active" properties of the daughter he identified with that side of himself which he found acceptable, whereas onto the son he seemed to project unconsciously his own weakness, and live this side of himself through the son. It was almost impossible for him to think of his son in any other kind of role. When the son went to the army, the father kept warning him that he might become a target of ridicule from other youths: "I didn't, I managed to get along well, but what about you, as you are so unable to defend yourself?"

Another feature of the dynamic picture of the family was that the mother's attitude toward the son was one of close and anxious attachment. This was clearly likely to arouse envy and aggressiveness in the father, for which his projective defense mechanism provided an unconscious outlet.

In my opinion, transactional defense mechanisms can also be used by relatively normal people, as, for example, in the interrelationships of married couples. However, they are used especially by persons characterized by a deficient integration of self- and object-representations, and then connected with narcissistic object relationships.

The parents of schizophrenics often belong to this category of ego pathology, as we have seen. The transactional dynamics of their relationships with their children may vary from an almost total narcissistic self-expansion (cf. a case report in Alanen (31)), to attempts at finding a substitute parental figure in their children, and to more specific and delimited projective identifications directed at them.

One starting point for transactional dynamics of this kind, especially in many mothers, may be formed by an initial projective identification with the child they are caring for. In this way they relive their own childhood. This is only normal and natural, but such an identification may also become pathological both in degree and duration, if the mother's way to get compensation for her earlier frustrations through the child becomes a permanent pattern. This is likely to lead to an unconscious resistance to the child's attempts at independent growth. In cases like this the parents' transactional defense mechanisms are used to avoid their own separation anxiety. They may also serve to avoid the formation of a real object relationship with the child. Both kinds of dynamics are often encountered during the course of family therapy.

It is important to note that defense mechanisms of a transactional nature are not always combined with an openly possessive parental relationship but can also be perceptible behind more negatively colored devaluating parental attitudes, such as in the case vignette presented above. This may form an answer to Arieti (67), who in the latest edition of *American Handbook of Psychiatry* suggested that encounters with excessively dominating mothers of the "classical type" may have led us to partly unfounded generalizations concerning the pathogenic significance of disordered parent-child relationships in schizophrenia, as such mothers constitute only a minority of these parents' mothers.

The Development of Schizophrenia as a Multiphase Process

The factors making for a proneness to schizophrenic illness in children who have grown up in interpersonal environments of this kind include a serious disorder of ego development, especially of the ego's capacity to form boundaries between the self and the persons in the outside world, so conspicuously manifested in the clinical schizophrenic state. This disorder of individuation and separation of the growing self is often very clearly influenced by the parents' possessive ways of relating to the child. Another important factor contributing to the child's disordered development and intimately connected with the first mentioned is the preservation of deep-rooted (if ambivalent) dependency needs.

Besides the experiences of many family and individual psychotherapists (51, 68-72), a study of the onset of psychosis by my colleague Räkköläinen (35), based on a sample of 68 parents, is pertinent here. He showed that, because of the fragility of their inner structure, these persons were prepsychotically dependent on a "world of self-objects" for their inner balance. They succeeded in retaining their integrity through the preservation of preponderantly narcissistic object relationships or fantasies; when these failed, Räkköläinen concluded, psychosis set in. Sullivan (73) described the onset of schizophrenia as a two-stage process reminiscent of this view. Räkköläinen's study also showed that in the majority of cases the schizophrenic psychosis had set in during some important developmental stage of transition in the patient's life: when he was faced with separation (often a delayed one) from his family of orientation, when he was attempting to establish a more adult-level interpersonal relationship than before, or when some significant change was about to take place in his psychosocial role. The break of the intrapsychic structure was thus very closely connected with interactional events.

It is legitimate to assume that the part played by the parents' cognitive disorders, stressed particularly by Lidz even in the '50s as a "transmission of irrationality" (20, 74), is also of great importance in the pathogenesis of schizophrenia in the offspring, although, I think, at a more secondary level compared to the interactions involving emotional relationships. Stierlin's (50) description of "cognitive binding," manifesting itself in phenomena such as mystification or misdefining the child's inner and outer experiences to him, shows, on the other hand, how closely emotional and cognitive parental attitudes may be bound together.

The obvious importance of continued transactional disorders is one of the reasons why I, like many other family investigators, find it difficult to accept those views of the pathogenesis of schizophrenia that place the critical point of schizophrenia-proneness almost exclusively in the early phase of the mother-child relationship. The parents' inability in these cases to differentiate the child from themselves, as well as the manifestations of their own separation anxiety, point to the crucial importance of the whole separation-individuation process in the developmental pathology of future schizophrenics. Likewise, the phenomena of the various forms of disordered parental cognitive communication will cause disturbances in the child's ego development only when the child has already begun to differentiate, organize, and integrate its conceptions of both its inner self and the external world—a stage which certainly is not limited to the child's first year of life, but coincides with the separation and individuation phase in its entirety. As Mahler says, the developmental phases have no sharp boundaries (46); they partly overlap, and one must not restrict attention to narrowly limited "critical periods," but consider also the severity and continuity of disordered interactions. One should then focus not only on separate mother-child or father-child relationships but on the family unit and its functions. Both parents, belonging to the same homeostatic circle, have an intense influence upon each other's emotional life, and they can reduce or increase each other's pathogenic influences, exerting compensating or reinforcing effects on them.

An important part in the pathogenesis—or the avoidance—of schizophrenia is also played by later developmental stages, especially the success or failure of identity formation in adolescence (a matter very much dependent on family transactions at that time). Among the later precipitating factors, problems linked together with marital relationships and families of procreation have a special importance. The development of schizophrenic psychosis is thus a multiphase process, presupposing a weakness of early individuation, but depending on later developmental factors, ranging from the continuation of pathogenic parent-child relationships to various interactional experiences in later life.

Notes on Family-centered Therapy in Schizophrenia

I have advocated reliance on the development of psychotherapeutic care along a wide front as the line to follow in the treatment of schizophrenic patients and their families. In spite of all their disturbedness, the possessive transactional relations which I have described have one clinically favorable aspect: They form a basis for the schizophrenic's frequent ability for a long-term relationship with another person, ambivalent and easily frustrated though this may be. The patient has had experience of a human relationship characterized by continuity. Most sociopathic persons, whose growth environments have often been openly rejecting, are in this respect in a less advantageous position. The basic attitude of the therapist of a schizophrenic has to meet certain conditions, however, which differentiate it from the classical psychoanalytic position. Simo Salonen (34), a Finnish psychoanalyst has used the concept of "holding," first introduced by Winnicott (75), to describe this kind of attitude, characterized by empathy and trustworthiness regarding its continuity.

A similar empathic basic attitude is called for in the case of these patients' families. On the basis of our knowledge, the disturbed attitudes of parents are to be seen as resulting from their own problems and difficulties, and a support-giving and understanding therapeutic attitude should be accorded to them. This recognition has directed our interests in the development of family therapy of our schizophrenic patients.

A conjoint family therapy is often necessary with the families of the youngest patients, in whom the developmental disturbance and the onset of psychosis usually is intimately connected with intrafamilial interpersonal relations, in the form of unresolved mutual separation problems. During the therapeutic process, the parents of these patients often will direct their dependent needs toward the therapist, and this in turn is likely to ease the psychodynamic position of the child patient and provide him with improved opportunities for personal growth. Interpretations, in the word's proper meaning, rarely have much importance, but the psychoanalytic concepts referred to earlier often help the therapist better to understand the manipulative ways of the parents' behavior and to sustain an empathic attitude toward them. In the most favorable cases, the conjoint therapy amounts to a process of growth of the extended family, in which matters are discussed and worked through at the levels of more than two generations; in other words, the parents' relations with their own parents will also be involved. The changes taking place in the parents' personalities are, according to my experience, usually not great; nevertheless, the family homeostasis may develop in a direction important to the patient, largely as a result of the parents' identification with the therapist and, also, with the therapist's attitude toward their child (cf. 31, 41).

A conjoint therapy of the patient and his parents is not called for in every case of schizophrenia (cf. 56, 76). In Turku we are currently conducting a treatment study, in connection with which an effort was made to formulate for each patient an optimal treatment plan consistent with the facilities of the municipal community psychiatric service (39). During the first stage of our study we regarded a growth-oriented conjoint therapy of the patient and his parents as indicated for 16 of 100 new, unselected patients in the schizophrenia group. This subgroup consisted chiefly of young patients. (It should be mentioned for the sake of comparison that an individual psychotherapy in a regular form was considered indicated in 25 cases in the same series.)

One interesting result was that conjoint sessions with the patient and his spouse, for the purposes of marital therapy or at least for exploration of the marital situation, were considered indicated in this study in 80 percent of those cases where the patient was married. This view reflects the important part that marital problems had appeared to play in the onset of illness in these patients. It corresponds to the findings of another study of ours (42), according to which a considerable number of spouses of such patients also have relatively severe personality disorders, often of a type likely to lead to a transactional exploitation of the partner. In many of these families, and particularly those in which the couple had children, the preventive value of a family-centered treatment was also clearly evident.

Despite the fact that conjoint therapy was considered indicated in only a section of the families in our series, we regarded a family-centered therapeutic orientation as important in nearly all of them. In only three of the 100 cases concerned was no kind of contact with the patient's family considered necessary. In many families not only the patient but also other family members were in need of care and support. Often the patient's individual therapy will also benefit quite substantially from contacts made with the other family members. And there are cases where, because of lack of treatment motivation in the patient, some of his family members' keeping in contact with the therapist or the therapeutic institution offers the only possibility for an ambulatory treatment.

In these families, as in individual patients, we almost always meet healthy psychological forces and endeavors besides and behind the pathogenic ones. In the family therapy and family-centered treatment approach, these healthy forces and resources can often be supported, and they may become a source of strength for the therapy.

REFERENCES

1. Markowe, M., Steinert, J., and Heyworth-Davis, F.: Insulin and chlorpromazine in schizophrenia. A ten-year comparative survey. *Brit. J. Psychiat.*, 113:1101-1106, 1967.
2. Niskanen, P. and Achté, K. A.: The course and prognosis of schizophrenic psychoses in Helsinki. A comparative study of first admissions in 1950, 1960, and 1965. *Monogr. Psychiatric Clinic Helsinki Univ. Central Hospital* No. 4, 1972.
3. May, P. R. A.: *Treatment of Schizophrenia.* New York: Science House, 1968.
4. May, P. R. A., Tuma, A. H., Dixon, W. J., Yale, C., and Potepan, P.: Schizophrenia—a follow-up study of results of treatment. *Arch. Gen. Psychiat.*, 33:474-486, 1976.
5. Kety, S. S., Rosenthal, D., Wender, P. H., and Schulsinger, F.: The types and prevalence of mental illness in the biological and adoptive families of adopted schizophrenics. In: D. Rosenthal and S. S. Kety (Eds.), *The Transmission of Schizophrenia.* Oxford: Pergamon Press, 1968.
6. Rosenthal, D., Wender, P. H., Kety, S. S., Schulsinger, F., Welner, J., and Ostergaard, L.: Schizophrenics' offspring reared in adoptive homes. In: D. Rosenthal and S. S. Kety (Eds.), *The Transmission of Schizophrenia.* Oxford: Pergamon Press, 1968.
7. Alanen, Y. O., Rekola, J. K., Stewen, A., Takala, K., and Tuovinen, M.: The family in the pathogenesis of schizophrenic and neurotic disorders. *Acta Psychiat. Scand.*, Suppl. 189, 1966.
8. Wynne, L. C.: Concluding comments to the section family relationships and communication. In: L. C. Wynne, R. L. Cromwell and S. Matthysse (Eds.), *The Nature of Schizophrenia.* New York: Wiley, 1978.
9. Goldstein, M. J., Rodnick, E. H., Jones, J. E., McPherson, S. R., and West, K. L.: Familial precursors of schizophrenia spectrum disorders. In: L. C. Wynne, R. L. Cromwell, and S. Matthysee (Eds.), *The Nature of Schizophrenia.* New York: Wiley, 1978.
10. Tienari, P., Lahti, I. A., Naarala, M., Sorri, A., and Väisänen, E.: Schizophrenics' offspring reared in adoptive homes. A family dynamic study. Paper read at the VI International Symposium on Psychotherapy of Schizophrenia, Lausanne, Switzerland, 1978.
11. Lidz, R. W. and Lidz, T.: The family environment of schizophrenic patients. *Amer. J. Psychiat.*, 106:332-345, 1949.

12. KASANIN, J., KNIGHT, E., and SAGE, P.: The parent-child relationship in schizophrenia. I. Over-Protection-Rejection. *J. Nerv. Ment. Dis.*, 79:249-263, 1934.
13. TIETZE, T.: A study of mothers of schizophrenic patients. *Psychiatry*, 12:55-65, 1949.
14. GERARD, D. and SIEGEL, J.: Family background of schizophrenia. *Psychiat. Quart.*, 27:90-101, 1950.
15. REICHARD, A. and TILLMAN, C.: Patterns of parent-child relationships schizophrenia. *Psychiatry*, 13:247-257, 1950.
16. ALANEN, Y. O.: The mothers of schizophrenic patients. *Acta Psychiat. Neur. Scand. Suppl.* 124, 1958.
17. FAIRBAIRN, W. R. D.: *Psychoanalytic Studies of the Personality.* London: Tavistock Publications, 1952.
18. HILL, L. B.: *Psychotherapeutic Intervention in Schizophrenia.* Chicago: University of Chicago Press, 1955.
19. LIDZ, T., CORNELISON, A., FLECK, S., and TERRY, D.: The intrafamilial environment of schizophrenic patients. I. The father. *Psychiatry*, 20:329-342, 1957a.
20. LIDZ, T., FLECK, S., and CORNELISON, A. R.: *Schizophrenia and the Family.* New York: International Universities Press, 1965.
21. HIRSCH, S. R. and LEFF, J. P.: Abnormalities in Parents of Schizophrenics. Institute of Psychiatry Maudsley Monographs No. 22. London: Oxford University Press, 1975.
22. KETTY, S. S., ROSENTHAL, D., WENDER, P. H., SCHULSINGER, F., and JACOBSEN, B.: Mental illness in the biological and adoptive families of adopted individuals who have become schizophrenic. In: R. Fieve, D. Rosenthal, and H. Brill (Eds.), *Genetic Research in Psychiatry.* Baltimore: Johns Hopkins University Press, 1975.
23. ALANEN, Y. O.: From the mothers of schizophrenic patients to interactional family dynamics. In: D. Rosenthal and S. S. Kety (Eds.), *The Transmission of Schizophrenia.* Oxford: Pergamon Press, 1968.
24. ALANEN, Y. O.: The families of schizophrenic patients. In: R. Cancro (Ed.), *The Schizophrenic Syndrome, An Annual Review,* Vol. 1. New York: Brunner/Mazel, 1971.
25. SINGER, M. T., WYNNE, L. C., and TOOHEY, M. L.: Communication disorders and the families of schizophrenic. In: L. C. Wynne, R. L. Cromwell, and S. Matthysse (Eds.), *The Nature of Schizophrenia,* Chapter 46. New York: Wiley, 1978.
26. WENDER, P. H., ROSENTHAL, D., and KETY, S. S.: A psychiatric assessment of the adoptive parents of schizophrenics. In: D. Rosenthal and S. S. Kety (Eds.), *The Transmission of Schizophrenia.* Oxford: Pergamon Press, 1968.
27. WENDER, P. H., ROSENTHAL, D., KETY, S. S., SCHULSINGER, F., and WELNER, J.: Crossfostering. A research strategy for clarifying the role of genetic and experiential factors in the etiology of schizophrenia. *Arch. Gen. Psychiat.*, 30:121-128, 1974.

28. ROSENTHAL, D., WENDER, P. H., KETY, S. S., SCHULSINGER, F., WELNER, J., and TIEDER, R.: Parent-child relationships and psychopathological disorder in the child. *Arch. Gen. Psychiat.*, 32:466-476, 1975.
29. ROSENTHAL, D.: Genetic transmissions in schizophrenia. Methods to decipher mode of transmission are presented. A mimeographed manuscript, 1977.
30. LIDZ, T., CORNELISON, A. R., FLECK, S., and TERRY, D.: Marital schism and marital skew. *Amer. J. Psychiat.*, 114:241-248, 1957b.
31. ALANEN, Y. O.: On background factors and goals in the family therapy of young schizophrenic patients and their parents. In: J. Jorstad and E. Ugelstad (Eds.), *Schizophrenia 1975.* Oslo: Universitetsforlaget, 1976.
32. ALANEN, Y. O., LAINE, A., RÄKKÖLÄINEN, V., and SALONEN, S.: Evolving the psychotherapeutic community:—research combined with hospital treatment of schizophrenia. Conference: Schizophrenia—the Implications of Research Findings to Treatment and Teaching. Washington: NIMH, 1970.
33. SALONEN, S.: The hospital ward from the standpoint of the patient's self-esteem. *Psychiatria Fennica,* 1975:325-331, 1975.
34. SALONEN, S.: On the technique of the psychotherapy of schizophrenia. In: J. Jorstad and E. Ugelstad (Eds.), *Schizophrenia 75.* Oslo: Universitetsforlaget, 1976.
35. RÄKKÖLÄINEN, V.: Onset of psychosis. A Clinical Study of 68 Cases. *Ann. Univ. Turkuensis,* Ser. D., Vol. 7, 1977.
36. SALOKANGAS, R. K. R.: Psychosocial progosis in schiozphrenia. *Ann. Univ. Turkuensis,* Ser. D., Vol. 9, 1978.
37. ALANEN, Y. O. and LAINE, A.: Development of a hospital centered community psychotherapy service for schizophrenic patients. Evaluation of the first phase. In: J. K. Wing and H. Häfner (Eds.), *Roots of Evaluation: An Epidemiologic Basis for Planning Psychiatric Services.* London: Oxford University Press, 1973.
38. ALANEN, Y. O.: The psychotherapeutic care of schizophrenic patients in a community psychiatric setting. In: M. H. Lader (Ed.), *Studies of Schizophrenia.* Brit. J. Psychiat. Spec. Publ. No. 10, 1975.
39. ALANEN, Y. O.: RÄKKÖLÄINEN, V., RASIMUS, R., and LAAKSO, J.: Indications for different forms of psychotherapy with new schizophrenia patients in community psychiatry. Paper read at the VI International Symposium on Psychotherapy of Schizophrenia, Lausanne, Switzerland, 1978.
40. ALANEN, Y. O.: The benefits of family psychotherapy in hebephrenic schiozphrenia. In: D. Rubinstein and Y. O. Alanen (Eds.), *Psychotherapy of Schizophrenia.* Amsterdam: Excerpta Medica, 1972.
41. ALANEN, Y. O.: On the foundations of family therapy—a clinical

and psychoanalytic view. *Psychiatrica Fennica,* 1977:155-166, 1977.

42. Alanen, Y. O. and Kinnunen, P.: Marriage and the development of schizophrenia. *Psychiatry,* 38:346-355, 1975.
43. Wynne, L. C., Singer, M. T., and Toohey, M. L.: Communications of the adoptive parents of schizophrenics. In: J. Jorstad and E. Ugelstad (Eds.), *Schizophrenia 75.* Oslo: Universitetsforlaget, 1976.
44. Goldstein, M. J. and Rodnick, E. H.: The family's contribution to the etiology of schizophrenia: Current status. *Schizophrenia Bull.* No. 14:48-63, 1975.
45. Spitz, R. A.: *The First Year of Life.* New York: International Universities Press, 1965.
46. Mahler, M. S., Pine, F., and Bergman, A.: *The Psychological Birth of the Human Infant.* New York: Basic Books, 1975.
47. Balint, M.: *The Basic Fault. Therapeutic Aspects of Regression.* London: Tavistock Publication, 1968.
48. Hartmann, H.: *Ich-Psychologie und Anpassungsproblem. Internat, Z. Psychoanal. und Imago,* 24. (engl. *Ego Psychology and the Problem of Adaptation.* Internat. Univ. Press 1958), 1939.
49. Stierlin, H.: Family dynamics and separation patterns of potential schizophrenics. In: D. Rubinstein and Y. O. Alanen (Eds.), *Psychotherapy of Schizophrenia.* Amsterdam: Excerpta Medica, 1972.
50. Stierlin, H.: *Separating and Adolescents.* New York: Quadrangle/New York Times, 1974.
51. Stierlin, H.: The dynamics of owning and disowning: Psychoanalytic and family perspectives. *Fam. Process,* 15:277-288, 1976a.
52. Alanen, Y. O.: Schizophrenia and the family. *Psychiatria Fennica,* 1978.
53. Kohut, H.: *The Analysis of the Self.* New York: International Universities Press, 1971.
54. Kohut, H.: *The Restoration of the Self.* New York: International Universities Press, 1977.
55. Brodey, W. M.: Some family operations and schizophrenia. *Arch. Gen. Psychiat.,* 1:379-402, 1959.
56. Lidz, T.: *The Origin and Treatment of Schizophrenia.* New York: Basic Books, 1973.
57. Kernberg, O.: Borderline personality organization. *J. Amer. Psychoanal. Ass.,* 15:641-685, 1967.
58. Kernberg, O.: *Borderline Conditions and Pathological Narcissism.* New York: Jason Aronson, 1975.
59. Bateson, G., Jackson, D. D., Haley, J., and Weakland, J. H.: Toward a theory of schizophrenia. *Behav. Sci.,* 1:251-264, 1956.
60. Wynne, L.C., Ryckoff, I. M., Day, J., and Hirsch, S.: Pseudomutuality in the family relations of schizophrenics. *Psychiatry,* 21:205-220, 1958.

61. STIERLIN, H., RUCKER-EMBDEN, I., WETZEL, N., and WIRSCHING, M.: *Das erste Familiengesprach.* Stuttgart: Klett-Cotta, 1977.
62. STOLOROW, R. D. and LACHMANN, F. M.: The developmental prestages of defences: Diagnostic and therapeutic implications. *Psychoanal. Quart.*, 47:73-102, 1978.
63. STIERLIN, H.: The transmission of irrationality reconsidered. In: L. C. Wynne, R. L. Cromwell, and S. Matthysse (Eds.), *The Nature of Schizophrenia,* Chapter 48. New York: Wiley, 1978.
64. ZINNER, J. and SHAPIRO, R.: Projective identification as a mode of perception and behavior in families of adolescents. *Internat. J. Psycho. Anal.*, 53:523-530, 1972.
65. ZINNER, J. and SHAPIRO, R.: The family group as a single entity: Implications for acting out in adolescences. *Internat. Rev. Psycho. Anal.*, 1:179-186, 1974.
66. SHAPIRO, E. R., ZINNER, J., SHAPIRO, R. L., and BERKOWITZ, D. A.: The influence of family experience on borderline personality development. *Internat. Rev. Psycho-Anal.*, 2:399-412, 1975.
67. ARIETI, S.: Schizophrenia: The psychodynamic mechanisms and the psychostructural forms. In: S. Arieti (Ed.), *American Handbook of Psychiatry,* Vol. III. New York: Basic Books, 1974.
68. BOSZORMENYI-NAGY, I. and FRAMO, J. L.: The concept of schizophrenia from the perspective of family treatment. *Family Process,* 1:103-113, 1962.
69. SLIPP, S.: The symbiotic survival patterns: A relational theory of schizophrenia. *Famliy Proc.*, 12:377-398, 1973.
70. SEARLES, H. F.: *Collected Papers on Schizophrenia and Related Subjects.* London: The Hogarth Press, 1965.
71. BURNHAM, J. L., GLADSTONE, A. I., and GIBSON, R. W.: *Schizophrenia and the Need-Fear Dilemma.* New York: International Universities Press, 1969.
72. SCHULZ, C. G.: An individualized psychotherapeutic approach with the schizophrenic patient. *Schizophrenia Bull.*, 13:46-69, 1975.
73. SULLIVAN, H. S.: The relation to onset and outcome in schizophrenia. In: H. S. Sullivan (Ed.), *Schizophrenia as a Human Process.* New York: Norton, 1962.
74. LIDZ, T., CORNELISON, A. R., TERRY, D., and FLECK, S.: The transmission of irrationality. *A.M.A. Arch. Neur. Psychiat.*, 79:305-316, 1958.
75. WINNICOTT, D. W.: The theory of the parent-infant relationship. *Internat. J. Psycho-Anal.*, 41:585-595, 1960.
76. STIERLIN, H.: Perspectives on the individual and family therapy of schizophrenic patients: An introduction. In: J. Jorstad and E. Ugelstad (Eds.), *Schizophrenia 75.* Oslo: Universitetsforlaget, 1976b.

Index